For Samina

To God belong the East and the West.
Wherever you turn the glory of God is everywhere.

—Holy Quran

ROCK and ROLL JIHAD

A MUSLIM ROCK STAR'S REVOLUTION

12 hit songs by Salman Ahmad and Junoon

SALMAN AHMAD

with Robert Schroeder

JAICO PUBLISHING HOUSE

Ahmedabad Bangalore Bhopal Bhubaneswar Chennai
Delhi Hyderabad Kolkata Lucknow Mumbai

Published by Jaico Publishing House
A-2 Jash Chambers, 7-A Sir Phirozshah Mehta Road
Fort, Mumbai - 400 001
jaicopub@jaicobooks.com
www.jaicobooks.com

Published in arrangement with
Free Press
A Division of Simon & Schuster, Inc.
1230 Avenue of the Americas
New York, NY 10020

ROCK AND ROLL JIHAD
with CD
ISBN 978-81-8495-118-9

First Jaico Impression: 2010

Printed by
Rashmi Graphics
#3, Amrutwel CHS Ltd., C.S. #50/74
Ganesh Galli, Lalbaug, Mumbai-400 012
E-mail: tiwarijp@vsnl.net

Contents

Introduction by Melissa Etheridge

The story you are about to read is the story of a light-bringer, a way-shower. He will be the first to insist that there is nothing special about anything that he has done. Yet there is no other that has gone before him and walked his path.

I had the blessing to cross the path of Salman Ahmad in December 2007, when we were in Oslo, Norway, for the Nobel Peace Prize Concert.

I had been on a life-changing adventure of my own. Diagnosed with cancer in 2004, I lay in bed for weeks on "dose-dense chemotherapy" (a new and intense form of chemo). And it was there and then that I found my meaning in life.

We are one.

I sent out a prayer to the cosmos. *Make me a channel for changing the world. I want to work with people who want to change the world. People who are through with the current paradigm that we have been agreeing to uphold day after day, people who know there is a great shift happening and that peace is the only thing that matters in the world.*

Before long, I received a call from former vice president Al Gore, asking me to write a song for his film *An Inconvenient Truth*. It was an opportunity for me to put out a call to arms, a chance to get people to "wake up." I watched as that one film single-handedly changed people; I saw it ignite a spark. I realized that one person's dream can make a huge difference to the whole world. I was surprised and honored to win an Oscar for the song I had written, "I Need to Wake Up."

In 2007, I was asked to participate in Live Earth, a concert raising awareness about global warming that was being held on 7-7-07, on all seven continents, all day long. It was an ambitious attempt to bring the world together though technology. I took this as a sign that finally we were all waking up to the need to understand our "oneness," and that for the first time, we might begin to rise as one to address and resolve the serious environmental issues facing this Earth right now. With excitement, I prepared a trilogy of songs to be played for my twenty minutes on stage. I planned to play two new songs from my not-yet-released album *The Awakening*, then end with the Oscar-winning song "I Need to Wake Up."

A couple of weeks before the concert, my manager told me that the organizers of the concert, acting, we assume, under pressure from their corporate sponsors, really wanted me to do a "hit" song. I could not believe my ears. On the one hand, the world was coming together as never before; on the other, I was being asked to sing "Come to My Window." Now, don't get me wrong: I love that song and am very grateful to have a hit or two under my belt, but the thought of turning this momentous occasion into a demand to roll out a hit song was starting to get me down. I told my manager that I would be doing the new songs or I would watch the concert at home. Eventually, the organizers backed off, and we agreed that I would perform the new songs.

The thought of having a live television audience, worldwide, for twenty minutes was exciting. Onstage at Giants Stadium, I chose to ask the question, "What happened to us?" I spoke about fear and change. I hoped to inspire somebody, anybody. I did not know it at the time, but Salman Ahmad and his family, who had arrived in New York City only months before, were at the stadium that day to watch this live concert event. I wish I could have seen them from the stage. As it was, I could only see a number of smiling faces, and a couple of folks who were really there to hear Bon Jovi and who also probably wanted me to stop talking and sing more (maybe that "Window" song).

As I left the stage, I took a good look at the corporate sponsors all around the stadium. With sadness I realized that this moment was brought to us by Verizon and a host of other "green-washed" companies, corporate hypocrites that seemed to jump on the green wagon just to sell more widgets. My heart really sank later, when I learned that not a note of my performance was shown on the three-hour NBC broadcast that night. Not even the Academy Award–winning song to the movie that got this whole thing going in the first place. All that made the corporate cut was my introduction, "Ladies and gentlemen, Mr. Al Gore."

This changing the world thing was going to take a lot longer than I thought.

Later that year, I received the request to join Mr. Gore in Oslo, where he was to receive the Nobel Peace Prize. I was asked to play "I Need to Wake Up" and one other song at the Nobel Peace Prize Concert. I found out that this concert was going to be broadcast on television to many nations.

Thanks to previous experience, I was feeling a little skeptical about just how much good a television show masquerading under the label of "A Concert" could do. I was starting to see that no matter how extraordinary an event like this can be, when it turns into television entertainment, you always hear the same thing over and over: "Let's bring peace to the world, shall we? And now, a word from our sponsor." What noble sentiment there is gets watered down, if not eliminated entirely, by the commercial interests that prevail over it. But I wanted to be there for my friend Al, so I said yes. I had been mumbling some of my doubts to my long-time tour manager and friend Steven Girmant on the plane ride over, when he said, *There is some reason you are here. You never know what might happen or who you might meet.* I hate it when Steven uses on me any of the spiritual pick-me-ups that I use on him. I decided to take my own advice and start looking for the purpose of my journey to a very cold place to perform on a TV show.

At the sound check, among the arena chairs I saw a beautiful couple, a man and woman. I sang my song to an otherwise empty hall. When I was finished, this strong man with amazing eyes approached the stage. He reached out both his hands to me. I bent down and grabbed them, and he gently told me in his Pakistani yet Americanized accent, "I love the vibration you are on." These words filled my soul. I had found another spirit who was searching for something more. I looked at him and said, "I live there." What a sweet smile he had. I met him again backstage, where he told me of his work. I saw him perform at the concert and was amazed by his vocal and guitar abilities. Here was this traditional Eastern sound that was rocking hard at the same time. We exchanged information, and I flew back to Los Angeles, satisfied that the universe knew what it was doing dragging me to Norway in December.

Salman and I made arrangements to meet up in Los Angeles. I told him we needed to write something together. He came to my home and we spent two days just talking. We could feel each other's vibrations, and again we were on the same wavelength, as we spoke of our dreams and each of our paths. I have a history of making choices that might seem brave to some. But when he told me about what had happened to him in Pakistan, the story that you're about to read in this book, I suddenly felt that my history paled in comparison to choices he made that could have resulted in his death. I was so inspired to create something in conjunction with this soul. He returned home and sent me some musical ideas. I found in one track a haunting guitar part that I kept playing over and over until finally the words started to come. "Whose God is God? Whose light is light? Whose law is wrong? Whose might is right?" This would truly be a song about peace. A song about finally ending the fear of differences.

I was recording a holiday album that I was calling *A New Thought for Christmas*. I wanted to bring out an alternative way of thinking about all of our religious differences. It seemed to me that a collaboration between a Sufi Muslim and a Midwestern lesbian might do the trick. I invited Salman to come to the studio, where he tracked with us for a full day. His smooth vocals and steady guitar playing made for a magical experience. We created a song, "Ring the Bells," and with the help of Deepak Chopra, the song became a movement of its own. I hope you hear it and are yourself moved to sound an alarm for peace and change in this world.

Peace in this world begins with peace in our hearts. Salman Ahmad has placed that peace in his heart and it now shines like a beacon for millions of people in the East, the West, and everywhere.

Read on, my friend, and know that his story is a part of our history. We are all connected, and as each day goes by, the connections become clearer.

Salman Ahmad inspires me to reach always for the greatest heights and never to fear. I am so blessed to know this extraordinary man.

—May 2009

ONE
The Taliban and the Guitar

On a cool, clear November morning in 1982, I woke up in my bedroom in Lahore, filled with anticipation. A little more than a year earlier, my parents, siblings, and I had returned to Pakistan after six years in America. That evening, I would finally break out my long-unused sunburst Les Paul and play before a live audience of my medical school classmates at our college talent show. My plan was to channel the eighties guitar hero Eddie Van Halen and perform "Eruption"—and to blow everybody away as only that classic one-minute, 42-second guitar solo could. Consumed by a musical passion, I threw on my white doctor's overalls and grabbed my anatomy and physiology books and headed for the door. I was eighteen years old.

The sweet smell of jasmine greeted me as I stepped outside and climbed into my beat-up, rusting yellow Mazda, the consolation prize given to me by my father for having taken me away from the life I loved in Tappan, New York. My parents and siblings had settled in the southern port city of Karachi while I had moved in with my mother's parents at 54 Lawrence Road for my studies. That hopeful morning, I drove down Mall Road, the main city thoroughfare, and into the cyclone that is Lahori traffic: an anarchic scrum of blue rickshaws, horse-drawn *tongas*, bicyclists wearing *shalwar kameez* (long shirt over baggy trousers), and Japanese motorbikes and cars all flouting the cops and running red lights. Navigating the chaotic roads, I motored past the palatial Punjab governor's mansion and Jinnah's Garden, the beautiful park known as

Lawrence Gardens during the colonial Raj. I gazed for a second at the gymkhana where I often played cricket. Its picturesque ground was encased in pine and eucalyptus trees and its pavilions were lined with red tiles. My eyes were still re-adjusting to the sights of Pakistan, and all of this looked like a scene right out of a dream.

My parents had enrolled me in Lahore's King Edward Medical College in the hope that I would give up my teenage fantasies of being a rock musician and adopt a respectable profession. They had been patient and even supportive when I joined Eclipse, our high school garage band in Tappan, founded by my Tappan Zee High School buddies Brian O'Connell and Paul Siegel. And they'd been sincerely happy when we won our high school's battle of the bands in 1980. But as I sat in the lecture hall that day, my old life in America was a world away and I was just another young Pakistani studying anatomy—albeit one who was constantly humming the chorus of "Helter Skelter" and "Revolution."

About two years earlier, my father's brother-in-law, Ismat Anwar, had visited us at our home in Tappan. At the behest of my parents, Dr. Anwar, a leading Pakistani surgeon, had a man-to-man talk with me about my career plans. I sat across from the serious-looking Uncle Anwar in my small room, focusing my bored gaze past him on the poster of Jimi Hendrix on my wall. With a shrug of my shoulders, I told my uncle that I didn't know about the future. But I knew that I wanted to rock.

"Rock? What does that mean, *beta* (son)?" Dr. Anwar asked in his Punjabi-inflected English.

I tried to explain in my New York accent. "Uncle, I just want to play guitar and be in a band for the rest of my life. That's my dream. Just like these guys," I said, pointing to the life-size posters of Led Zeppelin, the Beatles, the Rolling Stones, Hendrix, and Van Halen covering the walls of my room in our house on Lester Drive. My uncle took a look around at all the color posters in amazement, as Lennon and McCartney, Hendrix, Plant, Page, and Jagger seemed to strike poses of silent support.

Uncle Anwar pointed incredulously to the long-haired musicians playing guitars and exclaimed, "Salman *mian* [young man], you want to become a *mirasi* [low-class musician]? Your parents have high expectations of you and you want to waste the rest of your life playing this *tuntunna* [gizmo]?" He shook his open palms in the direction of my sunburst Les Paul, which rested proudly against the back of my guitar amplifier in the corner of my room.

Before I could answer I was saved by a car honking outside. It was Brian, come to take me to band practice. I ran out of the room carrying my amplifier in one hand and my guitar in the other. Freed from the interrogation, I yelled back, "I have to go, Uncle, our band Eclipse is rehearsing for the Tappan Zee High School battle of the bands!"

I escaped, but Uncle Anwar's words had unsettled me. It was only a matter of months until the other shoe dropped and my parents told me we were all going back to Pakistan. I was already reeling from two of my heroes' deaths, and now I had to face a forced march back to the motherland. That winter, I'd been devastated by the tragic killing of John Lennon, and had mourned the loss of drummer John Bonham of Led Zeppelin not long before. Both Zeppelin and the Beatles had been like close friends and teachers to me over the past six years. I had jammed with them with the head phones on, dissecting their guitar riffs. I had tried to mimic their impossibly cool fashions and belted out their tunes in front of my mirror at high decibels. I'd sung along with Robert Plant to Zeppelin's "Stairway to Heaven" or "Kashmir," and crooned "Day Tripper" or "A Hard Day's Night" by the Beatles. As a Pakistani kid who'd struggled with integrating into American life, rock and roll fed my soul and steered me toward a personal centeredness. Looking at myself in the mirror, I didn't see a Pakistani, an American, or a Muslim, or anyone who fit into a single label or category. I just imagined myself standing onstage, playing my guitar and making people happy. And that was all I wanted.

But in the summer of 1981, the clock was ticking. I dodged reality by spending more and more time jamming with my friends in Eclipse. As the August day of departure got closer, I felt more like a visitor to the U.S. from a parallel universe. I was leaving. But I didn't really know where I was going.

The America I knew was rock concerts at the Nassau Coliseum, Yankees games, and a close-knit group of teenage friends that made up a living mosaic of my adopted country. There was my Irish-American buddy Brian, my Jewish friends Paul Siegel and Michael Langer, and Frank Bianco, the New York Italian kid I perfected my ping-pong game with. And then there was me, a brown-skinned, Pakistani-American Muslim named not Brian or John or Shawn, but Salman. We were one big circle of light brought together by music, sports, and shared experiences. None of us cared about the made-up divides of color, culture, or religion. A month before I was to return to Pakistan, five of us had sped down the Palisades

Parkway in Cindy Shaw's father's red and white Oldsmobile, singing at the top of our lungs along with David Lee Roth to "Ain't Talkin' 'Bout Love." In that car, with those friends on my way to my final Van Halen concert, I shot footage for a mental movie of what I thought were the last days of my American life.

There was so much to leave behind. All around me, in 1981 in New York, kids had dyed their hair red or purple and identified themselves as punks after the movement spearheaded by Britain's notorious Johnny Rotten and the Sex Pistols. That year everyone wore dark sunglasses indoors. The musical-film *Fame* dazzled audiences. *Rocky Horror Picture Show* fans were doing the time warp. American hostages were finally brought home after 444 days of captivity in Iran, Pakistan's western neighbor. That spring, President Reagan had been shot in an assassination attempt in Washington. Bruce Springsteen sang about a hungry heart. Girls wore boots in the sun and high, open-toe Candies in the rain.

And then one day in August I was gone, sitting sullenly in the seat of a PIA 747 and jetting with sickening speed away from the New York skyline. I could see the cars zig-zagging on the highways, the tall buildings of Manhattan trying to kiss the sky, and the golden glint of the flame in the hand of the Statue of Liberty. Soon we left New York far behind and climbed higher over the Atlantic Ocean. I was full of resentment, frustration, and anger. But as I fell into dreamland, my journey—from East to West and back again—was really just getting started.

I couldn't pay attention in anatomy class that November day. I kept sneaking desperate glances at the clock to see when the session would end. Meanwhile, I threw knowing looks at my co-conspirator of the day—Munir, known to everyone as "Clint" due to his obsession with *Dirty Harry*. Munir was a quiet, bohemian guy whom I had quickly befriended when I learned that like me, he listened to bootleg tapes of Hendrix, the Beatles, and Zeppelin. He also happened to own the only set of drums I could find anywhere in Lahore—making Munir my only candidate for musical backup that night. "Clint" rolled his eyes as the assistant professor droned on about the heart's inferior and superior vena cavas, sino-atrial valves, and bundle of His. We weren't slackers, but that day we were ready to get as far away from campus as we could.

In fact, we couldn't get very far. In the Pakistan of the day, there wasn't much to do but study. In 1982, democracy was dead and a dictator, General Muhammad Zia-ul-Haq, was running the show. A war was raging in neighboring Afghanistan, and Pakistan, a U.S. ally, was being transformed into a virtual arms bazaar, with Kalashnikovs as common a sight as a squirt gun at a kid's birthday party. To me it seemed as if the body and soul of Pakistan had been snatched by aliens in Pakistani disguise. I still loved Pakistan for all the happy memories I had of growing up with my family and friends, and it was those childhood memories that kept me from losing my mind after I returned. But so much had changed. I couldn't, for example, even think about looking over at any of the handful of girls in class. In General Zia's Pakistan, male and female professors alike would call out and humiliate any amorous young man who took his eyes off the instructor and let them wander toward the pretty young women who sat together in the first couple of rows. The freewheeling country I knew had become dark, suffocated by religious extremism and gender-segregated. It felt like the last place in the world for an aspiring artist.

After three hours of anatomy, and another three agonizing hours of physiology, we were finally dismissed, and I raced back to Anarkali Bazaar to grab my car. It was mid-afternoon and the bazaar was packed. Girls dressed in colorful *shalwar kameez* walked past the merchants, who were hawking everything from cricket bats and balls, paprika, garlic, curries, lentils, and addictive *paan* (betel leaves). The shops displayed sparkling bangles, necklaces, and engagement rings. All of this was juxtaposed with a variety of live animals ready for the slaughter. Roadside fortune-tellers with monkeys and parrots offered to tell you the future for only one rupee, while the sky was alive with kites of all shapes and sizes, flown by young and old from the neighboring rooftops. I breathed in the intoxicating smell of the chicken kebabs from sidewalk vendors.

As I approached my car, I passed Mayo Hospital, where I was confronted by the stark suffering of the poor of Pakistan—as well as the collateral damage from the war raging up north in Afghanistan. Walking by, I saw old men and women from the villages of Pakistan pushed by interns on ramshackle wheelchairs. Afghan refugees with amputated legs and arms shuffled nearby. And then there were the little children suffering from terminal diseases, their eyes haunted and already half-dead. It broke my heart to know that many of these impoverished and unlucky patients would die, despite the best efforts of the doctors on staff.

Back at my grandmother's house, I quickly threw off the medical overalls and changed into black jeans and an AC/DC T-shirt. Around my wrist I wound a string of blue prayer beads favored by adherents of Sufism, the mystical branch of Islam. I dabbed some black paint under my eyes and put on my favorite necklace with a gold "Allah" pendant. I felt like a New Yorker all over again—except there was no mistaking that I was back in Lahore. I played "Eruption" in front of the mirror before I left, just for one last practice run.

While in America I'd lived the life of a suburban teenager—a life that I couldn't have imagined as a young kid in Lahore. I had arrived as a confused *desi* (South Asian) with my family in Rockland County, New York, in 1975. From 1975 to 1981 I had gradually transformed from an awkward, ill-at-ease Pakistani immigrant boy into a high school senior with a dream: I wanted to be a rock star. I would only whisper that to myself, afraid of saying it too loud in case someone overheard and burst my bubble. The rock and roll environment that had nurtured my starriest hope was now gone. But tonight was a chance, however small, to get some of that groove back.

As I stepped out of my small room, I saw my grandmother Aziza. She was a remarkable woman, full of love and life. She was one of the few women of her generation to be educated at the famed Aligarh University in India, and was always ahead of her time. Even though Pakistan had fallen under a cloud of military dictatorship and religious fanaticism, she retained her progressive values and vision. And like me, she loved music, TV, and movies. Seeing me dressed up in my makeshift rocker garb, the guitar on my shoulder, she smiled approvingly. I asked her to pray for me, to pray that tonight's performance would go well. She smiled and promised to do so. But as I walked away, she said something that I didn't fully grasp at that moment.

"Remember that everything which happens is a sign from God," she said. "We are all His instruments." She kissed me and said "*Khuda Hafiz*"—"May God's protection be with you." I didn't think much about her words at that moment, but they would take on profound meaning in a few short hours.

I threw my Les Paul in the back seat of the Mazda, along with my MXR distortion box and Crybaby wahwah pedal. In the Pakistan of the 1980s, where Western rock and pop music was considered as sinful, this guitar gear was as foreign as a *Star Trek* communicator from the future. I managed to emerge from the Lahore traffic in one piece and arrived at the site of our little talent show—The International Hotel. That regal-sounding place was actually pretty down at the heels, but I didn't mind. We had rented out a small ballroom for the show, and for a bunch of broke college kids it might as well have been New York's famed rock club CBGB.

At 6 p.m., the students started pouring in. About sixty kids from the freshman class showed up. We were excited about the turnout. If things went well, my friends on the organizing committee—mostly fellow "Overseas Pakistanis"—planned to do three more shows that year.

The night's performances began after a student named Timoo recited a verse from the Holy Quran in a beautiful voice. In the verse, God tells mankind that He created us as men and women from different nations and tribes so that we could get to know each other. It was a message that meant a lot to the students, who came from all over the world—the United States, England, Saudi Arabia, and Afghanistan—as well as a variety of cities and villages all over Pakistan.

Maybe Pakistan wasn't so bad, I thought as I watched the acts. A guy in glasses named Ali read Urdu poetry by the famous poet Faiz Ahmed Faiz, including a piece called "Speak." A series of Punjabi comedians had us in stitches, although they watered down some of their bawdy jokes out of respect for the girls in the room. Others performed skits mocking the stern professors and their idiosyncrasies. Then there was a juggling act and then it was my turn.

Fifteen months before that evening, I'd sat, rapt, inside the Nassau Coliseum in Uniondale, New York, watching my atomic punk hero Eddie Van Halen open his band's concert with a powerful performance of "On Fire." Eddie seemed to be playing just for me as he ran all over that Long Island stage, shirtless in Converse sneakers and white cargo pants and grinning like an impish captain of a guitar Olympics team. He never lost a beat even as he skidded on his knees, wrenching the notes out of his red-and-white striped guitar as he finger-tapped the finale to "Eruption." Thousands of breathless teenagers including me pumped their fists, stomped their feet, and paid loud homage to this axe legend. Looking at Eddie on that stage, I didn't just see him. I saw who I wanted to be.

And so in that Lahore hotel that November night, I summoned up the spirit of Eddie Van Halen and ripped into "Eruption." With Clint backing me up and the amp turned up to 11, I vented every ounce of pent-up frustration I had through my Les Paul and stunned the crowd with this blaze of heavy metal riffs. They'd never heard anything like it before. I closed my eyes and let my fingers do a dance of bliss on my instrument. All of a sudden, I heard cries and screams. Gratified by the response, I felt vindicated and energized, and I knew I was getting somewhere. I was, I hoped, on my way to being a rock star after all.

But when I opened my eyes, I realized that the cries were not of excitement coming from my audience of classmates. They were screams of rage. And they were coming from the angry mob of students—in Urdu, *taliban*—belonging to the college wing of religous parties who had broken into the hotel ballroom. They were outraged at what they protested was a den of sin.

"*Fahashi! Harami!*" they cried. Vulgarity! Bastard!

Somehow these bearded youths had learned about our little talent show. I stared, totally stunned, as these fanatics rushed inside, throwing burqas and chadors on the women and pushing them away from the men they had had the audacity to sit next to in the audience.

And then one of these youths, his eyes filled with a madness that has nothing to do with God, jumped onto the tiny stage. He tore out the amplifier, and then kicked over poor Munir's dusty old drum set.

A mighty anger welled up inside me and I found my voice. "What the hell is your problem?!" I yelled at the guy.

He looked at me and my guitar with contempt.

"Give that to me," he barked.

I stood frozen, unable to process what was happening.

He tore the Les Paul from my hands, and with a fury unlike any I had ever seen, proceeded to bash it on the green marble floor, wrecking it beyond repair.

I could not believe what I was seeing. Shocking as this act of wanton violence was, my first thought was that if anybody was going to smash my guitar it should've been me. Not these show-stealing thugs!

That guitar was my only link to a world I had loved and lost. I had bought it for $235 at Sam Ash Music in Paramus, New Jersey, in 1978, having diligently saved money from months of delivering newspapers and busing tables at Blauvelt Coach Diner on Route 303 in New York. It was the guitar that I had learned to play by jamming with Brian and Paul in Eclipse. It was an instrument of peace that had seen me through good times and bad.

I stood there, numb, watching the events that followed with a strange detachment. The music police threatened the medical students, warning them that the next time they tried to organize such an indecent display, the guns would come out and deadly tribal justice would be meted out in the defense of Islam.

I was a long, long way from suburban New York. Looking at my mangled guitar, I realized that I was now caught squarely in the middle of a cultural conflict the likes of which I'd never experienced.

I made a decision on the spot that November day. I silently vowed to fight the forces that could tear apart someone's dream with such casual cruelty. General Zia and his extremist sidekicks had distorted my beloved religion of Islam and were slowly asphyxiating Pakistani culture. Their target was music, poetry, and dance. They wanted to crush our spirits and destroy the creativity that I believe links mortals to God. I knew that Pakistan had a long, rich history, with ancient civilizations and the most beautiful love poetry and music. So nobody was going to tell me that there wasn't a place for rock and roll here.

Over the next several years, as I stayed in Pakistan and stuck with my musical *junoon* (my obsessive passion), the country would be ruled by a succession of leaders, some of whom were friendly to artists like me and some who weren't. Inspired by the incident at our talent show, in a few years' time, I began to wage a rock and roll jihad, or struggle, and began forming clandestine rock bands. They soon won fans among the youth of Pakistan, and a counterculture movement grew. The music eventually emerged from the shadows to confront the power of the mullahs in the streets. The angry, bearded young man's action had backfired. He inspired me to take my love of classic rock and the blues and mix it with the mystical music and poetry of Sufism, creating a new kind of "Sufi rock." He had his vision of Pakistan—no, of life—and I had mine. It was a vision that actually wasn't far from the spirit of harmony and happiness that I'd experienced back in New York with my high school friends. It is a cosmic oneness that sees no cultural boundaries.

Over the next two decades, I would be part of two of Pakistan and South Asia's most successful groups: Vital Signs, which I joined, and Junoon, which I founded. My music would be banned by hostile and repressive governments. I'd play in front of hundreds of thousands of fans in packed sports stadiums, concert halls, and colleges in South Asia, the Middle East, China, Japan, and the West. I would perform at the famed Royal Albert Hall in London and, one day, at the United Nations General Assembly hall in New York. In 2008, the kid who used to stand in front of the bedroom mirror jamming to Led Zeppelin would defy death threats from militants and play the first-ever rock concert in the war-torn state of Kashmir. I would also become the first Pakistani artist to perform at a Nobel Peace Prize ceremony, in December of 2007.

Picking up my bent, broken guitar that day in the auditorium, I was seething with anger. But amid the din of the departing students' voices, I heard a beckoning sound.

"Do you know what the music is saying?" asked the Sufi poet Rumi in the thirteenth century. "Come follow me and you will find the way."

TWO
Growing Up

One of my earliest memories is the sight of a man sitting cross-legged and barefoot at a wedding, singing about the oneness of God.

The man is a *qawwali* singer, and his voice is raspy and strong. He's wearing a black *sherwani* over white *shalwar kameez*. His leathery face and his mouth (filled with red betel leaf) contort with every note. Guests are dancing wildly and some are head-banging. I'm sitting in a corner, watching with an emotion I don't yet know how to describe. But I know that the song he's singing is traveling through my ears straight to my young heart.

Eighteen years before the bearded student broke my Les Paul, I was born in Lahore, an ancient city with a rich history of poetry, music, and culture. *Qawwali*, a popular form of South Asian Sufi music, was ever-present. So were the romantic films of the 1960s, my mother's paintings, and the azan, the sonorous Muslim call to prayer, echoing from a hundred mosques across the city five times a day.

Just after midnight on December 12, 1963, a Sufi holy man who was a friend of my paternal grandfather's whispered the words "Allahu akbar"—"God is great"—into my tender ears. I had been delivered by our family doctor just moments earlier at my mother's grandparents' home at 54 Lawrence Road because my mother, Shahine, couldn't stand the sight of hospitals. A cast of close family members was all around me. Abu (my father Ejaz), Aba (my mother's father), Ami Aziza (my mother's mother), Dada (my father's father), Dadi (my father's mother), and my mother's grandparents all had gathered at the simple, white colonial-style home opposite Jinnah's Garden. Earlier that cold night, they'd all assisted with towels, warm water, or prayers. The smell of homemade *zarda*, a sweet saffron rice reserved for special occasions, permeated the air.

There was also hope in the atmosphere that midnight hour, said the holy man, or pir, known as Sufi Sahib. He proclaimed to all who were present that my status as the first male grandchild on either side of the family would give me and my relatives *khush kismet*—good destiny.

The pir was right. The same day I was born, my father's childhood wish to fly and see the world was fulfilled. His acceptance letter from Pakistan International Airlines had arrived informing him that he'd been appointed passenger sales manager in PIA's Lahore office. To celebrate my birth and his new job, my father went out and bought a red Morris Minor—our family's first car. My maternal grandparents were similarly thrilled and distributed *burfis* and *ladoos* (traditional sweetmeats) and wrote letters to friends and family to announce the arrival of their grandson.

I was born 100 percent Pakistani and 100 percent Muslim, but I'm also the product of an ethnically mixed marriage. My mother, Shahine, is an Urdu-speaking Pashtun, while my father, Ejaz, grew up speaking Punjabi. There are also other important differences between them. Shahine is a *mohajir* (immigrant) whose more-liberal family fled west to Lahore from the Indian city of Patiala in 1947 during the violent partition of British India, from which Pakistan was born. They lost most of their possessions in the process. My father was born into a conservative and well-established family in Lahore in 1937. Abu, as I call my father, was the second-youngest child out of a family of four brothers and two sisters. My mother was only four years old when her family arrived in Lahore. She was the second of six children, three girls and three boys, born to my grandparents Habib Khan and Aziza Khanum. The name my grandparents chose for my mother means "falcon," and was inspired by a famous verse written by Allama Muhammad Iqbal—the poet and philosopher whose dream of a separate homeland for the Indian subcontinent's Muslims inspired the creation of Pakistan.

Having a mother whose name was taken from a poem was a good start for a future artist. And indeed, I got a lot of spirit from my mother's side of the family. Pashtuns are fiercely proud, self-confident, and family-loving people not easily blinded or fazed by money and fame. My mother had a passion for painting and music and her hands were often trying to paint a beautiful picture with a brush or coax a melody out of her sitar. Unlike her sisters Birjees and Nosheen, she had very little interest in dressing up, playing with dolls, makeup, or any other such "girlie" activities. As a teenager she took lessons in Kathak, the storytelling dance of India, and grew up in a household where discussion of Islam and politics was encouraged by her parents. One day, I'd use the very Iqbal poem that inspired her name in a Junoon song called "Khudi."

But the lively arts were nothing to aspire to in my father's family.

"Performing and jumping is only for street urchins," my paternal grandfather, K. B. Rashid Ahmad, would tell my father on occasion. "Only reading and writing will make you truly noble." That kind of attitude would frustrate my music- and cricket-loving, people-friendly father, who nonetheless looked up to his own father as a sort of mythical hero. And he was in fact an inspirational figure. My grandfather grew up in British India with little family wealth and rose to become secretary and advisor to the governor of Punjab. In his thirty-five-year service in the Punjab government, Rashid Ahmad served twelve governors—British and Pakistani—and oversaw the wrenching transition between British colonial rule and Pakistani self-governance. He was given the title "Khan Bahadur," roughly equivalent to "brave sir." Where my mother's family may have heard Sufi-inspired music, as Shahine learned her Kathak, my father's family often listened to British Indian army marching bands. Victorian anthems were the background music of my dad's childhood growing up in Dada and Dadi's annex next door to the Punjab governor's residence on Mall Road. And in pre-partition days, those anthems were performed at the governor's summer retreat, where Abu's family spent time in the cool Indian hills of Simla. Another sound in my grandfather's official residence was my grandmother reciting the Quran. She and my father's sisters wouldn't leave the house without wearing a burqa, in sharp contrast to the women in my mother's family, who worked, studied abroad, and didn't feel that their faith required them to cover their heads. My folks' families were mirror opposites in most respects, but it didn't stop my parents from falling in love after meeting through Abu's older sister. They married in January 1963.

If my life were a film the early songs on the soundtrack would be patriotic anthems, not Led Zeppelin. That's because my parents and I lived in Dada and Dadi's annex until January 1965. It was a fairytale home, complete with ducks and swans in the pond and tall wrought-iron gates designed by the British to keep unwanted locals out. Past the gates lay a circular gravel driveway lined with big red clay flower pots and huge green lawns dotted with trees bursting with oranges, guavas, apples, mangoes, and pomegranates. An army of servants looked after the estate round the clock. There were *chowkidars* (guards), gardeners, cooks, and turbaned waiters with starched white uniforms, who served tea, fruit juices, and snacks to the VIP guests and visitors who came from all over. During official banquets in the colonial era, a bandmaster and his orchestra playing European classical music accompanied the ballroom dancing of the Brits and their guests. By the time I was a child, the musicians were playing one of the world's newest national anthems, and Pakistani folk tunes. Looking out past those gates as a little boy, I could see the city that the British had loved so much and hated to leave. It was a city I would come to love as well.

Lahore raised me as much as my family did. Pakistan was a teenager when I was born, struggling to come to terms with its newfound freedom. But the ancient city of my birth has a four-thousand-year history that's been decorated and sculpted by the mists of time. It's multicultural, boisterous, and steeped in a natural poetic sensibility, much like Junoon's music aims to be. Lahoris say (in Punjabi) that anyone who hasn't seen Lahore hasn't started living. Though it's located in what is today a Muslim nation, Lahore actually began with a Hindu god. According to legend, the city was named after Loh, the son of Lord Rama, who is the eponymous hero of the classic Indian literary epic, the "Ramayana." Lahore has also seen invaders like Alexander the Great and passing holy men, including Islamic Sufis, Hindu *rishis*, and *fakirs* from all religions. The Muslim Mughal emperor Shah Jahan, the builder of the Taj Mahal, was born in the city. Lahore was briefly the capital of India during the reign of the great Emperor Akbar, Shah Jahan's grandfather. Sikh maharajahs and British colonialists have gone and come, along with writers like Rudyard Kipling and an untold army of poets and musicians. Lahore has witnessed countless stories of unrequited love, the most famous perhaps being the doomed affair between the beautiful courtesan Anarkali and Prince Salim, Shah Jahan's father. Lahoris have a long tradition of celebrating the heroic souls who sacrifice the world for their love and passion. Like the invaders, *badshahs* (kings), saints, sinners, and empire builders before me, I grew to love the indomitable spirit of Lahore. As a child I breathed in the air and sensed the city's carefree charm and old world grace. Later, I also felt a restless responsibility for its people to be celebrated by the world and recognized as second to none in poetry, music, sports, food, hospitality, and romance.

The Lahore I was born into owed its cultural richness to the times of Akbar, the great Muslim Mughal emperor. Akbar's reign (1556–1605) over the Indian subcontinent was a golden period of cultural pluralism, tolerance, and music, including *qawwali*, the devotional music of Sufism.

Sufism is one of the great influences in my life. Most basically, Sufism is about seeking truth and knowledge. It focuses one's attention on knowing God through knowing oneself. Using music, poetry, dance, and meditation, Sufis tune out the interference of the ego and merge with the divine. Sufis believe that in order to love God you have to love His people as well. The Sufi poet Bulleh Shah said:

> You can destroy the mosque, tear down the temple, break all that can be broken. But never break anyone's heart, because that's where God lives.

Sufis oppose violence and war and promote love, devotion, and social service. Many Sufi singers, poets, and scholars are women. Akbar himself was an ardent devotee of Sufism, and the activities in his time demonstrate that he practiced the tolerance that the Sufis preach. Hindus and Muslims in Akbar's court engaged in intensive dialogues and collaborations. They generated poetry, music, and dance that drew freely from the cultural traditions of all of the kingdom's people. The emperor got carried away near the end of his reign when he tried to start his own religion. But the cultural seeds that Akbar planted in the sixteenth century infuse the hearts of the people of Lahore even now. I owe my wedding memory of the cross-legged *qawwal* to the great ruler.

Lahore in the sixties and seventies was a fascinating mix of the old and new. Mughal-era forts, palaces, mosques, and shrines bumped directly up against British museums, high courts, schools, and universities. In Lahore, whichever direction you walked, you'd see gardens and fountains alongside domed tombs fashioned from sandstone and inlaid marble. On every visit to the ever-bustling Anarkali Bazaar—where my aunts and uncles went in their day to buy the latest 45- and 78-rpm records and Archie comics—I'd be overwhelmed by a rush of girls, boys, women, and men shopping for everything. They'd buy chai, milk, cakes, and more from turbaned, Peshawari-sandal-wearing vendors straddling bicycles. Smells of fresh fruit, tobacco, jasmine, and seekh kebabs hung in the air. And on any given day or night in Lahore, you could hear music, read poetry, watch dance performances, or gaze at art and architecture that was all home-grown and worn like a badge of honor on many a Lahori's sleeve. Pakistan, a young nation, had its cultural capital. I was living in it.

From the day I was born, I was taught to be a proud Pakistani. But the British had only been gone for sixteen years when I came into the world, and despite our independence and traditions, some colonial vestiges remained. One of those was my school, called Aitchison.

Thanks to my Dada's clout, I went to that elite British built public school in Lahore as a boy. It was, and is, a place for sons of Pakistan's wealthy landowning and established families to be groomed to become rulers of a nation of millions of poor rural villagers. But it wasn't just a place to learn math or English. The anglicized Pakistani teachers' aim was to make us students just like them. Having ruled over India for two hundred years, the British (known by the respectful title "sahibs") knew that they needed to recreate the local elite in their own image if they were going to have partners in their colonial venture. So it came to be that people who went to Aitchison and other high-class institutions (anyone, for that matter, who was educated in English) got stuck with the patronizing moniker "brown sahibs."

Neither I nor anyone in my family was going to take kindly to that name, especially after my mother and her relatives had suffered through the Brits' ill-executed Partition. But old attitudes die hard, especially those that had been around for more than a hundred years. Thomas Macaulay, a British member of Parliament in the nineteenth century, was the embodiment of this colonial attitude.

"I propose that we replace [India's] old and ancient education system, her culture," Macaulay said in 1835, "for if the Indians think that all that is foreign and English is good and greater than their own, they will lose their self-esteem, their native self-culture, and they will become what we want them to be: a truly dominated nation."

My mother's father, who escaped with his life from India, first told me about the speech when I was about ten years old. It went like this:

> We must at present do our best to form a class who may be interpreters between us and the millions whom we govern; a class of persons Indian in blood and colors but English in taste, in opinions, in morals, and in intellect.

As a newly minted Aitchisonian, all that sounded familiar to me. (My grandfather, meanwhile, would punctuate the end of the speech with "*Saala Bhootni-ka*!"—"Brother-in-law and son of a vile evil spirit!") The Aitchison idea was to turn us into factory presets of well-dressed, well-mannered, and disciplined Pakistani school boys with fake plastic British souls. I went to Aitchison from age six to eleven. Amid the school's majestic colonial architecture, the stern, black-robed, male and female teachers taught us to adopt a sense of superiority over the masses. We were the elite, they told us, and no weakness in character would be tolerated. It felt like we were in a military school—and with good reason: our British headmaster was Army Major G.D. Langlands. Every summer morning we would assemble in lines, wearing white half-sleeved shirts, khaki shorts, and white socks and black shoes. In the wintertime it was full-sleeved shirts, gray pullovers, blue blazers, gray shorts, matching knee-high socks, and black shoes. On Saturdays we'd also have to wear starched *pugharrs* (turbans) that were blue in the winter and gray in the summer. And if we ever needed a little moral support, all we had to do was look at our school badges, which bore Aitchison's motto: "Perseverance Commands Success."

Decked out in our uniforms, we would stand at attention for the national anthem and then be inspected by our "house prefects." Anyone caught out of line or talking would be made an example of with a caning or the task of doing "*bhetaks*"—exhausting squatting and standing exercises. I was often a usual suspect and had to bend over at least once and take a thrashing on my ass for repeating a bawdy joke I'd heard. It played on the Urdu word for "duck," which is *butukh*.

"A Lahori goes to a *gora*'s [Englishman's] house," I told a little audience of my peers when the prefects weren't looking. "He's looking to pay the lady of the house a compliment, Okay?" I'd continue as the kids looked at me expectantly. By this time the prefects must have noticed something was up and were heading over, but we were oblivious to their footfalls.

" 'Madam,' the Lahori says, your *goray goray* [fair] *butukhs* are very beautiful!"

The word was way too close to "buttocks" for the genteel English lady, and the pun could get a laugh out of any Lahori.

Any Lahori except my teachers. One of them promptly bent me over and whacked my own buttocks for being such an insolent wise-guy.

I got a good education at Aitchison despite the snobbery and took advantage of its excellent sports facilities, including a horseback riding school; beautiful green cricket, soccer and hockey grounds; and Olympic-sized swimming pools. But I constantly felt like a student from Pink Floyd's "Another Brick in the Wall" video, wanting to scream out, "Hey! Teacher! Leave us kids alone!"

By the time I started at Aitchison, I had moved off the governor's grounds to my mother's parents' place at 6 Napier Road, while my parents and younger sister Sania stayed on with my father's parents—a pretty typical Pakistani living arrangement. Once settled in Lahore after Partition, my maternal grandmother had taken up a job as a resident administrator at the girls' hostel at King Edward Medical College. The job provided the family with both an income and a new home, as on-campus living quarters were part of her compensation. My grandparents house was everything Aitchison wasn't: warm, relaxed, and fun. It was also, critically for my development, egalitarian. As an administrator to about five hundred girls from all over Pakistan and other Muslim countries like Iran, Afghanistan, Malaysia, and Indonesia, my grandmother encouraged her future women doctors to show compassion toward the poor of Pakistan. Every quarter, Ami also organized a camping trip for students, family, and support staff and their families to the Swat Valley. In that beautiful part of the country—which was taken over by the Taliban in early 2009—all of us (regardless of class or social status) inhaled the natural air and sat around campfires under moon and starlight. The extremists of the early twenty-first century wanted to take Swat back to the Stone Age by chasing out musicians, closing movie theatres, and destroying schools for girls. But in my boyhood, under my grandmother's supervision, boys and girls sang film songs, performed scenes from movies, and hiked all over the place followed by the curious eyes of monkeys, buffalo, rabbits, and deer. Those road trips were a lot of fun. My grandparents' love totally spoiled me. It also taught me to "share the love."

I feel like I lived a double life in those days, dividing my time between formal Aitchison and my grandparents' cozy home. My stress was compounded by the fact that my parents' marriage wasn't exactly perfect. The tensions between them seeped into my subconscious and on occasion made my behavior unpredictable. One day I'd be a charming people-pleaser and the next I'd be a self-centered bully. My mood swings would often lead to temper tantrums if I didn't get what I wanted. I would hurl things against walls and often bend and break spoons, forks, and plates. I'd rip up school books and fling pens and pencils across the room. An unknown rage would possess me, loosen my tongue, and make me expel the vilest Urdu and Punjabi curses aimed at no one in particular and at the whole world. My periodic outbursts shocked my family. Only my grandmother knew how to soothe me. She would often calm me down with an ice-cold, sugary red drink called *rooh afza*, run her hand over my forehead, and tell me stories of Ali Baba and Aladdin's lamp. Safe within my grandmother's bosom, my personal storms would subside as rapidly as they had come on.

Growing up at 6 Napier Road allowed me to explore life on my own terms. Life at the governor's mansion had been comfortable, but my heart always yearned for the much simpler, closer-knit red-brick home Aba and Ami Aziza kept on Napier Road. There, my grandparents, two teenaged uncles Javed and Junaid, their older sister Nosheen, an old widowed grand aunt, and I all slept in two medium-sized bedrooms with high wooden ceilings and giant fans hanging down low from the roof. During the summers, we would take our charpoys (beds) out in the open front garden next to guava and mango trees and escape the heat. Sometimes I'd lie awake at night listening to the sounds of crickets and the whirring rumble of the pedestal fan. On other nights I'd stare into the sky looking for faces of people or shapes of animals and kites by connecting the stars and slices of the moon.

My grandparents' was a small house, but it had a big impact on anyone who lived there or visited, especially if it was mealtime. Ami Aziza whipped up breakfasts of *aloo parathas* and tomato-and-onion omelets. Every morning, one of us would pour fresh water into a *garha*, a large round jug made of hand-fashioned pottery. Aba would bike over to Gowalmandi market and bring back delicious *halva poori* and *chanay*—a deep-fried chapatti with halva and chick-pea and potato curries. Lunch and dinner would come from the campus kitchen menu and alternate between *matar keema* (green peas and minced meat), *saag gosht* (spinach and spicy mutton), and *daal chawal* (lentils and rice). On some days we'd eat *aloo gosht* (meat and potato curry) and chicken *karahi*, a curry with thin chapattis; *dahi* (yogurt); and *achaar* (mango pickle). Anyone who set foot in the place felt right at home.

Roaming around and exploring the campus on my own, I soon mixed with and became best friends with the children of Ami Aziza's support staff. All these kids and their parents seemed to me like the living and breathing characters of the true Pakistan. Boota the school driver, Siddiq the *darzi* (tailor), Abdullah the *chowkidar*, Ghani the *maali* (gardener), Akhtar the soft drink salesman, and others all had kids my age, and it was from them that I learned to fly kites and play cricket, *pitthu gol garam* (a kind of dodge ball), and *gulli danda* (a *desi* innovation played with two pieces of wood, a stick, and a small cricket bail). They all lived with their families in tiny, one-room homes in the servants' quarters—but their generosity and kindness to me was limitless and I will never forget it. My stiff-upper-lipped teachers at Aitchison told us that playing with servants' children was beneath us. My mother's father instantly recognized that sentiment: as a subject of the Raj, he saw signs on British country clubs declaring "Dogs and Indians not allowed." But my friends from Napier Road were infinitely more real, as well as funnier and wittier than my supposedly superior peers at school. What's more, they looked at me as one of their own and didn't play any head games. They just asked to be treated like equals, with respect and dignity. I knew they'd put their lives on the line for that kind of friendship, and I learned more from them than any book I had to crack at Aitchison.

I didn't identify myself as a brown sahib but I still had a comparatively privileged upbringing in Pakistan. Seeing the poverty all around me got under my skin and burrowed into my conscience, leading me to take myself on punishing guilt trips even as a small boy. I knew I couldn't help or befriend everybody. But one Eid ul-Fitr, Allah showed me a sign in the form of one particular boy.

I was about eight years old and all my relatives had gathered for Eid, a day of thanksgiving after fasting for thirty days during the month of Ramadan. Custom has it that all children and teenagers are given *eidees*, or gifts of cash for the Islamic holiday. As the first grandson I received the unusually high amount of 100 rupees from my Dada's family. Playing cricket later that day on the medical college campus, I saw a boy about my age standing outside the front gate looking pitifully sad. He was shoeless, wore tattered and torn clothes, and had a mop of dirty hair. That sight is one of the childhood memories I carry with me even today. I went up to him and asked why he wasn't playing with his own friends and family on Eid.

"*Mein akela hoon, mera koi nahin,*" replied the boy, who said his name was Yameen. "I'm alone, I don't have anyone."

I didn't think twice. I took out the 100 rupee note and said "*mein jo hoon*" ("I'm there for you") and gave him the money. The smile on his face lit up the world and I felt thankful for the opportunity God had given me to help someone in need. I asked my grandmother if the boy could join us, and she just beamed and said of course. His joy was compounded when my grandmother took Yameen in and allowed him to stay on our campus and made sure that he went to school. Yameen grew up on that campus and years later got a job in Mayo Hospital.

On that holy day, which is about sharing and sacrifice and giving thanks for God's blessings, Allah made me realize something important. If I could help one kid to smile, I wanted to help others. Pakistan was a place of stark contrasts. The desperately poor lived side by side with the frightfully rich. But despite the disparity, even children who had nothing would gleefully run after kites, play cricket, and sing songs. They were no different from boys like me and they should have been in school, too. But because of fate and a colonial hangover, they were shunned by the elite, like untouchables. I soon figured out that if being "elite" meant keeping the poor down, I wanted no part of it. It was my grandmother, Aziza, who reinforced that feeling in me and all her children.

Every time Eid comes around, I remember Yameen's wide-toothed grin.

Pakistan saw its share of hardship in the years that I grew up. But it was also a time of joy and discovery for me. In the early seventies, Indian Amritsar television started broadcasting Bollywood films. Amritsar is just across the border from Lahore, so we could easily pick up the signal. But the only TV on campus was at our home, so each weekend night our small house would turn into a mini movie theatre, chock-a-block with girl students, relatives, and the families and children of the campus workers. Close to sixty or seventy people jammed into Ami Aziza's little place, claiming any spot they could on the floor or on laps. Huddled in with the rest of the neighborhood, sitting transfixed before the black and white Philips TV, my interest in Bollywood film music was first piqued. I had childhood crushes on Indian actresses like Sharmila Tagore, Mumtaz, and the seductive and risqué dancer/actress Helen. I gobbled up all the hit songs of the early seventies and filed them away in my memory bank.

There was also a very robust, if nascent, Pakistani TV and film industry at the time. One of the first Pakistani movie superstars was Waheed Murad. The campus girls would lose their minds at the mere mention of his name, and so would my Aunt Nosheen. Once, my mother's younger sister and her campus girl friends found out that the movie star was staying at the five-star Intercontinental Hotel in Lahore. He was in the city for the premiere of his blockbuster hit *Armaan*. I might have been about four years old at the time, but I remember meeting the actor because my aunt used me as her backstage pass. The security around the hotel was beefed up, so Aunt Nosheen came up with a plan. She and her friends whisked me off to the hotel and pleaded with a guard to be allowed to see the movie star for my sake.

"My nephew has to get Waheed Murad's autograph!" Aunt Nosheen told the guard. "Or he'll throw tantrums all night long!"

The sympathetic guard called the actor in his suite and convinced him to allow us in for a few minutes. Waheed Murad turned out to be a real gentleman, signing autographs, and offering his female admirers and young, star-struck me free tickets to his premiere the next evening. I was thrilled beyond words. The following night, at Lahore's Al-Falah cinema, I saw a man playing the guitar on the big screen for the first time in my life, performing a hit song called "Ko Ko Korina." The song's energy lifted me up out of my seat. The sight of the prancing Murad and his accompanying guitarist stuck in my head to the exclusion of everything else in that movie. It was the first signpost on the way to discovering my passion.

Waheed Murad was an Elvis-like presence in the Pakistan of those culturally rich times. But Pakistan would change, and Murad would come to resemble Elvis in more ways than one. The movie business took a nose dive under the military dictatorship of General Zia, and Murad died in his forties after losing a battle with depression and an overdose of sleeping pills.

The Zia era was the one that I would return to when I came back to Pakistan in 1981 from America. But if someone had told me as a kid in the late sixties and early seventies that a dictator would come along and squelch Lahore's musical kaleidoscope, I would have thought he was insane. Music was all around me, from the popular romantic songs of Urdu and Punjabi films to rollicking folk music to *bhangra*. It wafted into my ears every time my uncle Jadi rode around our neighborhood on his motorbike: his homemade horn played "Flight of the Bumblebee." Jadi *mamun* also had 45-rpm records of instrumentals like "Wipe Out," and a favorite tune, The Ventures' "Walk, Don't Run," always seemed to be playing at 6 Napier Road. Music was in the air and in front of my eyes. On a wall at our house, next to a print of the *Mona Lisa*, hung a painting my mother had done of an attractive flamenco dancer flanked by a long-haired, goateed troubadour. He was strumming an acoustic guitar with a cigarette jutting out of one corner of his mouth. It was another signpost. My passion was trying to find me.

But the genre that seized hold of me hardest and wouldn't let go was *qawwali*. "*Qawl*" literally means "to utter or to say," and *qawwali* singers typically have earthy and agile, rock-singer-like voices. Using mind-boggling vocal acrobatics, *qawwals* jam and riff on a repeating refrain and tease out deep emotions and the spirit of the musical moment. Harmonium- and *tabla*-carrying *qawwals* were often invited to our family weddings, to bless the union by singing Urdu and Persian poetry of Sufi saints like Amir Khusro and Rumi. They sat divided into a front row of lead singers and harmonium players and a back row of powerful percussive hand-clappers, chanting support vocalists, and *tabla* players. The dozen or so musicians, singers, and percussionists would comprise the *qawwali* band, which is called a party. I'd gaze at the *paan*-chewing, *topi*-wearing musicians from my seat with a feeling of awe.

The overwhelming emotion of *qawwali* is like the yearning intensity of gospel and blues. The aim of the *qawwal* is to create musical vibrations leading to a crescendo of ecstasy called *wajd*. Just like in a rock concert, the goal is to destroy the wall between audience and performer. I would watch intensely as my relatives and their guests, men and women, would lose themselves in the repetitious refrains of the *qawwals* and begin *jhoomna*, or swaying side to side. They would throw colorful 10-, 20-, 50-, or 100-rupee notes at the *qawwals* in appreciation of their music and poetry. Some guests would even step into a state of *fana*, a joyful, spiritual, and musical union with God. At those family wedding *qawwali* performances, I saw an enduring feature of my cultural heritage that has survived wars, religious fanaticism, colonial rule, and even Partition. I would develop a greater appreciation and understanding of *qawwali* later in my life. At the time, though, as an unself-conscious kid with a sense of wonder about the world, all I knew was that it moved my soul to hear it.

Music touched a special nerve in me from an early age. But in many ways I was just like a lot of other young Pakistani boys. I was completely mad about motorbikes, kite-flying, and cricket. Especially cricket. In addition to my parents and grandparents, I grew up with my uncles following the game. We knew the batting and bowling averages of all the Pakistani cricketers by heart and played our own games every day in the large front yard at the hostel. We'd also tune into the BBC and listen as radio commentators like John Arlott, Fred Trueman, Trevor Bailey, and Brian Johnston described the action at games. I would memorize and imitate John Arlott's rich Hampshire baritone or Fred Trueman's thick Yorkshire accent.

"In comes Willis," I'd mimic, "bowls to Zaheer . . . outside the off stump . . . and Zaheer square cuts magnificently! My word, that ball is traveling like a tracer bullet to the cover boundary. Glorious shot! Four runs to Zaheer and four runs to Pakistan!" For some reason it became my morning ritual to play cricket commentator while sitting on the commode. Resting comfortably with my shorts around my ankles, I'd get so into my imaginary game that my grandmother would have to bang on the door and tell me to hurry up or I'd miss school.

My summers and winters were spent listening to the radio cricket commentaries and playing school cricket at Aitchison. The more competitive cricket, though, was actually at home at 6 Napier Road with the kids of the campus employees. One of my favorite players growing up was the young and talented Imran Khan, who in 1992 led Pakistan to its first-ever World Cup victory against England. Long before then, cricket infused a just-born nation with passionate nationalism. Our chests would puff out with pride any time Pakistan beat England, Australia, India, or the much-feared calypso cricketers from the West Indies. Many years later I played first class (major league) cricket for Lahore and had to make a difficult choice between a career in medicine, cricket, or music. Fortunately for me, music enveloped all my passions and in time I found a way to work my love of the game, as well as my social activism, into my lyrics and melodies.

Being a Pakistani kid also meant flying kites, and taking part in the kite festival known as *Basant*. The year I turned eleven, I spent Basant atop a neighborhood roof with three beautiful Iranian medical students from the college, teaching them how to fly a kite. It was an innocent moment, but some men on top of neighboring roofs ruined it by making rude and obnoxious gestures at the girls. The Farsi-speaking Nargis Deliri, Lily, and Mehwish were reveling in the festival, which was a totally foreign concept to their Persian eyes. Miffed by the loutish display, the confident Nargis took me downstairs and called the Iranian students' association for reinforcements. In a matter of minutes, a bus full of male Iranian medical students arrived to avenge the slight to their sisters. These angry students ran right up to the Punjabi kite flyers who were trying to get fresh with the girls and a fracas ensued, including the use of two terms I'd never heard uttered as though they were curse words.

"Sunni!"

"Shia!"

Guys from other rooftops soon joined in and it turned into a typical gouge-your-eyes-out, fist-banging brawl. I ran to get Ami Aziza, figuring that the matronly "Apaji" (as the students called her) would command some respect. My grandmother soon arrived with campus security and calmed everybody down, ordering the warring parties to back off from each other in her firm voice. She also got the men to apologize to the three girls and made the Pakistani and Iranian boys shake hands with each other despite having bloodied one another's noses and blackened each other's eyes. In hindsight, the dust-up was almost quaint: in campus fights during the hyper-militarized 1980s, everybody had a gun of some kind and you'd have to collect dead bodies instead of clean up broken noses.

Later that day I asked my grandmother what the words "Sunni" and "Shia" meant. Ami Aziza put her arms around me and said, "That's just some people's stupid way of making themselves seem higher in status than others."

"What am I, Ami?" I asked.

"A Muslim," she replied. "We're all Muslims. The Prophet Muhammad was neither a Sunni nor a Shia. How could we be any different?"

THREE
Wandering Spirits

Before I took my music around the world, music took me on a journey.

From the time I was a little boy, I had the privilege of seeing diverse cultures and people up close and in person, thanks to my dad's airline industry job and its provision of free air travel for the family. I loved seeing the sights—in China, Kuwait, London, New York, and Denmark, to name a few places—but it was the music that had the most powerful impact on me everywhere I went.

My family's travels helped make a global soul out of a Lahori boy. But even as our family's world turned, I found a still center in sounds. In cities or countries as diverse as fashion-conscious Paris, freedom-loving New York, self-absorbed Washington, D.C., and faith-centric Pakistan, music filled my senses with a multicultural symphony conducted from beyond the known universe. I heard bohemian buskers singing folk and pop melodies, strumming guitars, sawing their fiddles, and blowing on saxophones, trumpets, and flutes. Standing for a few moments in the corners of the arched walkways of the London underground, I'd see struggling musicians lost in their own worlds and enveloped in private passions.

In addition to sightseeing I spent a lot of time traveling to see family. I lived for several years with my grandparents while my parents were abroad for my dad's job. Departing for the old Lahore airport from 6 Napier Road was a ritual that resembled Eid in its obligatory drawing of family together. My grandparents, uncles, aunts, and cousins would all put on their finest clothes and take me out for a meal, then shuttle me to the airport to make my connection for whatever destination was printed on my green PIA ticket. I walked down the tarmac alone but carried with me a zippered bag filled with cricket magazines, homework, and Enid Blyton books. Turning back, I'd see my family entourage waving frantically from behind the visitors' fence.

"*Beta, Khuda hafiz*, we'll miss you!" my grandparents would yell.

"Say hello to Ejaz and Shahine and Shehryar and Sania!"

I'd turn around one last time at the top of the flight stairs and see my grandmother wave before she'd start to bawl. On board, I'd get an adrenaline rush when the PIA airhostess announced in English and Urdu that the flight was ready to take off. "Please fasten your seatbelts and extinguish all cigarettes," a smooth voice said over the P.A. I was on a boyhood adventure, alone among adults. I looked out at the sky decorated with the stars, moon, or sun as the giant bird took me higher and higher above land and water.

Travel was always great fun for its own sake. But for Muslims, going on long journeys has a greater significance.

"In order to seek knowledge, travel to China, if necessary," the Prophet Muhammad said in the seventh century. The prophet was acutely aware of the need for all Muslims to enlighten themselves with both religious and secular education, and held up China's Tang dynasty as the seat of worldly learning.

My mother reminded me of those words in 1974, when she and I were walking step by careful step across the Great Wall of China. Earlier that day, with my mother and younger sister Sania, I'd seen a sea of Chinese men and women identically dressed in Mao suits pedaling to work on bicycles. We visited the ancient Ming tombs and watched a Chinese dragon dance, following along as the great beast blinked its eyes and shimmied in a circle. I loved the taste of the local fizzy orange drink and learning from neighborhood kids how to say "thank you, friend" *(xie xie pengyou)* and count from one to ten (*yi, er, san, si, wu, liu, qi, ba, jiu, shi*) in Mandarin. I'd keep repeating the numbers all day long like a mantra, as if I were channeling Dustin Hoffman in *Rain Man*, and drive my mother nuts.

In another mental snapshot I'm age six in Trafalgar Square with my mom, who is wearing a sari, her hair tied up in a bun. I'm sitting on top of one of the four bronze lions feeding the pigeons, and then, at Madame Tussauds, staring in awe at lifelike wax statues of King Henry the VIII and a composer, wearing a wig, called Beethoven. There were also four guys there with shaggy hair in suits, who would deeply influence me later in life: the Beatles. Soon after I was climbing up the Eiffel Tower with Sania and then recognizing a smiling woman at the Louvre, whose picture was framed at my grandmother's in Lahore. I learned that her name was Mona Lisa and that she was painted by a guy called Leonardo da Vinci. In Cairo, I saw the pyramids, where my mother told me the pharaohs were buried. I knew Egypt in spirit from the Quranic stories of the prophet Moses, whose staff could transform into a serpent and also part the waters. Even earlier, at age five, I sat on the steps in front of a giant sculpture of an American president called Abraham Lincoln, who was against slavery and had given his life to keep America united. In place after place, I saw and heard the diversity of God's creation and the artistic gifts He gives us.

Travel always gave me a feeling of exhilaration. I felt special and also overwhelmed. Special, because few boys my age had a chance to see our beautiful, wonderful world firsthand. And overwhelmed because, in my own eyes, I seemed totally insignificant compared to the vastness of the earth and the sky. Rumi put this feeling best. "O furious wind," wrote the poet, "I am only a straw before you; how could I know where I will be blown next?"

On all my wanderings, I'd stop and listen to musicians play whenever I could. The sight of their intense, ecstatic, and joyfully scrunched-up faces, seemingly in communion with an invisible force, would always stir something in me. Walking with Ami, I'd turn back and cast a longing glance at these troubadours, as if trying to recall a distant time in which, somehow, I might have known them.

These journeys offered up to me an infinite reservoir of sound sources. The ethereal though familiar sound of the *azan* was recited by muezzins in mosques from Pakistan to Jordan to Egypt to Kuwait. Hearing the lilting call of the five-times-daily *azan* struck a powerful, stirring chord no matter where I experienced it. Set to the *hijaz maqam* scale and echoing from loudspeakers, the prayer call washed over my young heart like an ocean wave soaking the sands and rocks of a parched shoreline. Music in the movies, music on the radio, music on the street all caressed my unsuspecting ears. The sitar, *tablas*, *dholak*, and harmonium grooved effortlessly inside my head with the Arabian *oud*, *daf*, and *doumbek*. They jammed alongside the guitar, bass, and drums of pop and rock music in a lush bouquet of vivid sound colors. I always felt it wasn't any accident why I was hypnotized by the vibrations of the 12/6 stringed guitar and the sympathetic ringing of the sitar. I was making up my own understanding of string theory. To my ears, we were all connected through music. These sounds were like seeds finding fertile ground in my young imagination.

The music had its deepest impact on me when I was going through emotional highs or lows. Vocals and sounds would harmonize my moods whether I was joyful, melancholic, angry, or ecstatic. I found tunes reverberating in my head and heart even during my sleep. The music was sparking creative impulses which were to mature much later, but I found myself getting addicted to *taala* (rhythm) and *raga* (melody) even at a very young age.

I loved traveling, but being elsewhere didn't make the tension between my parents—or its strain on me—any better. Even on some of these family trips, I wanted to escape back into my own world at 6 Napier Road in Lahore, with my grandparents.

Part of the reason I lived with Aba and Ami from 1970 to the middle of 1975 was that I'd turned into a *desi* Dennis the Menace and my parents decided I needed some discipline. When our family was living near McLean Gardens off Wisconsin Avenue in Washington, D.C., from 1968 to 1969, I ran away from home during one of my parents' arguments. I was five years old. My terrified mother eventually found me on a swing in a nearby park at dusk. It was the era of the Vietnam War. Sitting there on the swing, I saw other kids in the park dressed like soldiers, carrying toy machine guns and wearing green helmets, running around shooting imaginary communist enemies. But there was love in addition to war. I saw a young man and a woman locked in each other's arms, kissing each other with an open display of passion that was unthinkable in conservative Pakistan. I wasn't in Pakistan, though, so I wanted to try it. After we moved to the D.C. suburb of Alexandria, Virginia, I tried imitating the amorous couple with the six-year-old daughter of my father's boss. I gave it my romantic best and planted a slobbering kiss right on her lips, which had the unintended consequence of her reporting my Romeo-like indiscretion to my mortified parents.

From 1972 to 1975, my dad's job took the family to Kuwait, after a yearlong detour to London, where my brother Shehryar was born. I would only visit Kuwait from Lahore on holidays. Religion, food, music, traditional hospitality, and a generous spirit are what's common between Pakistan and Kuwait, but there are many differences as well. Where Lahore was lush and green, Kuwait was arid and sandy. Lahore had buffalo roaming on the streets and rickshaws sputtering on the roads; Kuwait had camels and big American cars. Lahoris had cricket mania; Kuwaitis were soccer obsessed. Lahoris spoke Punjabi and Urdu, while Arabic was the language of all Kuwaitis. *Dastasha*-wearing sheikhs in gas-guzzling American cars drove like Arab Schumachers on the highway, zooming past Bedouins riding on camels in the sand, making their way slowly toward the Arabian Sea. I didn't have what most people would call culture shock, though. By this time, I had vaguely figured out that although we might all look and dress different and speak in weird dialects, people were essentially the same.

During the seventies, a lot of South Asians emigrated to Kuwait to take up lucrative jobs arising from the booming Gulf economy. My dad was now a general manager for Pakistan International Airlines and he, Ami, Sania, and my younger brother, Sherry, lived in a medium-sized apartment in Salmiya, not far from Kuwait City. It wasn't easy re-adjusting to the rhythm of life with my family when I'd visit from Lahore. I had grown accustomed to having Aba and Ami Aziza's gentler nurturing indulgence—the opposite of the discipline I was supposed to be getting. My grandparents allowed me the freedom to discover the nooks and crannies of my personality and of life around me. But in Kuwait, Abu and Ami would make up for lost time and pour on the authority. I was essentially a free spirit and didn't like being told what to do, and my parents saw me as a wild horse that needed to be reined in. They felt, rightly, that my grandparents had spoilt their son and they were determined to discipline me.

That didn't always work well. Aitchison had fostered a strong aversion to authority in me and I continued to defy my parents. But that was just my way of trying to bring attention to my feelings. Rightly or wrongly I felt abandoned by them. But I loved them very much all the same and understood their difficult situation better than I let on. Ami Shahine had grown frustrated with playing the ill-fitting role of the society wife, constantly putting up with the travel and socializing that went along with my dad's job. Every day, she'd have to dress up for luncheons or dinners and entertain Abu's army of clients and his infinite circle of friends and acquaintances. Many of these people would appear unannounced at all hours, putting Ami Shahine through a trying ordeal that she hadn't signed up for.

Part of this twenty-four-hour party just had to do with who my father is. He's a proud Punjabi who, to this day, simply can't say no. In Punjabi parlance he is a *yaron da yaar* (a friend of friends). He extends his hospitality to anyone. But on many occasions, it went too far. Childhood friends and their wives would arrive suddenly and take my dad's car for days, borrow money, or live as guests in our house for weeks on end. A lot of Pakistanis treat their friends like family; it's just the natural and accepted thing to do. But for my mother, it was often difficult to cope with the constant comings and goings of my dad's extended entourage.

As a Pashtun, my mother felt more at home in the private company of her husband, children, and siblings. Abu's formal and conservative upbringing made it difficult to express his natural self at home, but in the company of his friends his personality bloomed like a wild flower. Abu would laugh, tell jokes, sing, and even dance. His *desi* charm and Punjabi wit was so contagious that his friends and colleagues couldn't get enough of him. Had *kismet* smiled and agreed, Abu—not me—would have been the professional entertainer in the family. Instead, fate had blessed him with friends and clients, including famous *desi* movie stars, singers, musicians, and cricketers. His face would light up with a smile whenever he met show business personalities, and he fondly recalled meeting Bob Hope and Danny Kaye at a lunch in New York City. His good looks and humor ensured that he was always the life of the party, but my possessive mother just couldn't stand sharing him with others. Being an introvert at home and an extrovert at social events created a chronic Jekyll-and-Hyde imbalance that meant he wound up spending far too little time with his family.

Not having my mother or father around in Lahore had made me tough and independent-minded, but it had also alienated me as a son. Years later the loneliness and separation anxiety often found expression in my creative work. My wife, Samina, a doctor and child psychologist, thinks that my passion for peace and conflict resolution can be traced back to this part of my childhood.

By the time I started spending summer holidays in Kuwait, I was a full-fledged problem child. I constantly got myself into trouble, including trouble with an Iranian family who lived on the top floor of my parents' apartment building. The Iranians owned a gleaming blue Cutlass Supreme. One hot afternoon, on a whim, I decided to go downstairs and let out all the air from the Oldsmobile's tires. As I was finishing the caper and making a quick getaway, I heard someone screaming from above in Farsi, and it sure didn't sound like love poetry. Our Iranian neighbor was glaring down, his face a beet red. The gist of his *fatwa* from the balcony was: "I am going to report you to the *shurta* (police) and tell your parents to teach you better manners!" Abu came home and gave me an earful and grounded me for a week.

A favorite game to pass the time at home was musical charades, which I'd play with Sania. I would hum a few notes from a Bollywood film song, *qawwali* or *ghazals* (Urdu love poems) and Sania would have to guess what it was. Then she in turn would do the same. The game made me focus on the melody and the marriage of notes within it, its rhythm structure, its emotional effect, and also the change in the melody if you speeded it up or slowed it down. Through these games I learned how to recognize scales from my favorite songs. One of the very popular Bollywood films of the seventies was called *Pakeezah*, and was based on the story of a courtesan who falls in love with a Muslim *nawab*. Many years later the images and sounds of that film inspired the music and video of Junoon's Led-Zeppelin-meets-Nusrat-Fateh-Ali-Khan tune "Yaar Bina" from our 1997 album *Azadi* (Freedom).

In Kuwait, Sania and I would spin the *Pakeezah* record over and over on the turntable, and it burrowed its way into the grooves of my brain. The composer, Ghulam Mohammed, had produced an amazing soundtrack. It was a treasure trove of classical *ragas* and *thekas* (grooves) tastefully and intelligently fused to make hummable, accessible commercial film music. I developed an elephant's memory for melodies, and these Bollywood soundtracks helped educate my ear and understanding of *desi* compositions. Even after I became a musician, I retained the ability to listen to music with a fan's ear. Some musicians over-analyze their own work and it just makes the music sound sterile and forced. I have a simple philosophy about tunes. If it sounds good and it's giving me goose bumps, I figure, it'll move others as well.

Being grounded had its musical advantages. But that didn't stop me from breaking curfew after only a couple of days and escaping to the beach to sulk. It was there one day, though, that my rebelliousness finally backfired on me.

I wasn't the only one with a bad attitude, I discovered. A large Bedouin in a dark blue *dastasha* was also sitting on the rocks by the seashore, smoking a cigarette. When he saw me standing alone skimming rocks off the still blue sea he looked all around and then surreptitiously walked toward me and said something in Arabic. I turned around and shrugged my shoulders and replied in broken Arabic, "*Ana la al-arabi*" (I no Arabic). The only proper Arabic I knew was memorized from the Quran. The mustachioed man with a sun-weathered face then reached into his pocket and held out several Kuwaiti dinars in his open sweaty palm. This wasn't a good sign, I thought—especially when he curled his right forefinger and thumb to form a hole through which he made vigorous back and forth movements with his other forefinger. This guy was a horny desert predator and I had unwittingly become a potential child target. My mother had warned me about strangers and stalkers lurking around and told me not to go anywhere by myself. Why didn't I listen to her? Why was I so stubborn?

Oh Allah, I prayed, please get me out of this awful mess, get me back safe and sound to my family. I promise I'll be good . . . from now on! As these thoughts and prayers collided in my eleven-year-old brain, I looked desperately to my left and right for help, but there wasn't a soul around in the burning summer heat of Kuwait. It was just the pedophile and me. Necessity being the mother of invention, I looked down and saw a jagged black rock peering out from the white sand. I picked it up in one quick motion and took several steps sideways and cocked my arm back, threatening to let fly at the pervert if he didn't back off. But the deranged man, blinded by his lust, guffawed like an evil *jinn*. Instead of taking evasive action he lifted up his loose *dastasha* to reveal a large and scary organ. How the hell did I manage to find myself in this crazy tangle? There was no time for reflection or self-condemnation. Offense was the only available defense. I took aim at his crotch and whipped the black projectile with all the might of an eleven-year-old—and then I ran like the wind. I didn't look around or stop for anything. Judging from the shrieks, howls, and curses I heard from behind me, I could deduce that my improvised missile had hit its mark square on.

I ran and I ran as fast as I could and didn't stop running till I reached home. I was breathless and my heart was pounding like a jungle drum. Later I recounted the incident to Ami and apologized for being insolent and audacious. That was the last straw for my parents. My mother told

Abu that I shouldn't be left on my own in Lahore and that from now on I was going to be with my immediate family.

By coincidence, this was just about the time that my dad got a new job offer. Kuwait Airways needed a manager for North America in New York. After almost four years in Kuwait with PIA my dad asked my mother how she felt about moving to the States.

"Let's ask the *bachchas* (kids)," my mother responded.

For me and Sania, moving to New York was a no-brainer. We desperately longed for a change of scenery for ourselves, our little brother Sherry, and Ami and Abu. Sania and I lobbied fiercely for our family to seek out the next frontier. Our enthusiasm was contagious. My parents agreed for once, and in August 1975, my father accepted the position of North American country manager for Kuwait Airways. For my dad, it was a job promotion. I just thought of America as the land of thirteen TV channels and the home of Bugs Bunny and all the McDonald's I could eat. My memories of the year we'd spent in Washington and Virginia included kindergarten and TV shows like *Batman*, *Wonderama*, *My Favorite Martian*, and *Road Runner* cartoons. But for my family, the meaning of America ran deeper than TV or fast food. It was also a country that had inspired and enlightened my mother not long before I was born.

Decision made, we all set off for New York from Kuwait in the summer of 1975. United as a family aboard a Kuwait Airways Boeing 707, all of us were excited and expectant. Pumped up about his promotion, Abu was in a good mood, and so was I. Waiting to take off, I sought to impress my sports-loving dad by discussing recent news about America and two sporting events that had captured the world's attention: Arthur Ashe's upset victory at Wimbledon over Jimmy Connors and boxing's upcoming "Thrilla in Manila," pitting world heavyweight champion Muhammad Ali against Smokin' Joe Frazier.

Our destination and all the sports talk led my mom to chime in, telling us about watching football games as an exchange student in Oakland, California, in 1961. I knew my mother had spent a year in America, but as the flight took off and the reality of our move sunk in, I began thinking less about sports news and more about family history.

High up in the air, we began playing hearts, and I asked Ami to tell me once more about her maiden visit to the United States.

"*Beta*, it was due to your grandparents that I got to see America," my mother began.

"Your father and I were engaged, and he wasn't happy at all to see me go!" she said with a quick glance at my dad to check his reaction.

Sania and I looked at each other as my dad began to protest that memory. But my mother quickly cut in and continued "*Beta*, I had to literally promise your father that I would come back within a year!"

We all laughed and then Ami retold her teenager's story as we flew through the cloudless blue sky.

At the young age of eighteen, Shahine took a train, a plane, and a ship to get to America, and yet another plane and a bus once on U.S. soil. She'd begun with a Lahore-to-Karachi train ride and then took a plane from Karachi to Tehran before flying on to London. All that traveling alone brought looks of amazement to the faces of me and my young siblings. Very few Pakistani girls in 1961 were allowed to go so far away from home on their own. But she could hardly contain herself at the memory of her big trip.

"Then after getting off at Heathrow in London, I got on a ship from Southampton to New York," she said, as Sania, Sherry, and I sat turned toward her in our comfortable seats. "We saw the Statue of Liberty and then I took a long, long bus and plane journey from New York to Oakland!" said my mother, grinning at the thought of it all. "It was a fun adventure!"

Now I knew where our passion for going to America came from. Over the years, my mother had been a walking, talking cultural ambassador for the U.S. I hadn't really dwelled on her stories until we were all embarking on our own American journey. I asked her how the whole experience came about.

In July 1961, Mom's younger brother Farooq brought home an advertisement for an American Field Service student exchange program. The AFS program offered a year in high school in the U.S., and Shahine was immediately intrigued—despite already being engaged to my dad.

"Were you in love with him?" I butted in as she narrated.

"Of course," she said, blushing, "ours was a love marriage.

"But I made up my mind to see America."

My reasons for wanting to go to America were simple: food and entertainment. But neither McDonald's nor Bugs Bunny seemed like a good enough reason to leave family and country for a whole year. So I asked, "Why America, Ami?"

"Well, *beta*, America has its problems," she said, like racial discrimination and economic disparity. "But Americans always root for the underdog and they fight for civil rights and freedoms."

America was a place, my mom said, where people of all colors, cultures, and religions could go and fulfill their dreams.

"Even me?" I asked.

She smiled and said, "Yes, even you, Sania, and Sherry!"

It's hard to imagine many Pakistanis saying that today. But before 9/11 and George W. Bush's war on terror decimated U.S. relations with the Muslim world, feelings like my mom's were totally commonplace. Bush's "war on terror" made Pakistanis view the U.S. as a country to fear or resent for its racial profiling of Muslim-Americans or its torture of Muslims at Guantanamo Bay or Abu Ghraib. Up until very recently, for most Pakistanis America was simply the land of opportunity. Hopefully now, we're getting back on track: President Barack Hussein Obama's June 2009 speech in Cairo was a great inspiration. Obama said he was seeking a "new beginning" between the U.S. and the world's Muslims, based on "mutual interest and mutual respect." It's important to translate those words into deeds.

My mom had to clear some hurdles, she said. America was almost eight thousand miles away, too far and too costly for her meager family resources. She was a single Pakistani Muslim girl who wanted to travel alone to an alien land filled with cowboys, super heroes, movie stars, and big shiny cars. Aba agreed immediately. But, asked Ami Aziza, was she sure about making this long trip? Wouldn't she get homesick within the first few weeks? Shahine had never been away from her family. How would she deal with the day-to-day issues of school and adapting to a new culture?

She met every parental query with a confident response. No, she wasn't afraid to go, she said. She wouldn't get homesick. Adapting to school and American life wouldn't be a problem, she told them. It turned out that the cost wouldn't be a problem, either. To the great surprise of both my mother and grandparents, it would only cost $104.50 for Ami to spend a year in the U.S. The deal was sealed when my mother said, "Allah will protect me, there's no need to worry." No one could argue with that.

So Ami lived in Oakland from August 1961 to the summer of 1962, spending six months each with two different American families, the Coles and the Mortensons. The Coles were Catholic and the Mortensons were

Protestants, but each had a big family with six kids. That year, Shahine listened to Pat Boone and Chubby Checker, learned how to do the Twist, drank Coca-Cola, watched *Perry Mason* on TV, and was elected Oakland High's homecoming queen—the first young woman to win the title who didn't have a date.

"I was loyal to your father," she explained.

Most Pakistanis looked to secure themselves financially and strengthen their roots and family ties. But my mother wanted to transcend the predictable future of the demure housewife. She wanted to play a greater role in serving the poor and needy and dispossessed. It's from her that I probably got my first lesson in social service. Watching the day-to-day struggles of millions of her poor countrymen left an indelible impression on her heart and mind, and it was America's commitment to higher ideals of social equality and justice that beckoned my mother to travel there and learn and absorb how Americans lived, laughed, and dreamed.

Among those Americans was the country's president, John F. Kennedy. Just days before she was to return to Pakistan in June 1962, my mother and other AFS students sat on the White House lawn. She remembered watching and listening to Kennedy with the same kind of excitement and hope that my family and I have about Barack Obama today.

Kennedy's optimism and universal vision greatly inspired my mother. Just months before I was born, in that fateful year of 1963, Kennedy spoke to AFS students for the last time. "When you go home," Kennedy said, "you will not be (just) a friend of the United States, but rather a friend of peace, a friend of all people.

"You will desire to see good will among all nations, and . . . you will stand in your community, in your state, and in your country for those principles which motivate us all, all around the globe: a chance for everyone, a fair chance for everyone. And also for a world in which we have some hope for peace. If we're able to do that, this will be the most remarkable generation in the history of the world."

My mother believed in that fair chance for everyone, too. Fondly recalling Kennedy's spirit, my mother sank back into her seat as we flew toward New York. Our game of hearts was long forgotten.

My mother probably doesn't fully recognize it, but she is my hero. Over the years we might have had disagreements over faith and politics, family obligations and professional life. But we also agreed on social service, respect, and dignity toward the friend as well as the stranger.

Her idealism and optimism flowed into me. Her actions, like spending months by the side of terminally ill relatives and friends, stirred a similar compassion to address the poor and suffering of Pakistan and the world through my music and social work.

I would learn to take the good with the bad and internalize the positive currents of my early childhood. Today those boyhood strolls through London or Egypt, or listening to the *azan* or the guitar, and the experience of hearing my mother speak excitedly about the hope and possibility she imbibed in America echo back at me when I'm playing before a crowd in Los Angeles or Lahore. Looking out, I'll often see faces that appear nothing like mine. But it's times like those that I'll remember myself as a nine-year-old, seeing the world for the first time and gazing on in wonder. My cross-cultural journeys began with my parents.

Life back in America would be another trip altogether.

FOUR
American *Desi*

Tappan, New York, is a quiet, leafy colonial town 16 miles outside of New York City. It's got a population of just under 7,000, an area of 2.8 square miles and one of the country's oldest taverns. George Washington used the town as his Revolutionary War headquarters. On the Fourth of July, the stars and stripes burst into view and on Sundays people go to the Tappan Reformed Church to pray. In 1975, Tappan was the picture of small-town America, where most everyone was one color and there wasn't a mosque or a Muslim in sight.

Tappan is a world away from the megalopolis that is Lahore, and from steamy Karachi or the Kuwaiti desert. But it was there that I would live for six of the best years of my life, from 1975 to 1981, making friends, playing baseball, and throwing mind, body, and spirit into learning about rock and roll and the art of the guitar. Along the way, I would live as American a life as a Pakistani boy could.

Though I'd lived in the U.S. from 1968 to 1969, this time I was older and more conscious of my surroundings—and in America to stay, or so I thought. Much in the same way that my mother had set off into the unknown in 1961, I was going to dance my way into this New York life and meet my destiny. By the time I had to go back to Pakistan in 1981, I didn't want to leave Tappan. But I now see that it was all part of God's design for me and my life. And one day, much later, after unspeakable terrorist attacks changed our world, I would come back.

I came to love living in New York as a boy. But it took a while.

My initial cultural shock was middle school in South Orangetown. My *desi* accent was unintelligible to most of my classmates and caused great hysteria and hilarity every time I spoke.

"Dear sir (or madam), may I please be excused to attend the bathroom?" I would earnestly ask my teachers, sounding like Peter Sellers's Indian actor character in *The Party*. My name was sliced from Salman to "Sal" no matter how many attempts I made at correcting people. "It's 'Sull-man,' you see?" I'd say. "It sounds like salmon or like the prophet Solomon. It's very easy." Nobody got it. My American name was now Sal.

There were other adjustments. It was no longer mandatory to dress in winter and summer uniforms as we had at Aitchison, and there were no prefects checking the length of my hair, the dirt under my fingernails, or any potential ring around the collar. That's because in my new middle school there were no collars: everyone wore T-shirts and jeans or shorts in the classroom. Students could put their feet up or rest their heads on their desks and the teacher wouldn't even blink. At Aitchison you could get a brush on your butt for such insolence. At the end of my first week in seventh grade, my social studies teacher, a flower-power Beatlemaniac named Gary Johnson, asked me to see him after class. I immediately wondered what I'd done wrong.

"Are you feeling okay, Sal?" he asked. "Is anything bothering you?"

No, not at all, I said. Everything's fine.

Then why, Mr. Johnson wanted to know, was I getting up from my seat every time he walked into or out of the classroom, or when he asked me a question?

In Pakistan, I explained, getting up for the teacher was a sign of respect. It was also about saving your ass. If you didn't get up when a teacher addressed you, I told Mr. Johnson, you could get caned. Mr. Johnson laughed and said that teachers in America could get fired, or, worse, have charges brought against them if they physically or verbally abused a student. Mr. Johnson wasn't above a little ribbing of the new kid himself: he'd labeled me "Guru Mahesh Yogi Bear," in a crazy mingling of the names of the Beatles' spiritual guide and the cartoon character. He and other teachers would crack up when I stood at attention. But in Johnson's ribbing was a sign of affectionate respect and friendship. I took that respect for kids to heart.

Meanwhile, my new middle school had power dynamics of its own. I got picked on regularly by the other kids. One day someone would hide my books and on another day kids would punch my back in the halls, then run away when I turned around to see who did it. The bus journey back home from school was also the scene of a few incidents. Some of the boys used to take my school bag and throw it out the window and make me get off the bus to go retrieve it. All of this was pretty typical stuff, but in my case it was made worse by racial slurs.

"Come on, Pac-Man, what's the matter?" went one. "Lost your shit again!"

I also put up with nicknames like "eight ball" (for my dark skin) and "wacky packy." But I was hardly the only one getting picked on. Instead of "Shia" and "Sunni" taunts, I heard kids referred to as "Hebes," "Micks," "Krauts," and "Dagos." The bullies on my bus called both Muhammad Ali and Joe Frazier "Niggas" when the Thrilla in Manila match had boxing fans mesmerized in October 1975. I tried to keep a low profile, but it wasn't easy. Kids would kick my bag farther and farther away when I tried to retrieve it, laughing at the bumbling brown foreigner. I took all this in stride and put it down to a learning curve and adjustment to a new environment. But these trials by fire made me homesick for Lahore and all the things I loved, like cricket, kite flying, spicy food, and most of all Aba and Ami Aziza.

During those early, difficult months my two best friends were the TV and the radio. In my free time I hung out with Fonzie from *Happy Days*, and Vinnie Barbarino and Arnold Horshack from *Welcome Back, Kotter*. On *Star Trek*, meanwhile, I found a world of diversity. To Jim Kirk, Mr. Spock, Bones McCoy, and Lt. Uhura, color was no barrier. *Kotter* similarly appealed to me with its cast of playful characters. Deejays like Jay Thomas of 99X FM introduced me to tunes like KC and the Sunshine Band's "That's The Way (I Like It)" and "Get Down Tonight," as well as War's "Why Can't We Be Friends?" and the Bay City Rollers' "Saturday Night." I memorized that War song and felt like those pop tunes were giving me both an emotional anchor and a cultural compass in my new hometown. I was a Pakistani version of Woody Allen in *Sleeper*, with songs on the radio throwing me headlong into the unknown future.

After a while I started making friends with some unlikely characters. One of the tough guys on my bus was a boy called Frank Bianco. I used to dread getting off at my bus station near Mallory Lane, because that's where Frank lived. But Frank surprised me when he approached me one day and said, “Hey Sal, I heard you know how to play ping-pong well. Do you?”

“I know how to play table tennis, Frank,” I replied coldly. “That’s what they call it where I come from.”

Frank gave me a puzzled look and said, “Well, whatever. I need to practice and was wondering if you want to stop by my place and play a few games.”

Tappan instantly became a new world.

Frank and I became best friends in middle school and played ping-pong day after day and night after night like two miniature Forrest Gumps. Frank was an Italian-American Catholic and his father Frank Sr. had been a singer in the fifties and sixties in the mold of Sinatra. I taught Frank how to perfect a killer spin serve in ping-pong, and he returned the favor by getting me hooked on baseball and football. Thanks to Frank I became a rabid Yankees fan and in 1976 I watched Chris Chambliss hit a playoff-winning home run against the Kansas City Royals at Yankee Stadium. After the game I watched the New York fans go totally berserk and tear up the seats, the turf, and the bases. Their excitement bordered on chaos, and for a minute I flashed back to the crowds I’d seen going similarly nuts at cricket stadiums in Lahore. This was a display of New York’s spirit of unbridled freedom and passion and I lapped it up. Here was a city suited to my rebellious heart.

But in America, I soon realized, immigrants can sometimes be hated before they are loved. Like many others, I had a heavy burden to prove myself. Frank was one of the most popular kids in school and life got a little easier after he befriended me. But it didn’t solve all my problems. Frank told me that Americans love winners and not whiners and you need to stick up for who you are. Otherwise you’ll get kicked around, beat up, and called a loser. It wasn’t long before I did have to fight for my identity.

One of the advantages of going to a British school in Lahore was that my English was pretty good, in spite of the unusual way I spoke. I frequently got top marks on my vocabulary tests in my seventh-grade English class, to the delight of my teacher, Mrs. Stevens. Young and hip, Mrs. Stevens took a liking to me and used my grades to try to motivate the other kids to do better.

“Here’s a kid from Pakistan putting all of you to shame in English,” Mrs. Stevens scolded. “You people need to brush up on your vocabulary skills.”

That naturally enough made me feel good but had the opposite effect on my fellow students. One kid in particular, Robert, grew livid and decided to put me in my place. Robert had always gotten a sadistic thrill out of bugging me, but this time he made a big mistake when he tried to mete out my punishment for being so good at his own language.

Mrs. Stevens had temporarily left the room. Robert walked over to my desk, picked up my geometry box and instruments and chucked them across the room directly at the blackboard. The box broke into pieces. The old geometry box wasn't expensive but it was a farewell gift from Ami Aziza and when I saw it break I flipped out.

I jumped on Robert and grabbed his neck and started choking him like a possessed spirit as the entire class chanted "Fight! Fight!" Robert's face was beginning to turn blue as Mrs. Stevens came back into the room and sent both of us to Principal Risseto's office. Our punishment was detention. In the detention hall Robert kept looking over at me and saying "dead meat" and that he'd meet me after school. Fine, I said, we'll settle this on Schaeffer Field.

News about the Salman-Robert match spread on the bus as though it were a major sporting event, and by the time I got to the field that evening a big crowd of kids had gathered to watch the fight. Before going to the duel I stopped at home to drop off my books and grab my Thrilla in Manila T-shirt bearing a picture of Muhammad Ali.

Just as I was walking out the front door, my mother asked me where I was going without having dinner. I set my jaw and said, "I've got some unfinished business at school, Ami." But she knew something was up and made me tell her the whole story. Then she asked me one question.

"Is this boy fighting you because you are a Muslim?" she asked.

No, I said, repeating that he'd antagonized me by breaking my geometry box. I was seriously expecting some parental support. My mother just shook her head.

"So it's your personal vanity you're going to go fight over?"

"Yeah," I said, "I'm going to kick his butt."

Then Shahine laid down the law.

"You are a Muslim," she said sternly. "You cannot fight someone unless your religion is being threatened or attacked. That's what Islam teaches us."

"You don't understand!" I protested. I would look like a coward if I backed down from the fight, I told her.

"You won't be a coward in the eyes of Allah," she said.

But I slipped out and went to Schaeffer Field to face Robert anyway. The kids were screaming for blood and guts and Frank was there to give me moral support. There I was, standing eyeball to eyeball with my nemesis, ready to pummel him with everything I could. But then I remembered what Ami had said. The words spilled out of my mouth.

"I'm not going to fight you, Robert," I said, shocking the crowd into silence.

He narrowed his eyes and said, "What's the matter? You chicken? Are you a pussy?"

"No, I'm not a chicken or a pussycat," I said in a serious voice as I heard everyone laugh at my choice of words. "I just don't want to fight you over something really stupid."

That wasn't what he wanted to hear. He pushed me to the ground and pinned my shoulders with his knees. I got ready for the fist he was about to feed me when something totally unexpected happened.

He punched the ground next to my head.

"Screw it," he said. "I don't feel like fighting either. Let's call it a draw."

Like a lot of other young immigrants, I came to live a double life in New York—although it was very different from the split existence I'd had to lead back living at Ami and Aba's and as a student at Aitchison. At home with my parents, I was still a Pakistani kid, a Muslim, and a member of the family, but outside was a 100 percent American suburban cocoon that could beat me down if I didn't try to fit in.

So that's what I did. From the summer of 1975 to the summer of 1977 I attempted to get used to a new way of teaching and meld into a totally diverse cultural vibe of jocks, nerds, nature-loving "organics," artsy types, and the dreaded losers. In Pakistan there was greater emphasis on learning by rote and essay-style exams. But in my new middle school, most tests were multiple-choice and the focus was on a conceptual understanding of problems.

More important, though, was the social environment. I was already out of place as a foreigner and being dubbed a loser would have killed me. I tried to blend in with the jocks, but that wasn't easy. There was so much sports trivia I was completely unaware of. Every kid seemed to know the names of all the players in the NFL, NBA, and NHL, as well as all the racy details of the players' salaries, scandals, and girlfriends. Talk about girls occasionally led to other things. In seventh grade a kid named Howard, who boasted about his sexual exploits, shocked me by showing me graphic pictures of the "pets" in *Penthouse* magazine. I had never seen frontal female nudity and went into an uncontrollable, high-pitched fit of laughter, shrieking "holy shit!" multiple times in front of the whole class. That earned me an instant detention. Howard winked at me as I was leaving the classroom and said, "Don't worry, man, you're cool now." My protective mother would have had a cow had she known the kind of things I was learning and the company I was keeping.

Robert and Howard were two characters who made up the colorful mosaic of my junior high school. As time went on I met other kids, Irish, Italian, and Jewish. I gradually fell in with the jocks and spent the first two years of my New York life with them. Most of the kids in my neighborhood were sports fanatics, and I quickly got into playing baseball, football, and basketball. Because of my cricket-playing skills, I found baseball easiest to adapt to. But there were some key differences. I just could not get used to fielding with a baseball mitt. So as a right fielder I caught balls with my bare hands, just like in cricket. Watching this crazy action by a mutant *desi* freaked out my Little League teammates, but it won me respect. I'd catch most high fly balls and line drives safely by just making a basket with my hands and rocketing the ball back to the infield, much to the annoyance and astonishment of the hitter and the opposition. Some of the members of my team, The Reds—Frank Bianco, Sean Russo, Mitch Norotsky, Jerry Colby, Charlie Garavanta, and Jeff Bergman—were Yankee fans and through them my baseball education turned into an obsession as I joined them in following the Yankees religiously. Watching TV, I got a kick out of seeing baseball managers and players arguing bad calls and kicking dirt onto umpires. I stared in fascination at dugout-clearing brawls between opposing ball clubs. This kind of passion appealed to my Sagittarian heart. Baseball certainly wasn't a "gentleman's" game! I loved the down-to-earth nature of the sport and watched every Yankees game I could. The 1977 season was broadcast on WPIX, Channel 11, and I discovered a whole new world of sports announcers like Phil "The Scooter" Rizzuto and his famous "Holy Cow!" line, as well as Bill White and Frank Messer. Just as John Arlott or Fred Trueman gave cricket play-by-plays on the BBC, Rizzuto and the others filled me in on all the details and finer points of baseball, but with more relaxed and informal deliveries. I also got my Yankees history lessons, starring the likes of Babe Ruth, Lou Gehrig, Joe DiMaggio, and Mickey Mantle.

It was an exciting time to be a Yankees fan. The team had started to find its winning ways, with one of the most exciting and volatile teams in baseball. Reggie Jackson, Thurman Munson, Lou Piniella, Mickey Rivers, Catfish Hunter, and Sparky Lyle were some of the star players, led by a junooni manager, Billy Martin. The team's unpredictable brilliance on the field was matched by its spectacular infighting off the field. Billy Martin's and Reggie Jackson's egos were too big even for the gigantic Yankee stadium, and their shouting matches gave me an insight into the eclectic cultural mix that is America.

Back in school, I learned a lot about team spirit and self-belief from my gym teacher, Mr. Dorni. Despite my reticence to play basketball, simply because I was no good at it, Mr. Dorni would regularly pick me and encourage the better players to keep passing the ball to me. I'd usually lose it pretty quickly. In one eighth-grade interclass game, our team was losing by two points with only seconds to go and I found myself with the ball. I was mid-court and had no time to pass it to my teammates. But Mr. Dorni yelled out, "Take the shot, Sal!" I didn't have the confidence to score a basket from that distance, and I hesitated as the clock wound down. Mr. Dorni screamed, "Sal, you can do it, just take the shot!" And so without thinking I chucked the basketball over the sea of hands that were trying to grab it from me. My three-pointer won us the game and my teammates went into a wild frenzy, congratulating me with high fives and back slaps. I'd finally been recognized by my peers, and sinking that shot was a huge boost for my self-esteem. Still, I downplayed it. I just stood there shaking my head.

"That was a total fluke," I told everybody.

Mr. Dorni wouldn't hear it. He asked us all to stay after class and made that shot an object lesson in the importance of self-belief. Sal scored this basket, Mr. Dorni said, because he was willing to go beyond his imagined doubts. That was the mindset required to succeed in anything in life, he said. It was a lesson I'd draw on many, many times in the years to come.

Music, books, and film also bolstered my confidence in those early New York years. I loved books like S. E. Hinton's *The Outsiders*, Ray Bradbury's *Fahrenheit 451*, and the James Bond thrillers of Ian Fleming. During America's bicentennial in 1976, Frank Bianco and I went to see *Rocky*. If there was ever a movie which captured the meaning of the American dream, it was this powerful tale of the underdog boxer Rocky Balboa. I saw the film a half dozen times. Being an overweight, under-confident teenager, I endlessly played Bill Conti's "Gonna Fly Now" theme in my head as I struggled to jog around my neighborhood and tried to get myself into some kind of respectable shape.

I was also very aware of my brown color and intuitively understood that I was "the Other" in this white man's world into which I'd moved. Being a Muslim made it a little more complicated, especially since I was still learning my own faith. Seeing a film called *The Message*, starring Anthony Quinn, set off a new round of questioning. The movie is about the birth of Islam and Prophet Muhammad, but he doesn't once appear in it, owing to Islam's prohibition of physical depictions of Allah's messenger. Quinn plays the Prophet's uncle, Hamza, but history's greatest role model for Muslims was completely invisible throughout the movie. His absence made him into a mystery, and my teenaged curious mind began to conjure up all kinds of images of the Prophet, none of which I could relate to. All I knew was that I was expected to feel a deep reverence for him, just like my family and the wider Muslim community. But I wasn't cut out for blind worship. I had a lot of questions about my faith and my Prophet, but they lay dormant for many years because I didn't know how to articulate them. I was also emotionally split between Pakistan and America, and my identity crisis was just compounded by someone whose job it was to help me. "You people," my guidance counselor said to me, need to try extra hard to fit in here in America. To her, it was that simple. Conform or be cast out.

In fact I still had one foot back in the world I'd come from. There were no mosques in Rockland County and no places for my parents to buy halal meat, so on weekends and special occasions we would go to Queens or Manhattan to pray, buy groceries, and occasionally watch Bollywood films. The Islamic holidays and festivals of Eid ul-Fitr and Eid ul-Azha were also celebrated in New York City with Muslims from around the five boroughs of New York and some from New Jersey. In Lahore, we usually spent Eid with our large extended family of aunts, uncles, nieces, nephews, cousins, grandparents, and close family friends, chatting in Urdu and bound by our shared Punjabi culture. Celebrating Eid in America, on the other hand, was a mind-bogglingly diverse affair. At the mosques, we'd join men, women, and children who were African-American, European, South Asian, Chinese, Indonesian, Malaysian, and

Middle Eastern. Black, white, and brown all came together in a rented, improvised mosque in Manhattan to bow in unison toward the Kaaba (House of God) in Mecca. The cube-shaped Kaaba was built by Prophet Abraham and is the holiest of Muslim places of worship in the world, where millions come to perform the annual Hajj pilgrimage. In Manhattan, on Eid, we were all strangers to each other but we were bonded by our common belief in the one, supreme, divine essence of God.

Going to the mosque on Eid, though, was about the extent of our family's contact with other Muslims living in and around New York. Everyone was scattered throughout the area and involved with their families, jobs, and school. Our disconnectedness worried my mother. She fretted that once I got into high school, I'd lose my religion if I didn't stay in regular touch with it. But I think she was overcompensating for losing something else in her life.

In 1978, Abu's employers at Kuwait Airways decided to transfer him from New York to Copenhagen to run their office in Denmark. The move was actually fine with Ami and Abu. They needed a break from each other. In 1981, the arrival of my baby sister, Scheherezade, would begin to heal the rift. But in 1978, they decided that perhaps it was better to live apart for a while. Ami stayed back with me, Sania, and our little brother Sherry in Tappan so as to prevent another disruption in our schooling. Abu, meanwhile, would see us all in Copenhagen over the summer and winter holidays. There wasn't much I could do about my parents' marriage or the new family living arrangement but it caused me immense angst and frustration all the same. With my father gone, my mother laid down too many rules for me, and my response was to rebel against all of them. I resentfully lived as a caged *desi* at home but gradually grew to resemble some kid out of *Fast Times at Ridgemont High*. I drove my mother up the wall by not saying my prayers five times a day or reading from the Quran. And when it came to the opposite sex, I was a total lost cause in her eyes.

"As a Muslim," Ami Shahine would say, "you need to lower your gaze anytime you see a girl walking by you in school."

That was just laughable. And had I done it, the mockery at school would have gotten worse. There was no way I could lower my eyes, when, walking down the school halls, there'd be girls clad in shorts, T-shirts, and jeans that looked painted onto their legs. I had to figure this culture clash out on my own and Ami's anxiety was just cramping my style.

One day, my mother came up with a new plan. In order to keep in touch with our faith, we kids would all go to a makeshift Islamic school at a family friend's house in New Jersey on Sundays. Sania and Sherry were always obediently on board, but it destroyed my weekends. I'd sit there reading the Quran in Arabic (not understanding the language, like many non-Arab Muslims who read the holy book) and fume that I was missing neighborhood baseball and football games. I didn't care at the time, but I recognize that it was the only chance my mother got to socialize with other Pakistani families and to see her children learn their faith.

My mother actually didn't need to force Islam on me. My faith in God was always strong, and I was constantly praying for all kinds of things. Throughout middle school and later, into high school, I asked Allah to heal my parents' marriage—and sought divine intervention for both the Yankees and Pakistan's cricket team. I prayed that girls would like me and, most of all, that I'd be a great guitar player. I felt a warm presence around me which guided my choices and communicated itself through dreams and signs. As a teenager, I had figured out my own approach to the riddle of culture and religion: life was simply about being a good person, having good intentions, working hard, and letting go of the results, God would take care of the rest.

By the time I got to eighth grade, I'd settled in to my life in Tappan and had made some buddies whom I valued. But that 1977–1978 school year, I also made four friends who would become lifelong companions: John Lennon, Paul McCartney, George Harrison, and Ringo Starr.

The Beatles were the main band in Ms. Graph's music appreciation class, and with them, my Western musical education truly began. I'd heard of the Beatles and listened to their song "Yellow Submarine" a bit in Pakistan. My Aunt Nosheen had told me about the times the Beatles had touched down in Karachi during the sixties en route to India. Just like in America, scores of teenagers had flocked to the airport to catch a glimpse of them. But it wasn't until the spring and summer of 1977 that I fully recognized their huge influence on the world of music and on Western pop culture. Ms. Graph, a child of the sixties, gave me a crash course in all things Beatles. Sitting in that class, explosions went off in my heart and mind. I was mesmerized by the overwhelming cascade of positive sound vibrations in the music. Every day we would hear different songs, all recorded within an astonishingly short period of time, 1962 to 1970. Ms. Graph had the red 1962–1966 and blue 1967–1970 Beatles compilation albums, which I also later bought at Korvette's discount department store. Those albums saturated my brain that school year. From "I Want to Hold Your Hand" to "All You Need Is Love" to "Revolution" to "Come Together" and on and on. Ms. Graph would ask us to listen closely to each and every instrument, to dissect the melody, analyze the lyrics, and become aware of chords and harmony. It was a total revelation.

Beatles arrangements were in sharp contrast to the mostly linear and modal *desi* music I had been exposed to. My curiosity was also piqued by the obscure subliminal sounds and effects in songs like "Strawberry Fields Forever," "I Am the Walrus," and "Tomorrow Never Knows." Ms. Graph's class was my journey through the looking glass into the Wonderland world of the Beatles. There was a unity of vibrations which I heard in songs like "A Day in the Life," "Within You Without You," and "Norwegian Wood." It seemed as if all the sounds I had heard from different cultures growing up had been embraced by the Beatles. They used string quartets as well as sitars, harmoniums, tablas, and dilrubas. All that was in addition to folk, country, and blues sounds, and for me the Beatles' music formed a sonic harmony similar to the visual harmony I was seeing with the multicultural cast of *Star Trek*. Their message of peace, love, and unity resonated in me with the same emotional intensity and familiarity of *qawwali* and Bollywood music.

I was still just a music appreciator, though, and not yet a musician. I knew songs, melodies, and lyrics but had never attempted to play any instrument. I just didn't think I had the talent required to learn drums, bass, or guitar. But I overcame that reticence once I met a guy with whom, on the surface, I had nothing in common.

I met Michael Langer through Jeff Bergman, one of my Tappan Reds teammates, after Jeff heard of my newfound love affair with the Beatles. Mike was an exceptionally talented singer and multi-instrumentalist whose garage band Apple Corps was a Beatles tribute band. The band's guitar player was Paul Siegel, another teenaged relic from the Woodstock era, with whom I and my buddy-to-be Brian O'Connell would later play in the garage band Eclipse. Mike was a Paul McCartney fanatic and a walking, talking Beatles encyclopedia.

I wish every naysayer who thinks Muslims and Jews are doomed to unending internecine warfare could have watched my friendship with

Michael Langer develop. Our love for the Beatles and the Yankees bridged the religious and cultural differences between us. And Mike could understand where I was coming from on other levels: he was very well-informed about the world for a thirteen-year-old. Unlike most other kids in school—who couldn't even find South Asia on a map—Mike knew a fair bit about Pakistan, India, the Middle East, and Islam and was completely nonjudgmental about Muslim culture. After we got to know each other better, I taught him Urdu, Punjabi, and Arabic phrases like "*kya haal hai*" (How are you?) and "*Salaam aleikum*" (Peace be upon you), and, of course, the choicest of Punjabi and Urdu curse words. Mike sent me into fits of laughter when he fired off those racy, procreative swear words following a classroom scolding from a teacher or too much homework.

Mike also took me along to Beatlefests in New York City. These annual gatherings of Beatlemaniacs were usually held from dawn until dusk at a Manhattan hotel and were hosted by New York disc jockeys like WPLJ's Jimmy Fink and WNEW's Dennis Elsas. Entering the room, we'd walk into a world where everything Beatles was on display. We'd see wigs, posters, rare pictures and film clips, as well as magazines, old concert tickets, and signed autographs. There were also Beatles movies playing nonstop. The only thing I could compare it to was a Sufi *urs* celebration, except that at this *urs*, everything "Beatles" was for sale: the Beatles had broken up and the fans had created a kind of moveable shrine to them.

These *urs* were also frequented by friends and acquaintances of the band members themselves, like Klaus Voormann, Victor Spinetti, and Billy Preston. It was during that period that I saw *A Hard Day's Night*, and watching the Beatles being chased by girls and having so much fun playing their music made me want to go to the next level of my musical journey.

I became possessed by the thought of becoming a musician. I was so possessed, in fact, that I didn't even consider what my parents would think. It was unheard of for a thirteen-year-old Pakistani kid to contemplate asking his parents if he could play a rock and roll instrument. I didn't even know which instrument I wanted to try. Drums or piano seemed to be the easiest to me, because it looked like all you had to do was bang down on the skins or the black and white keys and make a musical sound. The guitar had the most appeal to me but also looked the most difficult to play. I searched my heart over whether I should just try to stay happy as an Apple Corps groupie or pick up an instrument and boldly go where no Ahmad had gone before. But as summer approached and I prepared to transition from middle school to Tappan Zee High School, a sign was revealed to me.

Danny Spitz, also a talented guitar player in our school who would later become a member of the hugely popular 1980s thrash metal band Anthrax, had an extra ticket to a concert at Madison Square Garden. I'd never heard of the band before, but the ticket I bought from Danny turned out to be a ticket to my own personal musical ride.

The band was named Led Zeppelin.

On Monday, June 7, 1977, I bounded off my school bus clutching a red ticket bearing the words "Led Zeppelin, Live in Concert."

I walked home from the bus stop through the cool late afternoon air and stepped into my house to find Ami Shahine sitting there, waiting for me. Her nervousness was all over her face. Rock was a little-known phenomenon in Pakistan and my mother was pretty freaked out about letting me go to my first-ever concert. The way my family imagined it, these long-haired musicians were wacked out on drugs and alcohol and just made noise and, worse, vulgar gestures on stage. Ami thought that Elvis had been bad enough, but these hard rock bands I was listening to (like KISS and the Rolling Stones) were "amoral and depraved," she said. Ami was worried to death that her thirteen-year-old son was going to be eaten alive in this hedonistic world of sex, drugs, and rock and roll.

"*Beta*," she said, "keep an eye on your money and ticket. There are pickpockets roaming the streets of New York. Don't ever talk to strangers, and most important, do not buy anything from them!"

Then she paused. I knew what was coming.

Staring hard into my eyes she warned, "And for Allah's sake don't do any drugs or I will disown you!"

"*Ji*, *Ami* [yes, Mother]," I replied as she vigorously ran a comb over my head, "but you're pulling my hair out!" I was both excited and apprehensive about going to the Garden by myself, but I tried hard not to let on how I felt.

"*Fiqar mat*, *Ami* [Don't worry, Mom]," I said, "It's only a music concert!"

I understood her concerns. But I couldn't stand being in my *desi* cultural shackles much longer. Having grown up with a lot of freedom at 6 Napier Road, I was aching to get back to exploring and experimenting. I was a Pakistani version of the teenaged William Miller in Cameron Crowe's movie *Almost Famous*, whose eccentric, overly protective mother tries to smother his natural instincts. Like him, I was itching to discover the side of American life still hidden to me. And I was yearning to share the excitement of millions of other young people about music and pop culture. Ami Shahine interrogated me silently with searching, skeptical eyes as she ironed my clothes for the evening: a yellow flowered dress shirt and red and white striped pants with a black belt and matching polished shoes that Abu had gotten me in Kuwait. I cringe when I think of that outfit. My parents' rules were to dress well at public events—but I wasn't going to a friend's birthday party at Jinnah's Garden. I was going to see a band called Led Zeppelin! My hopes and passions and my mother's anxiety and fears were clearly on a collision course, but that evening, I gave in to her choice of clothes. She was, after all, driving me to the Garden and would pick me up after the show after visiting a friend in the city.

My excitement built as we drove into New York. The city has always held out a mystery and a secret promise of adventure. Going from the safe and serene surroundings of Tappan into Manhattan was like a journey crossing from one world into another, from Hobbiton to the center of the Earth, via the tree-lined Palisades Parkway. As Ami and I travelled over the gigantic steel structure of the George Washington Bridge, Manhattan loomed over the sunlit horizon. Ami drove cautiously, with the red needle stuck on my parents' dark blue Buick's speedometer at 55 miles an hour. I knew next to nothing about Led Zeppelin, but I'd become familiar with New York City. My parents and siblings and I had visited the top of the Empire State Building and gazed together over the sprawling Gotham. We saw the Statue of Liberty welcoming millions of immigrants—just like ourselves—from distant shores, people who spoke an untold number of dialects and celebrated their cultural heritages with colorful parades. The city never turned its back on those who had the courage to follow their dreams, big or small. It held out its expansive arms and embraced all as one.

It was a balmy summer evening as we drove along the Hudson River on the West Side Highway toward downtown, passing Forty-second Street. The road was filled with pot holes as we got closer to making a left turn into the bumper-to-bumper traffic leading to Thirty-third Street and Seventh Avenue. Finally we arrived. Saying goodbye to Ami and slamming the door behind me, I stepped onto the concrete sidewalk into a sea of thousands of boys and girls wearing bell bottom jeans and Led Zeppelin T-shirts. Some were dazed and confused and others were hyper and expectant. I entered the Garden and through a haze of smoke saw hundreds of peace signs worn by freaks with flowers in their long hair. My clothes must have seemed like a psychedelic illusion to them. After we had waited patiently for an hour—as smokers and non-smokers alike got high off the grass smoke–permeated air—the lights went down and a powerful roar greeted the four members of Led Zeppelin as they strode onstage.

The minute the band started to play, I knew why I'd come. The excitement I felt as Led Zeppelin ripped into its set began at the base of my spine and enveloped first my heart and then my head. I didn't know any Zeppelin songs but it didn't matter. Celtic, Indian, and Arabic melodies combined with the blues with effortless ease, glued together by John Paul Jones's bass and drummer John Bonham's powerhouse percussion. Robert Plant and Jimmy Page ruled the stage with incredible visceral energy and oversized personas. Standing on my feet in the sixty-third row of a jam-packed Garden, I looked over the heads and shoulders of a teenage wasteland and watched as the distant exploding stars foretold my musical destiny.

For most of the night my eyes were transfixed on the guitar player, Page. He had an otherworldly presence, coaxing, bending, squeezing, bowing, and physically summoning mystical sounds out of a two-headed guitar. He was dressed in a white satin shirt and pants with dragons painted on them. Red, blue, and green laser lights formed a pyramid around him as he played, totally soaked in sweat and bathed in an admixture of color and sound. Everywhere I looked around me there were smiling, happy young people, swept up in this menagerie of deafening sonic thunder and blinding lights. I had never experienced such an assault on the senses, and I felt fully awake despite the fact that everyone around me was swimming in the depths of dizziness. The tornado of guitars, bass, vocals, and drums made this brown-skinned boy boogie woogie! And to think I'd come to the concert on a whim. I was a still-fresh immigrant, and Led Zeppelin could've been the Bay City Rollers, for all I knew. I had no preconceived notions about the band, so I just listened to the music. But when Jimmy Page switched his red twelve- and six-string Gibson double neck for a sunburst Les Paul and tore into the signature riffs of "Moby Dick" and "Whole Lotta Love," I entered another realm. I never came back.

From "In My Time of Dying" to "Stairway to Heaven," from "Rock and Roll" to the hypnotic and climbing "Kashmir," rock and roll irrevocably lodged itself in my heart that night. The show was nearly three hours long, but it seemed to fly by in a wink of an eye. That Zeppelin concert gave me an audio-visual blueprint for the distant music I was hearing in my head. Sitting in the Garden, I saw a vision for my future crystallize. I wanted to play music for the rest of my life. Period. I had found my passion and now I wanted to connect with it, share it, and change the world with it. By the end of the night my shoulders, head, and feet were in a state of *fana*. I was one with the music. I didn't just like rock and roll. I loved it.

Nine months later, I would finally have the money to buy a guitar. I spent hours locked inside my room every day, jamming with Led Zeppelin, Jimi Hendrix, Santana, and Beatles records. I listened to the solos at a slower RPM so I could hear every last note. I played and played, to the point that my fingers bled onto the strings and then toughened into calluses. I drove my mother mad.

Over the next four years, my life changed dramatically.

The summer after the Led Zeppelin concert, I left South Orangetown Middle School to begin life as a freshman at Tappan Zee High School. With visions of Page still in my mind, I signed up for guitar club—though I still owned no instrument. TZHS seemed to be swarming with an army of guitar and bass players who would ritually gather once a week after school with their instruments. They brought Gibson Les Pauls, Fender Stratocasters, twelve-string Ovations, Taylor acoustics, Rickenbackers, and Hofner basses. Everybody got a chance to trade licks and riffs and share information about new gear and upcoming bands and artists. It was like a gathering of bikers on a mountaintop. Except none of us was even old enough to drive.

In guitar club, I reconnected with the always-smiling and mellow Paul Siegel. Paul had moved on from Mike Langer's garage band Apple Corps and joined forces with a tall, lanky (and tormented) Irish-American guitar player by the name of Brian O'Connell. Brian was a quiet guy, and when we first shook hands, neither of us could have imagined that we would be rocking the world with Junoon tunes a decade or so later, with me on lead guitar and him on bass. Paul had an Ibanez copy of a Les Paul, the same kind of guitar I had seen Jimmy Page play at Madison Square Garden. I'd been in love with the guitar's cool sunburst color, shiny finish, and shapely curves ever since that concert. I asked him to let me hold it just to see how it felt. At first touch, the guitar seemed to hug my body as I held it gently in my arms, and I felt a bond with it even though I couldn't really play a note or a chord. I just plucked the open strings E-A-D-G-B-E over and over with my fingers, and even those most basic of sounds were heavenly to my novice ears. The six steel strings wound tightly parallel upon a rosewood neck seemed to be communicating a secret message: "You've finally found me after all these years. I'm the one that you were looking for." I was hypnotized.

Paul and Brian were playing in their garage band Eclipse and were both accomplished musicians. They'd even written their first original composition, called "Guadalajara." I could get hooked just watching Paul and Brian play dueling leads. On one particular day at guitar club, though, I took a leap and asked Paul if I could play his Les Paul for just a few minutes. The applause from the other club members had died down after they finished jamming, and I reached for the guitar. But like an overly eager Frodo grabbing at his precious ring, I dropped the Les Paul and sent it crashing to the ground. All the blood ran out of my veins. Everyone looked at me as if I had just committed murder. But no damage was done except for a small wooden chip that fell off the head stock, which ruined the guitar's finish and my beautiful day. I expected Siegel to totally lose it. But Paul, always the unruffled, easygoing one, told me very calmly but firmly, "Sal, man, I think it's about time you got your own guitar."

He was totally right. It was time. But an original sunburst Gibson Les Paul custom, like the one Page played, was completely out of my price range. Everything was; I had no money at all. I appealed to my parents, but Ami Shahine just said, "You're in high school now. Work and save up enough money to buy your guitar."

So that's what I did. Obsessed with my goal, I worked as a bus boy at the Blauvelt Coach Diner for $1.25 an hour plus tips and did a paper route. An original Les Paul was too expensive. But by April 14, 1978, I'd saved up $200, enough to buy a copy made by Carlo Robelli. Paul came with me as Ami drove down Route 4 to Sam Ash Music in Paramus, New Jersey, to buy my first-ever guitar.

I was like a toddler walking into a toy store. The place had everything. I saw stacks of amplifiers—Marshalls, Fender Twin Reverbs, Ampegs, and Hiwatts. There were stomp boxes, tone changers, and foot pedals. There were MXR phasers, equalizers, and flangers. In another corner sat fuzz boxes, Memory Man delays, and chorus and wah-wah pedals. Column after glorious column of gleaming, colorful guitars hung from the store's walls. I anxiously located the Les Paul. But I'd miscalculated. It was $235. Ami looked at me, smiled at my restless, doglike eyes and said, "OK, *beta*, here's the rest of the money, let's get you your guitar." I gave her the tightest, biggest hug and kiss that I could muster and then proudly headed out of the music store with my baby in my arms. It was a relationship that would last forever.

I practiced like a madman and basically taught myself to play. I didn't have an amp so I hooked the guitar up to my dad's stereo and Akai reel-to-reel recorder and just played. When I wasn't playing, I would hang out with Paul and Brian and go to watch Eclipse rehearse or perform at birthday parties, garage sales, open houses, barbecues, and school prom–like "ring night" events. Back then Brian and Paul were light years ahead of me as guitar players, and I learned a lot just watching them. Paul showed me a few chords and Brian, who along with Dan Spitz was amongst the best guitar players in school, showed me bending techniques, hammer-ons, pull-offs, and Eddie Van Halen–style finger tapping techniques. I listened to Hendrix, Clapton, Jeff Beck, and Santana in my basement, and I became so proficient that within six to eight months, I was asked to join Eclipse as a replacement for the band's bass player, Rich Silverman. Then one day in the middle of practice, Paul said, "I think I'll take over on bass. Sal, why don't you and I switch roles?" I looked at him incredulously. I was happy just to be in the band. Apparently Paul, Brian, our lead vocalist Jeff, drummer Scott, and keyboard player Joy had come to the conclusion that my guitar playing had developed so rapidly that I had fast overtaken many guitar players in school. From then on, Brian and I alternated lead and rhythm guitar on different songs.

Being part of Eclipse was like being reborn. In high school, where image mattered, I had a new identity as one of the cool kids—something I couldn't have imagined as a fresh-faced immigrant just a few years before. But I was still struggling with my identity and I found myself drawn to others with whom I shared a common passion. Sharing faith with my friends helped, too. When Paul and Brian would come over to my house to jam, they'd often see Ami praying and would feel comfortable enough to talk about their beliefs. Originally from the Bronx, Paul's Jewish family kept a kosher kitchen, I learned. He went to Hebrew school and had recently had his bar mitzvah. Brian, whose family were devout Christians, was born in Queens and had moved to Rockland County when he was a child. Having both moved to Tappan from elsewhere, Paul and Brian felt like outsiders as much as I did. Brian was a sensitive soul and I instinctively felt protective of him. At that young age, the friendships we had were pure and we just accepted each other. Our different family backgrounds were part of our teenaged dreams and fears and they only made our bond tighter.

Eclipse was a safe haven for me. We played all the hits of the sixties, seventies, and early eighties note for note: "Free Bird," "Stairway to Heaven," "Jumping Jack Flash," "Smoke on the Water," "(I Can't Get No) Satisfaction," "Like a Rolling Stone," "Purple Haze," "Back in Black," "You Really Got Me," and others. We could play "Sweet Home Alabama" better than Lynyrd Skynyrd, or so we thought, and even won the 1979–80 Tappan Zee High School battle of the bands. Playing guitar in front of people made me feel very special. Although I was basically a shy person, the stage would bring out an alter ego. I would wear a *kurta* over jeans and an Allah necklace, and perform barefoot to feel the earth beneath me. I naturally connected with the band's energy and with people in a hall or auditorium. Living inside the notes, I let the music flow through me and felt safe and protected.

In addition to Paul and Brian, I also made friends with John Alec Raubeson, a TZ graduate who knew Brian. Like me, he'd seen his share of family issues. Debilitated from illness and pain-killing drugs, John's father shot himself when John was only seven. There was further tragedy in John's family when his tormented older brother also committed suicide when John was a teenager. But music had proven therapeutic for John, too, and he was thoroughly grounded in music theory and recording. Our difficult home lives as well as our common musical passion brought all of us together. John and I became very close and I always saw him as an older brother. John was a constant pillar of strength. After high school I would remain in touch with both Brian and John from Pakistan. We all wanted to be musicians, but if anyone at that time had suggested that Brian and John would later join me in Pakistan and become a part of my musical journey I would've thought that person was mad.

I made one more unlikely musician friend, and that was Joy. Joy Schloss was a goddess to me, and her long black hair, dark mascara-lined eyes, and all-American smile had me hypnotized. The sneaking whisperer on my shoulder would say, "Forget it buddy, she'll never like you, you're brown, Muslim, and totally uncool." Joy was Tappan Zee High School's prom queen and homecoming princess, a cheerleader, captain of the gymnastics team, and Jewish. But I was some kind of Sufi mutant even back then, like the boy Jamal Malik in *Slumdog Millionaire* who falls for his childhood sweetheart Latika. I'd wait each day in school by my locker to see her pass me by with her girlfriends. Even while walking in the halls and eating in the cafeteria, I'd try to catch a distant glimpse, but I was always too *desi* shy to catch her eye or say "hi." But one day after I'd joined Eclipse, I heard a hesitant voice asking a question at a party we were playing at.

"Hey, do you guys know how to play 'Riders on the Storm'?"

I looked up and it was Joy. Mindlessly I replied, "No sorry, don't have any keyboards in the band, just guitar, bass, and drums, like to keep it real and simple. Why do you ask?"

"Well . . . I have a Fender Rhodes keyboard . . . and I learned how to play that song . . ." said Joy.

"Oh wow!" I said. "I love the sound of the Fender Rhodes. John Paul Jones plays that on 'No Quarter.' Tell you what. Doors songs are real easy for us to play. I'll tell the guys that you'll sit in on 'Riders.' It's in the key of E minor, right? By the way, I'm Sal." Joy joined the band and another Muslim-Jewish, brown-white, East-West barrier fell to pieces.

By my senior year at TZ, I was reveling in my newfound identity. For the past five years I had traveled a long and bumpy road from immigrant Pakistani boy to a rock and rolling American teenager. I was now also a naturalized U.S. citizen. I had gotten over my shyness and lack of confidence and to my surprise was voted "most friendly" senior in my high school yearbook. Dan Spitz signed my yearbook by saying, "Sal, see you underneath the Garden lights, don't ever stop trying, dude!" I was settled, happy, and felt at home.

But this was when Ami dropped the bombshell.

"*Beta*, you're going to be so happy to know that Abu and I have decided we're all going back to Pakistan and you're going to become a doctor!"

I had to fight to keep silent. My mother was pregnant with Shezy at the time and I didn't want to upset her. But inside I was seething.

Abu was being transferred from Copenhagen to Pakistan and we were all going to become one united family again, my mother told me. I saw the relief in my mother's eyes and I was genuinely happy that Ami and Abu were trying to make things work. But all my dreams of becoming a musician seemed to crumble as I heard Ami's words. I wanted my parents to come together, but not at the expense of my future. But I was left with no choice, and nobody paid any mind to my strong and deeply emotional protests when I finally spoke up and begged my parents to stay in New York. Ami, Abu, and Uncle Anwar spoke in unison.

"*Beta*, you can't become a *mirasi*! Being a doctor will give you respect and nobility."

So I resigned myself to my fate. Throughout that final year, I constantly listened to Led Zeppelin's plaintive "That's the Way," and I put a music video together in my head reliving all my best memories. In my mind's eye I played ping-pong with Frank Bianco in his basement; went to Beatlefests with Mike Langer; hung out all night at rock clubs with Ricky Herskowitz; saw Van Halen with Brian, Cindy Shaw, and Nikki Kessaris; jammed with Paul, Brian, Jeff, and Scott in Eclipse; and nursed my first big crush and subsequent heartache over Joy. I watched the Yankees win the World Series two years in a row. I remembered saying all five prayers on the day of the historic one game play-off between the Yankees and the Red Sox at Fenway Park in 1978. Allah must have heard my prayers because Bucky Dent hit a home run over the green monster to help win it for the Yankees. I watched John Alec and Brian talk animatedly about going on to become musicians and I asked Allah to somehow help me find my musical destiny.

But as I prepared to go back to Pakistan, there was no answer. Worse, discouraging and ominous signs began to appear. At the end of the year, a grumpy social studies teacher took the hard-earned wind out of my sails by writing this in my high school yearbook:

> Dear Sal: In many instances your social status as far as friendship among your peers and being one of the "gang" appeared to have priority over the serious purpose of gaining a sound education. In

about three to five years from now, you will realize the price you have paid for this happy time at TZ. It will hit you pretty soon and I hope you can take the shock. Best of luck.

The September of my senior year, John Bonham of Led Zeppelin died. And on December 8, 1980, my hero John Lennon was murdered by a crazed fanatic, Mark David Chapman. I heard the news that night on the radio and immediately drove with Mike Langer into Manhattan to lay flowers in front of Lennon's Dakota apartment. Mike and I saw an amazing sight that night. Thousands of fans just like us had blocked the streets and filled every nook of the building with flowers. I thought of the Dakota as a *dargah*, or shrine, for Lennon, who to me is like a Sufi poet from a rock and roll canon. All of us strangers hung out together singing our blues away with "Imagine," "Help!" and "Give Peace a Chance," feeling a unity and peace in our collective mourning. "To God we belong and to Him shall we return," Ami said to me that evening, quoting the Quran. I had to struggle to keep back the tears which were welling up because of the loss of a great artist, as well as my impending departure.

The final farewell was set for August 1981. After six years in America, I was going back to Pakistan. America had helped me discover myself and my passion for music. And now I was terrified I was going to lose both, forever.

FIVE
Finding My Way

On a hot summer afternoon in 1982, I stood among a crowd on Mall Road in Lahore, watching future men and women doctors from all three of the city's medical colleges peacefully protest the Punjab government's policies about medical jobs.

I was a first-year student at King Edward Medical College that June day, and I stood watching the senior students raise slogans in front of the same governor's mansion where I'd spent a small part of my childhood. Nepotism was rampant throughout the country, at all levels. General Muhammad Zia-ul-Haq's hand-picked cronies in the Ministry of Health and the Punjab Public Service Commission would arbitrarily pass or fail students and fire or hire medical graduates. None of the students liked this, of course, so they had taken to the streets in their white overalls and stethoscopes to protest. All this looked familiar, even though I'd been away for several years. When I was a child, my uncles and aunts had participated in boisterous and impassioned—but mostly peaceful—political rallies and campus protests just like this one. So I just sat back and watched the display of dissent unfold.

That was when the riot police arrived.

All of a sudden, it looked like a new colonialism was bearing down on my fellow medical students. Just as the British had during Partition, the riot police started to shove and baton-charge the protestors. The future doctors tried to protect themselves with their books and hands but were mercilessly beaten, thrashed, and handcuffed by the cops. Not even the women were spared. Men who tried to protect their female colleagues—including my future brother-in-law, Imran—had their heads smashed open by police *lathis*. Watching from my safe post, I could see the women and men defiantly holding their ground even as the police had them trapped and surrounded in the middle of daytime traffic. Some of the students' overalls were stained a scarlet red. The concrete sidewalk was wet with blood. The police actions were ruthless and coordinated. And the looks on the cops' faces and the might with which they swung their batons suggested that their orders were to show zero tolerance for anti-government rallies and congregations. The students never had a prayer. A big part of me wanted to do something to help. But I was paralyzed by the ferocity of the violence and the fear it struck in all who witnessed it.

I looked on in horror. What had happened to my Pakistan?

There had been a whole lot of changes since I'd last been in Pakistan.

Once tolerated, dissent was now deemed unpatriotic. But there were many more rules to Zia's game than that. The dictator had taken power in a military coup in 1977, later hanging the democratically elected Prime Minister Zulfiqar Ali Bhutto and sending his daughter Benazir and her family into exile. Zia's plan wasn't just to be an interim military leader. He had a long-term view to change the political, religious, and cultural destiny of the nation. Forging an unholy alliance with the religious right, Zia went on a campaign to take Pakistan back to a year zero of his own design. The entire establishment—from the president down to the ministers, judges, police, and TV and radio executives—was obsessed with stamping out *fahashi* (vulgarity) and *uriani* (obscenity). Music, song, and dance were considered corrupting tools of Satan that weakened the Muslim heart and mind and had to be wiped out of the national memory.

Gender segregation also became official state policy. Overnight, women and men risked jail for merely holding hands walking together in parks. Brothers and sisters couldn't sing standing side by side. State control over radio and TV made certain that even fathers and daughters couldn't touch each other in commercials or TV programs. Just as Charles Ingalls was about to hug or kiss his wife or daughter on *Little House on the Prairie*, for example, poof! He'd get within inches of them and disappear from the screen. In the government's twisted logic, Soviet-killing American bombs, guns, and rockets were celebrated, but innocuous U.S. family-oriented TV shows were deemed dangerous. Ditto the worldwide broadcast of the *Live Aid* concert in 1985. The bearded board of censors cut out anything that sounded licentious to their bionic ears—though of course, most of it was completely tame. Sufi poems and poets vanished because they promoted cultural and religious harmony. Even speeches by Pakistan's founder Muhammad Ali Jinnah about the separation of mosque and state were withdrawn from public view.

All of this couldn't have been more different from the environment I'd lived in as a child. At my grandparents' house, we'd watch *The Man from U.N.C.L.E.*, *The Fugitive*, and *The Saint*, starring Roger Moore, without any interruption whatsoever. But no more. Ragas like "Durga" couldn't be performed, owing to their Hindu-inspired names. Shia, Ahmadi, and other non-Sunni Muslims were targeted in McCarthy-era-like witch hunts. Physicist Abdus Salam, Pakistan's only Nobel laureate, was barred from starting a science school or even working in Pakistan because General Zia disapproved of his Ahmadi denomination. Anyone from non-Sunni communities who held a high post in the government, media, bureaucracy, or armed forces was demoted, transferred, or fired. It was as if General Zia had taken a page out of the dictatorial Mughal Emperor Aurangzeb's playbook in trying to force Islam down the throats of the Pakistani people. The difference was that this wasn't seventeenth century India—Pakistan was already more than 90 percent Muslim. The whole country was being prepared for war against its short history.

Zia's Islam wasn't the Islam that I—or a majority of Pakistanis—knew. Most Pakistanis' beliefs are inspired by tolerant Sufism. But Zia imported Wahabbism, the extreme, puritanical, violent strain that emerged from central Saudi Arabia in the nineteenth century. Zia divided the nation into a passionately centrist but powerless majority of Pakistanis and a Wahabbi-wannabe, armed-to-the-teeth minority of "Allah's soldiers" and student militias working under the umbrella of the ISI spy agency (Inter-services Intelligence, Pakistan's equivalent of the CIA) and the various religious parties, like the Jamaat-e-Islami. The connection with Saudi Arabia didn't end at Wahhabism. According to Pakistani author Ahmed Rashid's book *Taliban*, along with the covert support of the CIA, Saudi petrodollars partly funded Afghanistan's jihad against the Soviets. All of the weapons and money went through the generals in Islamabad.

Zia and his henchmen controlled the state media, the madrassahs, and the college campuses, including my new school, King Edward Medical

College. The influx into Pakistan of Kalashnikovs and rocket launchers and the rise of student-morality police had transformed college campuses into virtual war zones, resulting in campus shootings and sometimes death for anyone who stood up to the jihadi brigade. I was lucky to escape my college days with just a mangled guitar and a death threat. Violence was everywhere. Daily newspapers like *Jang*, *Dawn*, *The Nation*, and *The Pakistan Times* were filled with stories of eighteen- and nineteen-year-olds killing and wounding each other in gang fights over trivial events like fender benders or someone looking at somebody's sister or fiancée in the wrong way. College students kidnapped teachers and rival students just to disrupt exam schedules. Poor people caught stealing food would have one hand amputated while those who were rich, with connections, plundered the country. (Zia, in his great benevolence, decreed that anesthesia had to be administered before anybody got his hand sliced off.)

Drug addiction was also rampant, as kids had practically nowhere to turn for entertainment. Cheap heroin and hashish were always freely available on college campuses. During my early years back in Pakistan I saw a few friends self-destruct by trying to create a drug-induced illusion of normality. But nothing was normal.

It was beyond my comprehension how this mustachioed dictator, who had taken Pakistani society into the dark ages, could be considered a friend of the United States. All the values that I had associated with America were being violated daily in Pakistan. But Zia wasn't stupid. While helping America fight the Cold War, he also allowed some (controlled) cultural exchanges in order to maintain the façade of a tolerant Pakistani society. Those exchanges had one purpose: to appease the westernized Pakistani elite and Zia's American and Western allies. Once or twice a year the American cultural center organized Hollywood film screenings and tours for jazz and classical musicians. I was lucky enough to get a pass to see Kevin Eubanks and the Charlie Byrd Trio, who played to packed audiences of about five hundred people. But I was sitting with a hand-picked audience full of foreign diplomats and kids of high-ranking officials. Zia had learned the colonial way of governance: keep the natives suppressed, divided, and under control while supporting the corrupt feudal elite. As long as the elite were happy, there'd be no revolt and no biting the hand that generously fed it.

But anyone could see what was really going on. And what was worse, Zia was laying the foundation for decades of conflict at home and abroad.

With the CIA's help and Saudi funding, the ISI helped to create, arm, and train ruthless warriors known as the mujahideen. The Taliban later rose to prominence fighting mujahideen warlords. And from the mujahideen "freedom fighters" there rose a tall and cunning man called Osama bin Laden who, along with the mujahideen, helped defeat the Soviets and win the Cold War for the West. Many years later, he would turn his sights on his former patrons and send terrorists to fly planes into buildings on September 11, 2001.

Looking around this barren, violent landscape, I felt that my musical dreams were dead on my arrival back home. I couldn't see how I could be a musician in this now-alien country. But with the help of one woman and one athlete, I found redemption—and a new way of fitting into my old country.

One year before the music police broke my guitar at my medical school talent show in 1982, I attended my Uncle Fareed's wedding in Rawalpindi. Pakistani weddings are all-consuming cultural events: three-day celebrations filled with song, dance, and merriment. They were some of the few bacchanals of joy that General Zia's dictatorship had thankfully failed to quash. Women don their most beautiful clothes and jewelry, spending days preparing their hair and painting their hands with intricate designs in henna. In most families, weddings are the one event where boys can have an all-access pass to mix with beautiful girls, and are the breeding ground for many secret trysts and romances that never would have a chance to develop in an otherwise segregated society.

Uncle Fareed's wedding was a revelation for me, as a Pakistani who'd just returned from America. It showed me another face of Pakistan. Behind the veil, there was a rich and vibrant society that embraced laughter, beauty, music, and song. Looking at the girls wearing exotic earrings, shimmering temple ornaments, rings, and necklaces, their curves wrapped in sensual, multi-colored *shalwar kameez*, *tang-pajamas*, and *ghararas*, I realized that I'd only seen the surface of a society under the boot of General Zia. Most people still managed to privately hold on to their cultural traditions and progressive values despite the interference of the government and its cronies in the public sphere.

The sight of a seventeen-year-old girl singing a traditional wedding song gave me even more hope. She was sitting in the center of a circle of young women and her beautiful voice gently recited a classic melody composed by Amir Khusro.

I was entranced by the young woman's rendition of Khusro's timeless love poem. A delicate scarf hung from her right shoulder and her black hair was plaited down to her waist like the lovely Layla from the famous Arabian tale of Layla and her mad lover Majnun. Unlike many of the other girls, she wasn't wearing a lot of makeup and jewelry. Here, I thought, was the promise of romance amid the fearful, segregated society to which I'd returned.

Back in high school I'd made friends with girls like Joy Schloss, Cindy Shaw, and Nikki Kessaris. But they'd become simply friends. This girl I was looking at was someone I immediately knew I wanted to pursue in a different way. I was back in Pakistan now. The rules were different. I didn't know how to approach her. I didn't have the chance to, anyway, not yet. In a flash she was swallowed up into the crowd and I saw her no more that day.

I spent the next two days desperately trying to find out who she was. Uncle Fareed's wife, my new Aunt Hina, immediately saw an opportunity to put her *rishta* (match-making) skills into action. The girl I had seen was named Samina, Hina told me. She was a soldier's daughter. She and her family had come from Lahore for the wedding. Samina had a love for singing, painting, reading, and dancing. She was also deeply spiritual. She had, amazingly, already accompanied her mother on the *hajj*, the Muslim pilgrimage to Mecca. In Pakistan, it was very rare to see a girl so young take the strenuous journey and possess the spiritual discipline required to perform the *hajj*. Hina—whose family were old friends of Samina's parents—gave me more details about this beautiful wedding singer. Since childhood, Samina had loved Barbra Streisand and The Carpenters as well as *ghazals*. She liked to sing duets with her dad, who was a Nat King Cole fan. She'd also learned spiritual discipline from her parents. At his Christian school, her father had won a gold medal in Bible study. Her mother, Nina, was a *hafiz-e-quran* (one who's learned the Quran by heart). Samina had learned the Quran in translation and regularly kept up with daily prayers, observing thirty days of fasting during Ramadan.

By all appearances, she was the easy-listening FM to my rock and roll. And yet, there were similarities between us. Like me, Samina was studying to be a doctor. And she'd seen her share of parental problems. Her father, a former brigadier in Pakistan's army, had served as military secretary and later as Pakistan's ambassador to the emirate of Abu Dhabi during the late Prime Minister Bhutto's government. He was a charming and worldly man with an unfortunate weakness for the ladies, and had left Samina's mother for another woman. Samina had to make the difficult choice of deciding which parent to stay with. She loved her father very much but chose her mother, and moved in with her, along with her two sisters and older brother. Her parents' divorce also meant that Samina had to give up the luxurious, privileged diplomatic lifestyle that she and her family had been accustomed to. Samina, with her mother and siblings, had to start life all over again in a modest home in Lahore with no air-conditioning or car. In those early difficult days, Samina's faith gave her the strength to overcome the trauma of her parents' split. Being well-versed in the Quran also helped her grow as a woman and made her more aware of her rights. She learned that she had the right to an education and to knowledge. She also had the right to economic independence, to an inheritance, and to the choice of a life partner. If the need arose, Islam also gave her the right of divorce. She empowered herself with that knowledge so that she could protect herself and other women from the pain that she saw in her mother's eyes. Pakistan was filled with such stories of helpless women living in a male chauvinistic society. For women, it was a society deeply rooted in the rituals of religion but largely devoid of *haqooq-ul-ibad* (rights toward humanity). Samina was determined to make a different path for herself.

In Hina's pencil sketch, I sensed a strong similarity between Samina's personality and that of both my mother and my grandmother Aziza. I became even more restless to know this mystery girl. But Hina warned me to tread carefully around Samina. She was protective of her and sensitive about her fatherless household. Still, Hina promised she would introduce us the next time Hina was in Lahore.

But next time proved to be a lifetime.

Amid all the chaos of military dictatorship, there was but one inspiring figure to look up to: Imran Khan. Samina motivated me to go on a spiritual odyssey. But through the *desi* obsession called cricket, Imran Khan held up an example of a modern-day leader to emulate. The captain of Pakistan's cricket team, Imran Khan was a living legend. He was a combination of Michael Jordan, Muhammad Ali, David Beckham, Roger Federer, and Babe Ruth all rolled into one. His exploits on and off the field made magazine and newspaper headlines worldwide. He was as bold off the field as on, too, seen with leggy blondes, Bollywood actresses, English heiresses, and Middle Eastern princesses.

Imran amazed me, though, long before I was even aware of girls. I particularly remember watching black and white footage of Pakistan playing against the mighty Australians at Leeds in the first cricket World Cup, held in England in 1975. The white-flannelled, fair-skinned, fiery twenty-two-year-old Pashtun ran in and bowled to the seemingly indestructible Aussie batsman Greg Chappell, forcing him into error and sending him back to the Headingley pavilion. In the same game, I saw Imran face off with the long-haired, dreaded, and fearsome Aussie speed merchant Dennis Lillee. Imran displayed an almost arrogant calm, confidence, and poise—traits not typically associated with a Pakistani cricketer's temperament. Being from a family of Pashtuns on my mother's side, I instantly recognized his aura and felt a tribal bond with him. It's part of tribal folklore that Pashtuns are loyal and courageous and will not barter their honor for anyone or anything. They also don't forget to repay the smallest kindness, and will aggressively avenge any slight aimed against them. It's always good to have a Pashtun as a friend but never as an enemy.

I came back to Pakistan in time to watch Imran's demolition of India's cricket team, in the spring of 1983. Being at the Pakistan-India matches during the two countries' dramatic face-off that year was like being in the Coliseum in Rome. Except all of us felt like we were the emperors. We were united whether we were rich or poor, male or female, soldier or civilian. We produced a deafening roar at the fall of every Indian wicket or a boundary hit by a Pakistani player. (But even the Indian players and public were in awe of Imran Khan.) The strong partisan nature of the crowd was awe-inspiring, like New York fans sitting in Yankee Stadium watching the Bronx bombers take on the Red Sox. But instead of hot dogs, beer, and "Take Me Out to the Ball Game" or "Charge!" chants, we had spicy seekh kebabs, Coke, and Pakistani men, women, teenagers, and kids screaming out "Allahu Akbar" slogans.

In some ways it was actually like seeing Led Zeppelin at Madison Square Garden: total intensity. This was the kind of thing I missed. At the matches, girls screamed and cheered and held up players' placards and Pakistani flags; sang Bollywood songs; and created a rock concertlike atmosphere in a country where all public gender mixing was discouraged. (There was no way the morality police could keep hundreds of wives and daughters from rooting for the home team alongside husbands and brothers.) No Pakistani rock band yet existed. But these same stadiums would reverberate with Junoon's music a decade or so later. Even before I got started playing music again, I recognized the passion of the girls and understood their yearning for their own natural cultural identity: modern and Pakistani. The joy and happiness of the crowd was a total negation of the false "sober" shackles that had been affixed by the police state. I wasn't alone, I realized, in feeling alienated. I could feel young people's unrest and also a cultural vacuum that had to be filled.

There were very few homegrown cultural figures left in General Zia's Pakistan. The exceptions were folky pop singers like Alamgir and Shehki and the pop diva Nazia Hassan and her brother Zoheb. But their popularity was mostly dependent on the odd television performance, and they didn't hold big concerts in Pakistan. Cricketers and their charismatic leader had the opposite experience. Imran Khan would go on to do humanitarian work and even start a political party. For me, it was his larger-than-life mythic sporting image which burned into my consciousness and that of every other Pakistani.

I first became aware of Imran Khan at the age of ten. Like me, he had grown up in two cultures, Pakistani and British. He faced the same tug of war between the West and Islam. We were both Aitchisonians. He had gone on to Oxford University and become an internationally celebrated sportsman. But what was more crucial for me was that he felt proud to be a Pakistani. He inspired millions of his poor countrymen and women to aim for the stars. People like Imran Khan provided me and others with an alternative, progressive vision of Pakistan, completely at odds with the joyless, dark, Cromwellian version enforced by the mullahs and their military enablers. The competing visions were like huge, grinding tectonic plates, and they would continue to clash throughout my musical career and my life. Through Imran's cricketing example I saw another side of Pakistan: excellence-driven, stylish, and resting on a foundation of hard work and merit. It was an example I was going to follow.

By going to all six Pakistan-India matches in 1983, I got to know Pakistan again. I travelled with friends, relatives, and scores of rabid fans by car, bus, and plane to all the games across Pakistan. From the northern Punjabi cities of Lahore and Faisalabad to the southern port city of Karachi and neighboring Hyderabad in Sindh, I saw a multicultural, multiethnic mix of Punjabis, Sindhis, Baluchis, Pashtuns, Memons, Parsees, Hindus, and Christians being ruled by men in khaki and men in beards.

Watching those games filled me with pride. They also helped pass the abundant time on my hands. In New York, we had sometimes seen Bollywood films, and I'd missed the likes of Waheed Murad and the romantic comedy-dramas he'd popularized. So one thing I had looked forward to after coming back was watching those kinds of films again.

Forget it. Pakistani movies in the 1980s were a joke. Gun-, hatchet- and *gandasa*- (Punjabi axe-) wielding action heroes shot and sliced up the screen in low-budget flicks, mirroring the violence on the streets. Murad and his genre died a slow death as Zia starved the Pakistani film and music industries. Meanwhile, Zia and his family were known to love watching Indian movies on the presidential VCR. The "anti-India" dictator even hosted Bollywood star Shatrughan "Shotgun" Sinha as an official state guest in 1981. (Zia's daughter was a Sinha fan.) While Sinha enjoyed Zia's hospitality in Islamabad, Pakistani artists and poets languished in cultural jails. Besides the shoot-'em-up fare in the theatres, most Pakistanis had no choice but to watch pirated Indian and Hollywood films on home VCRs. The Pakistani dictator's cultural apartheid made Indian actors like Shotgun Sinha, Naseer ud din Shah, and Amitabh Bachchan the only *desi* cultural icons for millions of Pakistanis. It was as if Zia's state policy was to create a nation of voyeurs, spectators, and hermits.

As I traveled to see the cricket games, Zia's "cultural vision" was everywhere. Pakistan was swarming with mullahs and army majors, colonels, and generals. Mosques were named after Saudi kings. Rockets aimed at India bore the monikers of Islamic warriors. Soldiers were encouraged to grow beards if they wanted to be promoted. All female newscasters on state TV had to cover their heads, as did even PIA air hostesses. In the 1960s and 1970s, women had choices. Now it was the general's way or the highway.

The only places General Zia couldn't touch with his propaganda machine were the cricket grounds. All stadiums that spring of 1983 were jam-packed with tens of thousands of delirious Pakistanis singing, dancing, banging *dhol* drums, and blowing horns in a mass patriotic fervor. The celebrations were as much an up-yours signal to the military dictatorship as they were about trying to trounce Pakistan's much larger, more celebrated, separated-at-birth neighbor and "mortal enemy," India.

I'd missed seeing and playing cricket while I was away in Tappan, and now my love of the game came back in full force. While studying in med school, I joined the Lahore Gymkhana cricket club. The club was managed by Imran's mother's family and the superstar himself would come to train and practice there from time to time. Hordes of fans and admirers followed him. From a close vantage point I would watch him hit colossal sixes out of the ground and over the trees with effortless ease. Gathering speed like an Olympics javelin thrower he'd race in from a distance of 30 to 40 yards and hurl the five-and-a-half-ounce red thunderbolt at more than 90 miles per hour, curving it in the air at will. Most batters would have no clue which way the ball would move, and many international players saw their careers end due to Imran's lethal bowling. But the speed and the strenuous effort required to sustain it took its toll on Imran. In 1983, he suffered a shin fracture which took him out of the game for almost three years, and from his immortal platform he fell to earth and was shunned and reviled by his enemies in the cricket establishment and the Pakistani media. Some disgruntled mullahs and gossip circles insinuated that his leg injury was Allah's curse on him for his sexual appetite and playboy image. But *kismet* would bring him redemption, and bring Imran and me closer together.

Before traveling the country to see the cricket matches in 1983, I was still sullenly accepting my lot in life. In the winter of 1982 I focused on my studies in medical college and rekindled my passion for playing my favorite sport. I hoped that by becoming a doctor, as my parents fervently wished, I would be able to find a way back to the life I left in America. I missed jamming with Eclipse, and I still dreamed up ways to break into the American music scene. The obsessive passion that had built inside of me needed release. I realized that if I didn't find an outlet for the frustrations dammed up inside my heart, I would end up lonely and depressed.

I needed an emotional rescue. And, in an ironic stroke that the *taliban* wouldn't have appreciated, I partly had my guitar to thank for getting to know my soul mate. A few days after my humiliation at the talent show, my Aunt Hina came to visit my family in Lahore. She mentioned that she was planning to visit Samina—the girl I'd glimpsed a year earlier at Hina and Fareed's wedding—and her family that afternoon. Hina didn't have to remind me who Samina was. I immediately canceled all my plans for the day and volunteered to drive Hina to Samina's house.

Samina was just like I remembered her: elegant and soulful, needing no gaudy jewels or splashy makeup to attract attention. She walked into her living room serenely, wearing a white *tang-pajama*, her long ebony hair tied in a plait. Any fears that the impulse I had felt at the wedding a year before was just a shallow infatuation were instantly dispelled.

I tried to think up a way to start a conversation with Samina. The major problem was finding some way to distract her mother Nina, who was talking nonstop about the virtues of Samina's brother Imran, a surgeon in training. That was to be expected: she was her kids' greatest champion and pillar of strength and had had to be strong for them and herself after the divorce. But her words sounded far off and garbled to me, like the incomprehensible speech of the adults in Charlie Brown cartoons.

I finally managed to find my voice and spoke directly to Samina. "So . . . er . . . um . . . how's Allama Iqbal compared to King Edward?" Asking about her medical school wasn't much of a line, but it was all I had.

Samina smiled at me and started to answer when Nina interrupted.

"What could she tell you, Mansoor?" she said. Now I smiled. Who was Mansoor?

"She's such a modest girl, Mansoor," Nina continued. "Let me tell you how hard she works . . ." and went on and on and on. Somehow Samina's mother had either wrongly heard that my name was Mansoor or had just arbitrarily chosen a name for me.

I must have looked like I was in pain. Hina finally intervened. "Aunty, maybe Samina could tell us about some of her experiences at school?" she said hopefully.

Aunty Nina tried to speak again but this time Samina managed to cut in. She looked at me directly and asked me what I thought of my school, King Edward Medical College. I stammered something stupid about the professors being very strict about grading and the fact that there were only thirty girls out of three hundred students in my class.

"We have parity between men and women at Allama Iqbal," Samina said. "But the boys are pretty dumb, of course."

Everyone laughed, but alarmed by the possible direction this conversation was heading in, Nina quickly steered toward other topics that had nothing to do with gender or sex. Playing her role as my go-between, Aunt Hina proudly mentioned that I was the best guitar player back in Tappan Zee High School and that I would've been a world-famous rock star had I not left America to come study medicine in Lahore. That was an exaggeration but I took the compliment. It also took my fate in a whole new direction.

Samina's brother Imran perked up. "Really?! You know, I've always wanted to learn how to play the guitar," he said, with real excitement in his voice. This was my chance.

"I can teach you," I said, watching Aunty Nina and her three daughters look at me with the first signs of interest. I didn't want to appear over-eager, though, so I said in a deeper, skeptical voice, "But let's talk about it. I'm usually very picky about taking students. In your case I could make an exception, since your family is so close to Aunt Hina." For the first time that afternoon, I had managed to impress Aunty Nina. Nevertheless I had to play it cool and struggle to hide my own excitement. Here was a way to get close to Samina at last. Imran and I agreed that our first guitar lesson would be next week.

I knew I couldn't pursue Samina the way I would have tried to pursue Joy Schloss back in high school in Tappan. There is no concept in Pakistani society of just calling a girl up or asking her out. There was no way Samina and I would be going to see a *Friday the 13th* movie or a Van Halen concert. On the drive back home from Samina's house, I was in a daze. I had met my soul mate and now had to figure out a way to her heart. This will probably sound insane to most Westerners: an eighteen-year-old boy contemplating marriage to a girl he's just met. But in Pakistan, that is the cultural norm in most cases. When a boy and girl are attracted to each other, the only socially acceptable way for them to be together is as husband and wife. And besides, I had always been a deeply intuitive person. I believed that God had brought me to Samina.

I asked Hina what I should do. She told me that the best thing was to write Samina a letter. "Use the fact that you are both in medical school," she advised. "You have that in common. Make it your excuse to get to know her better." But she warned me to tread carefully. Samina did not have a father to protect the dignity of the household, and her reputation could be easily destroyed in Lahore's vicious gossip circles. I rushed home and locked myself in my room. My wastebasket was soon full of dozens of failed attempts to get the words right. I finally settled on a simple and straightforward message:

Salaam aleikum, Samina.

It was great seeing you again. Although we weren't formally intro-

duced back then, I first saw you at my aunt's wedding a year ago. I'm writing this letter because I didn't want to offend you by calling. I've grown up in New York, where speaking to a girl on the phone is not a taboo. I hope you won't mind my audacity! I just want to convey to you that I am an admirer. Your voice, your smile, and the way you carry yourself have touched me very deeply. I hope that we can get to know each other, inshallah [God willing]! Khuda hafiz, Salman.

I carefully folded the letter into a blue envelope and wrote Samina's name on the front. Then I hopped into my Mazda and immediately drove back to her house. Since she didn't have a mailbox, I threw the letter over the gate, and prayed to God that no one except her would read it. I drove home with my hands sweating. I didn't know if I was doing the right thing. I didn't know if this was acceptable in Pakistan or not. But I didn't care.

The day of Imran's (known to me by his nickname "Kim") first guitar lesson filled me with great anticipation as well as terror. I would finally see Samina again, and would know whether my feelings were reciprocated. I arrived only to discover that Samina wasn't home. But Imran was there, enthusiastic and ready for our lesson. The thought entered my head that Kim might have learned about my clumsy efforts to court his sister and would teach me a lesson. This was not just an idle fear. In Pakistani culture, brothers will ruthlessly avenge any slight against the honor of their sisters—seriously wounding, debilitating, or even killing any potential troublemakers, no questions asked.

But thankfully Kim appeared oblivious to my intentions. I hoped that I would see Samina during our next lesson, but again, no luck. Almost four weeks of lessons went by without any sight or sound of the girl I was pining away for. I was despondent. Had I screwed up by writing the letter? Was there some rule I'd broken?

When I arrived for Kim's next lesson, he met me and ushered me into his room. As is the custom in Pakistan, guests are usually greeted with snacks and cold drinks, and Kim called out to his sister Ayesha to bring me some fruit *chaat*, *namak paras*, and mango juice. Ayesha apparently wasn't home, but then another voice called out from downstairs: Samina's voice. She said she would bring us something. But her footsteps receded into the distance after putting the food outside Kim's door. That was more than I could take. I had to talk to her. I turned to Kim. "I left something in my car. Be back in a minute."

I ran out of his room, hoping to catch Samina before she disappeared downstairs. As I raced toward the staircase, I was suddenly greeted by loud and angry barking. Max, the family's ruthless terrier, came racing toward me with hate glowing in his little eyes. He was barking like mad and I thought he would bite my ankle at any moment.

I was standing, pinned against the wall by this ridiculous little dog, when Samina appeared to rescue me from my tormentor. Dressed in a simple *shalwar kameez*, she picked up the angry mutt, who immediately became a docile puppy in her arms. Embarrassed at having been held hostage by a tiny dog, I tried to regain my machismo. I gathered up the courage to speak from my heart and . . . completely ran out of anything to say.

Samina looked at me as if I were some curious little creature that had crawled inside the house. I stared at her, mouth agape, before I finally found some words.

"I . . . I need to get something from my car. . . . could you . . . er . . . open the gate . . . please?"

Samina shrugged and led me to the gate. She opened the latch and turned to leave, and I realized that it was now or never.

"Um . . . did you get my letter?"

She stopped.

"What letter?" I heard a hint of caution entering her voice.

"It was in a blue envelope," I said, my heart sinking. What if she never got it? "I dropped it off about four weeks ago."

Samina turned to face me. And my heart sank further. Instead of love, joy, modesty, desire, or any of the other emotions I hoped for, her face was cold, stern. An ice sculpture.

"You wrote that letter?"

I nodded meekly. Suddenly I wanted this to be a bad dream from which I would awake at any moment. Her eyes narrowed further.

"I've been wondering who 'Salman' was," she said, looking me over suspiciously. "I thought it was one of the boys from my college, but I don't know any Salman there."

"That's me. Remember, I came over with my aunt that day . . ."

She suddenly laughed, and I felt even more stupid than ever.

"I thought your name was Mansoor!"

At that moment, I felt like a total moron for not correcting Aunty Nina when I had had the chance.

"Let me explain . . ."

But Samina didn't give me a chance. She immediately exploded at me.

"What kind of girl do you think I am?" She said fiercely, her arms crossed in defiance. "We gave you respect, let you into our home. And then you try to pick me up like I'm some dumb blonde from a cheap Hollywood film!"

I desperately tried to explain that I wasn't trying to "pick her up."

"Then what do you want from me?" she asked, her anger overheating.

I don't know how it happened. I tried to stop the words even as I heard them coming from my mouth. To this day, I have no idea who or what took over my vocal cords and made me say the words that would change my life.

"I want to marry you."

Samina's eyes went wide. And then she laughed.

I realized that I was drowning. I should have cut my losses and gotten the hell out of there with whatever shred of dignity I still had. But then the dam around my heart burst and it all came flooding out. I was suddenly like Aunty Nina, my mouth moving faster than the eye could see. I told Samina that I was in love with her, that I needed her, and that I couldn't live without her.

She looked at me like I was insane. Which, of course, I was. Anyone who has ever fallen madly in love knows exactly the mania that had possessed me.

But before Samina could respond to my desperate pleas of affection, a loud honk startled both of us.

A car pulled into the driveway, and her mother Nina emerged, a smile on her face.

"Oh, look. It's Mansoor."

Romance in Pakistan was proving to be difficult. It could also be hazardous to one's health. I was relatively safe pursuing the object of my affection from within the confines of a family friendship. Outside, though, General Zia had introduced medieval laws which made women vulnerable to accusations of adultery and wrongful fornication. Poor people would be lashed in public for adultery or the "crime" of getting caught in a romantic rendezvous. The torturers would whip the unfortunate souls until they lost consciousness—a barbaric practice that had no precedent in the Lahore I knew from before or even in the history of the Islamic Republic of Pakistan. I only saw such images because the papers would defy Zia and print them.

As I was spinning my wheels trying to pursue Samina, I continued to find sustenance and inspiration in cricket, and Imran Khan's example. My longstanding obsession was just growing stronger. Even when I'd been totally hypnotized by the Beatles and Led Zeppelin, I would follow Imran's and the Pakistan cricket team's fortunes through BBC World Service radio programs. Like my father, I felt an ownership over and immense pride in the Pakistan cricket team, just as I had with the New York Yankees. Imran Khan's heroic performances around the cricketing world were the fuel for intense dinner table conversations for the whole Ahmad family in Tappan. Imran was one of the few things that both my parents agreed upon, and our family couldn't wait for the day he became captain of the Pakistan cricket team. As a special treat, my father flew with me to London to witness the historic Pakistan win over England in 1982 at the famed Lords Cricket Ground. I was watching a true Pakistani hero whom even General Zia could not rein in. Imran was an object lesson in the power of non-political public figures—one I'd internalize and draw on as I became a musician who clashed with the government. You didn't want to be on the wrong side of the Pakistani public's love for Imran Khan, even if you were a military dictator.

When it came to girls, though, I was no Imran Khan. After my failed attempt to talk to Samina, I wrote her dozens of letters and threw them over the gate of her house. Again I confessed my love, the depth of my feelings, my insecurities, and my fears and hopes. I told her that she was my soul mate and that I would do anything for her. I left her my phone number and begged her to call me so that I could talk to her in person. I heard nothing back.

I was on the verge of despair when one day my mother's cousin Tasnim came in to my grandparents' living room, looking concerned for my well-being. She told me that I had a phone call from a "Doctor Samina." I ran to the phone, which was unfortunately located in the least private spot in the house—the dining room, right by the front door. I cradled the phone close to my ear as my family members shot me concerned glances. They assumed I had some medical condition that I was keeping secret. Why else would a female doctor be calling my home?

"Hello." I held my breath.

"So what do you want to talk about?" The voice on the other end was stern, formal, but not cold.

For the next two and a half hours, I told her everything. My life in America. My love for music. My high school band. My dreams of playing guitar again before the crowds. The pain of trying to integrate into an alien and repressed society.

She listened and asked me questions abruptly, like an interrogator making sure to get the truth out of a subject. And then finally, Samina opened up to me. She wanted me to know that she was taking a great risk with her reputation by even calling me. I told her I would support her until the day I died. But I felt I had to warn her that I had faults and flaws. My travels had made me appreciate the planet's diversity, but I felt like I didn't really belong anywhere in this world. I just managed to live between the cracks of different places and cultures and had always felt like a complete unknown. For years, I had been wondering why God brought me back to Pakistan, but now I understood.

There was a long silence on the line. And then Samina finally spoke.

"Next week, *inshallah*, you will be officially invited to my house for tea," she said softly. "You can make your case to my mother then."

Samina hung up. I stared at the phone in wild, happy shock. But a cruel twist threw up one more obstacle between me and my future wife. Crossing it taught me a lot about love, and about Pakistan.

On the same spring day in 1983 I was set to go to Samina's house and propose, I came home to find a large gathering of young men inside my house. It was a *jirga*, an informal council called by my mom's younger brother Junaid. Juni *mamun* was only a few years older than me. Seeing the expressions on the men's faces, I realized something was terribly wrong.

"What's going on?" I asked.

Juni *mamun* looked at me with intense emotion in his eyes. "Someone's trying to steal Ami's land," he said.

That's when I knew how serious the *jirga* was. Real estate is like gold in Pakistan. It's not unusual for a 500-square-foot plot of land to appreciate fifty times or more its original cost within a span of a few years. That's why land-grabbing mafias working in tandem with corrupt cops, lawyers, and judges are a menace to Pakistani society. Their common targets are law-abiding citizens like Ami Aziza. My grandmother wasn't wealthy, but she owned a small parcel of undeveloped land that was one of her few assets. Apparently a criminal gang had broken in through the gate and taken possession of the property.

I sat down, stunned, and listened as Juni *mamun* and his college buddies plotted how they could retake the land and restore the family's honor. The idea that anyone would try to hurt my grandmother or steal from her ignited my *junoon*. So if there was going to be action, I was going to be part of it.

The young men, mostly medical students who were friends of Junaid's, hatched a plan to take the land back by force. Looking back, it was clear that we all had watched too many bootleg copies of *Rambo*, but at the time it seemed like the natural thing to do. A massive show of force would be enough to scare off the thugs who were squatting on the property. So we went to kick the bastards off my grandmother's land.

I don't know what I could have been thinking. My relatives and I had to be at Samina's house for tea later that day. But I convinced myself that this would be a quick little operation. I would beat up the bad guys, salvage my family's honor, and then wow Samina and her mother with stories of my bravery.

That Tuesday afternoon we drove off on our mission. There were thirteen of us in two separate vehicles, with a few AK-47s thrown in the trunk. Automatic weapons were totally commonplace in Pakistan at that time as a side effect of the war in neighboring Afghanistan. We brought along the guns more for show than anything—we weren't killers and only wanted to scare off the thugs who had taken possession of Aziza's land.

The plan was to kick the thieves out and then hold the property until the cops (whom we'd tipped off earlier) came. Junaid had brought the original deed to show the police, and we figured the matter would end there.

We drove up to the mud wall that surrounded the property in Model Town. The only way in was the front gate. We got out and saw that there were just a handful of scrawny-looking men inside, near a ramshackle hut that had been hastily erected by the squatters. All of us in our little posse smiled, surmising that this was going to be easier than we thought.

The thirteen of us broke through the gate and raced inside screaming with outrage and vengeance. When the thieves saw us, they bolted, climbing over the wall like terrified monkeys. That made me grin and think, "No problem at all!"

Having easily regained control of the property, most of my uncle's friends soon took off. Four of us stayed behind, unarmed, waiting for the police to turn up. Once the cops arrived, we would show them the deed and all would be well.

I stood by the main gate, looking out for the police. The gray, overcast April sky rumbled with thunder, and heavy rainfall soon turned the dirt road where I was standing into a river of mud. I looked at my watch. Where were the cops? I wanted to get this over with so that I could get home and change out of my rain-soaked *kurta* and get ready for my big evening with Samina's family.

A car suddenly turned around the corner and slowly approached the gate. But it was a dusty old Toyota, not a police cruiser. Something wasn't right.

As I watched warily, the car pulled up to the gate. I saw three men inside, as well as a large woman wearing a black *chador*. A door opened, and the veiled woman emerged alone. The car quickly sped off as the woman approached me.

"Get out of my way!" she ordered. "This is my home!"

I realized she was working with the criminal gang and stood my ground. "This is my grandmother's land," I said as forcefully as I could.

All of a sudden the woman made a break for the gate. I blocked her, and she rammed me with the force of a rhinoceros. I felt all the air explode out of my lungs. Somehow I managed to stay on my feet and pushed her back. But she just charged me again and again.

I wasn't going to hit a woman so I did a Muhammad Ali "rope a dope," taking all her punches. I felt incredibly stupid. Here I was, a tall, healthy young man, having the crap knocked out of him by a middle-aged woman. This wasn't the kind of heroism I wanted Samina to hear about.

The woman responded to my "rope a dope" moves by striking her glass-bangle-covered forearms against the gate until the jewelry shattered and blood streaked her wrists.

Suddenly she fell to the ground and tore her chador to shreds with her fingernails. She grabbed a handful of mud and smeared it across her face and clothes.

"I've been dishonored!" she screamed. "I've been raped! Rape!"

At that instant, a flashing blue light made me raise my head. The cops had arrived just in time to witness this moment of infamy. Three cops led by an SHO (station house officer) carrying a *lathi* emerged from the police jeep.

"What's the problem?" they asked the writhing woman.

She showed off her bloody forearms and her torn clothes, weeping big tears as she luridly described how I had prevented her from entering her property and then attacked her.

I tried to explain what really had happened, but the cops (whom I soon realized had been paid off by the gang) were not interested. As Junaid, my cousin Amir, and Khalid, one of Juni *mamun*'s friends, emerged from inside, we desperately tried to tell the police that we were medical students, not criminals.

The station house officer shook his head in mock despair.

"If a healer can ravage a woman, what is our country coming to?"

"No, you don't understand!" I shouted. "This is my family's property!"

Junaid tried to show the crooked cop our deed to the land, but the SHO shrugged dismissively.

"That's just a piece of paper, son," he said. "It doesn't mean anything."

With those words, I realized that the rule of law was truly dead in Pakistan. I began to protest, but my speech was cut short as the cops took out handcuffs and bound my wrists.

The only thing I could think of as the corrupt cops pushed us inside the jeep and drove us off to jail was Samina.

We were taken to a holding cell in Model Town police station, a small dingy room that housed several hardened criminals with cruel eyes. The air was rank and infested with aggressive mosquitoes. As our jailers handcuffed us to each other and then turned to leave, I called out in fury, "I want my phone call!"

Ugh. I guess I had watched too many cop shows in America. An officer looked at me with contempt.

"What phone call would that be, doctor *sahib*?" Then he disappeared.

As the rain pattered down on the roof above, I hung my head in despair. My uncle Junaid's response to this crisis was to seek refuge in a happy delusion. He had convinced himself that this was all a mistake, and the cops he had called earlier in the day, who had seemed so sympathetic when he told them about the men who had stolen his mother's land, would show up any minute. They would corroborate our story and we would be released. It didn't occur to him that the cops he had spoken with were the very same ones who had arrested us under false pretenses.

I let him keep his fantasies as I looked around the small room. I avoided the intense eyes of the real criminals and focused my attention on the small hole in the ground that would serve as our communal toilet. Whenever an inmate used the latrine, he could call for the guards to give him some water to cleanse himself, as is the Islamic custom. Then a sadistic little man in uniform would arrive with a jug. Instead of pouring the water onto the hands of the prisoners, he enjoyed throwing it in their faces.

We spent one day and two nights in that holding cell each with one arm handcuffed to our rickety beds. Finally we emerged from the nightmare and were taken in front of a magistrate. My relatives had learned what had happened and had come to bail us out. But the magistrate, also bought off by the gang, decided to remand us to the Civil Lines jail near Regal Chowk. Because rape would be hard to prove, the charge against me was reduced to unlawful entry and criminal harassment.

Just when I thought it was going to end, the bad dream continued. I spent two more nights in prison, my only companions a pair of malnourished cats that would slip inside the bars, looking at me with hungry eyes. I shook my head and felt totally defeated. I had fallen so low that even these cats had more freedom than I did.

Finally, negotiations between my uncle and the SHO boiled down to a simple equation. The cops knew we were innocent and they had to let us go—but they wanted something for their troubles. Pay less now and get out of jail without a record, they told us, or try Pakistan's corrupt justice system and get stuck in the courts for generations while clearing our names and securing our property. The charade came to an end when my uncle agreed to pay a token sum to the dirty cops and we were let go without any criminal records.

As I was led outside the jail, the newly enriched station house officer smiled.

"Keep up the studies, doctor *sahib*," he said shamelessly. "The country needs good men like you."

To this day that plot of land that my grandmother inherited is still disputed real estate. And my uncle Junaid hasn't given up trying to legally claim it on behalf of his late mother Aziza.

After five days in prison, I immediately drove home and called Samina. She hung up on me at once. Desperate, I called again.

"Don't hang up! Let me explain!"

"I'm listening," she said. This time her voice was deathly cold.

I told her the whole story. Even as I spoke, I realized how completely improbable the entire incident sounded. But I held onto the hope that she would believe me.

When I finished, there was a very long silence. Then Samina finally spoke.

"You Americanized guys think we Pakistani girls are so naïve," she said with real anger. "What kind of stupid story is that? And the rape thing is not funny."

"No! No!" I cried, my hopes plummeting. "It's all true!"

"So you want me to tell my mother that my prospective fiancé has a criminal record?"

"Don't worry," I said. "There's no record. We paid off the cops."

That made her hang up again.

But I wasn't going to give up that easily. I ran to my Mazda and drove for thirty-five minutes until I reached Samina's home. I banged on the gate until her brother Imran opened the door. He looked at me, perplexed, and asked if we had a guitar lesson scheduled for that day. But I didn't have time for his questions or anything else.

"I'm here to see your sister," I said, storming past him. I knew that I was violating every rule of Pakistani etiquette and was risking finding myself back in jail for trespassing and home invasion. But I bumbled through Samina's house like a drunken man until I found her inside the drawing room. She looked at me, shocked, and asked me what I was doing. At that point I just spilled my guts.

"If you don't see me, I have nowhere to go. I'm lost."

As Aunty Nina and Samina's younger sister Ayesha watched from the next room, we sat down and talked.

After our first real heart to heart, Samina arose, indicating that it was time for me to go. It was late, and she couldn't be entertaining young men in her house at night.

I hadn't even bothered to acknowledge her mother and sister, and Aunty Nina walked into the room saying "Mansoor, *beta*, is everything alright, why are you here so late?" Nina had obviously trusted her daughter's judgment in allowing me into the house despite the night-time hour.

Samina cut in and said "Mama, 'Mansoor' is actually 'Salman,' and he has just come over to study the cardiac cycle for his physiology exam next week. I'm just going to show him out." With that she came outside and turned to me one last time.

"I won't meet with you again without being engaged or meeting your family," she said in a serious voice. "I have to protect my reputation."

I looked at her in a daze.

"So do you mean . . . ?"

She nodded.

"I will tell my mother that I am ready to accept your family's proposal," she said simply.

Ever since that night, Samina has been the solid ground that keeps me standing. It says in the Quran that men and women are a garment for each other and it's true. Samina covered and enveloped me completely.

My grandmother Aziza taught me that God's signs are everywhere, if we only know how to read them. I knew that meeting Samina had been a sign. Whatever my destiny was, Samina would be a part of it. Pakistan was still overrun with fear, violence, and corruption. But God had rewarded me with love.

And yet still there was a void in my life.

I continued to study medicine and play cricket, but my music remained silent. My spare Fender Stratocaster sat unused and unplayed in my closet. Kim gave up his guitar lessons to focus on his studies; besides, he'd already played his role as an agent of destiny in bringing his sister and me together.

I took comfort in being engaged to Samina and also in watching Imran make a comeback after his shin injury.

One spring day I visited him at his parents' house in the tree-lined residential area of Zaman Park. I had come equipped with a tape recorder to interview him for my college sports magazine. As I began to question him about his personal life and whether he had any plans to marry, he turned the question around and asked me if there was anyone special that I had seen in Lahore. I switched off the tape recorder and told him that I was engaged to Samina. He looked at me incredulously.

"Logie," he said, using the nickname he'd given me after a famous West Indian cricketer, "don't make the mistake of falling in love and getting married!"

I was naïve to believe in true love, Pakistan's greatest sporting hero told me in his deep, loud, and authoritative captain's voice.

"Logie, all my friends, Western and *desi*, are divorced!"

I mustered the courage to contradict him and replied by saying, "Skipper, she's my soul mate!"

That just made him even more determined to set my head right.

"Believe me," Imran said, "I saw it in a dream. Marriage is the end of all hope!"

I didn't convince him but he did enjoy my defense of soul mates. I first met Imran as a fan, but over time I became like a younger (though fiercely independent-minded) brother to him. During his injury and recovery period I pulled examples from medical books showing him how modern sports medicine had helped athletes like Martina Navratilova recover from physical and psychological injuries. I sensed that he needed positiveness around him and knew that he was capable of making the supreme effort required for a powerful comeback, even after everyone in the country had written him off. His rehabilitation gave me personal hope as well. His recovery was a powerful example of overcoming adversity and taught me how transient fame can be. One day your head is in the skies, and the next day you can just as easily crash and burn. These truths would bear themselves out soon in what was to become my own unpredictable career in music.

It was around this time that I began to think it was my destiny to play cricket professionally. On a cold day in December 1985, I played a friendly match against Imran at the gymkhana. It was at once exhilarating and fear-inducing: exhilarating because I'd be able to tell my future kids I actually had batted against one of the greatest fast bowlers of all time, but fear-inducing because of the litter of injured players Imran had left in his wake. What if I suffered a fractured skull, broken jaw, a bloody nose, a cut eye, or a smashed finger, as had so many other, more accomplished players before me?

"*Allahu Akbar*," I whispered to myself. I padded up and left the red and green gymkhana pavilion and strode onto the middle of the lush green Bagh-e-Jinnah ground to open the innings.

I stood side-on in my crease and saw him race in like a tiger, with the white sight screen behind him. It was a breathtaking sight to see his hunter's eyes only 22 yards away and see him taking the final jump toward his prey. The crimson leather-covered Gray-Nicolls ball he released hurtled toward me like a piece of menacing, moving poetry. Imran bowled flat-out, testing his rehabilitated leg. The first few balls whizzed past my head like heat-seeking missiles. Imran had his toughest game face on. He would give no quarter to any batsman on what was for him a battlefield. I was initially nervous, but I managed to focus by reminding myself of my grandfather's saying, "It's better to live one day in the life of a lion than a hundred years as a lamb!" That thought sufficiently inspired me as I scored an unblemished and solid knock of sixty-odd runs, including a few confident straight-and-cover drives against the Tom Seaver and Cy Young of cricket.

The ball hitting the middle of the bat with a sweet, sharp "thwack" psyched me up and gave me the same adrenaline rush as a guitar player feels when he's timed a fast and explosive triplet run over a relentless groove. But my little victories didn't sit well with him—I earned the wrath of Khan and got hit a couple of times by his punishing in-swerves and darting red cherries aimed at my ribs and thighs. Fortunately for my future three sons—the youngest of whom is named after Pakistan's king of cricket—my family jewels were well-protected from potentially irreversible damage. It hurt, but these were war wounds to be proud of. I survived and had a great story to tell everyone I knew.

That day told me that cricket and I were seriously made for each other. Imran only cemented that feeling when the next week, he came up to me during practice and said he was impressed by my courage and defensive skills. To my complete surprise, he told me he was picking me to go to Bangladesh with an unofficial Pakistan cricket team that included talented young players like Wasim Akram, Saleem Malik, Rameez Raja, and my friend Zakir Khan. It was a formidable bunch. These were some of the players who would help Pakistan win its first World Cup title under Imran's leadership in 1992. As we rode a PIA flight from Karachi to Dacca, I embraced what I thought was my destiny in the sporting life.

We were the first Pakistani team to visit Bangladesh since the bloody war of 1971, after which Bangladesh was born. Prior to 1971, Bangladesh was called East Pakistan, and what's now Pakistan was named West Pakistan. Before the war, Bengali Muslims were treated like second-class citizens in their own country by the Pakistani government and military, stirring up deep animosity. Muslim was pitted against Muslim in the war, and the world was outraged by the bloody fratricide. India opportunistically helped Bangladesh gain independence, widening what was a civil war into a regional battle between Pakistan and India. Fourteen years after that bloody conflict, our manager, the late great cricket commentator Omar Qureshi, was now warning us to conduct ourselves carefully in public in Bangladesh. We stepped off the plane with trepidation, not knowing how we'd be welcomed.

All our worries vanished the moment we emerged from the airplane. The airport was 100 percent positive pandemonium. The whole of Dacca, it seemed, had come to welcome us. Crazy Bangladeshi fans were screaming "Im-RAAN! Mighty Im-RAAN!", making it blissfully clear that the power of sports and cultural celebrities trumps that of divisive and fear-mongering politicians any day. For those next two weeks, Imran and the Pakistan team were treated like rock stars instead of sportsmen. We were invited to countless parties in Dacca, where beautiful Bengali women constantly hovered around us. Sade's "Smooth Operator" was the theme song of our tour, and we also jammed to Tina Turner's "We Don't Need Another Hero" and "What's Love Got to Do With It?" We felt like princes, putting up at the luxurious Sonargaon Hotel in Dacca.

One evening, after the day's play was over, I wandered into the hotel's sumptuous lobby to find a Bangladeshi cover band unloading their guitars and drums from a van. It was New Year's Eve, 1985, and the band was setting up to play at a party being held in our honor. I stopped in my tracks when I saw the gear. It was if a landed fish had seen water.

Quickly recovering, I ran up to the guitar player as he started the sound check.

"*Salaam aleikum*!" I said, eyeing his instrument. "I'm with the team from Pakistan. Can I play your guitar?"

The guy just looked at me and laughed.

"You should stick to cricket, man," he said. "A guitar is nothing you hit sixes with. This thing is really delicate."

I smiled at him and asked who his favorite guitar player was.

The Bengali musician instantly said, "Carlos Santana."

"Does your band play any Santana songs?" I asked.

"Yeah," he said, "we play 'Black Magic Woman' and 'Oye Como Va.'"

"Alright," I said. "If I give you free tickets to our game tomorrow will you let me play?"

That was an offer he couldn't refuse. He handed me his well-worn red Gibson SG and I jammed out the intro to "Black Magic Woman." The band joined in and for the next half hour, I played my heart out while the Bangladeshi band members looked at me in disbelief. It was cultural diplomacy in action, with Bangladesh and Pakistan coming closer together through a Latin American guitar player's ode to a spell-weaving woman! On the spot, the band invited me to play during their evening set and agreed to keep it a secret from my teammates until show time.

That night, we dressed in suits and ties for the official function. As the local elite crowd milled about in colorful saris, suits, and shiny boots, the sight of European tourists wearing skirts and high heels shook up the joint with the Pakistani boys, as the Bengali cover band blasted out The Bangles' "Walk Like an Egyptian." During the middle of their set the band leader took the microphone and introduced me.

"Ladies and gentlemen, we've got a surprise for you this evening. Salman Ahmad of the Pakistani cricket team is going to play guitar for you!"

Imran and my other teammates looked at me quizzically.

"How much did you pay them, Logie?" quipped Wasim Akram, my teammate and probably the greatest southpaw fast bowler of all time.

I paid his ribbing no mind. Stepping onto the stage, I strapped on the SG, flicked the toggle switch to the lead pickup, and turned up the amp's volume. I gave the Bangladeshi band the cue by picking out the seven soulful bluesy opening guitar notes to "Black Magic Woman."

The band followed me and I launched into a long solo, reaching into the depths of my heart and letting it bleed all over the finger board. Eyes closed, oblivious to the world, I blew away the cobwebs that had gathered over the last four years and re-entered the mystical realm that Jimmy Page had unveiled for me that electric night at Madison Square Garden. The exploding stars that had guided my destiny to this place were charting a new path for me. God's universe would continue to conspire to make me succeed well beyond that New Year's Eve in Dacca. I swayed my body with the rhythm and played 'til my hands ached.

For the rest of that trip, Imran referred to me as "the hit kid," and Wasim transformed from a competitive teammate into a lifelong buddy. He, like Imran, would become one of the biggest fans of Vital Signs and Junoon. I'd gone to Bangladesh thinking I'd come back even more dedicated to cricket. Now something told me I had to follow my musical dream. The Bangladeshi audience had gone wild for my performance with the band. I knew that Pakistani kids had the same musical passion inside of them. And I was confident I could start the same buzz among them as I had in that hotel in Bangladesh.

The Pakistan I returned to was still shrouded in darkness and violence. But a musical butterfly would soon begin to flap its wings.

SIX

Rock & Roll Jihad

Dreams often lie dormant, sleeping inside of ourselves after their fuel has run out or we've grown too tired or defeated to nurture them. Life, too, has a habit of getting in the way of our following our passions, much like a giant iceberg appearing out of nowhere and sinking our ship of dreams.

But sometimes, thanks to luck or fate or circumstances we can't control, a catalyst will come along and reignite the *junoon* inside of us. For me, that impromptu Santana jam on New Year's Eve in Dacca was just the key I needed to unlock my highest hopes of playing music. As I played with the cover band that night and watched the members jam on stage, I felt like the curtain was being drawn back to reveal a beautiful possibility. Here were *desi* Muslims playing rock music without the government or religious leaders giving them an ounce of crap. Why couldn't Pakistani musicians enjoy the same freedoms back home?

Others, I soon discovered, were thinking along parallel lines.

Back in Lahore, I was pumped up and ready to start scheming up a way to play music again. Following the debacle at my college talent show, I had restrained myself by just playing at home, and I'd made a decision to sell some of my guitar effects, figuring there was no use for them in Pakistan, yet. I kept my Stratocaster, but I didn't think I'd need my chorus, echo, distortion, or other foot pedals. Having heard about me through the Lahore college grapevine after the talent show, a couple of Beavis and Butthead look-alikes turned up at my house to inspect my gear. But as I plugged in my Stratocaster to demonstrate how the pedals worked, the kids told me why they'd really come.

"Actually, Salman," said Beavis, "I want you to teach me how to play 'Smoke on the Water'!"

"And 'Stairway to Heaven' and 'Black Dog,'" said Butthead.

These guys wanted to hear Van Halen, AC/DC, and Aerosmith riffs played live! So I spent a whole afternoon jamming out song riffs and blues scales for these die-hard rockers. Their passion impressed me. But better yet was what they told me. They had friends, and a lot of them, who had formed a secret society of young Lahoris who were seeking out ways to learn the guitar and bass and keyboards, and to sing. These kids were right in my midst and I hadn't even known it. They were going to the same colleges as everyone else: King Edward, Forman Christian College, Government College, National College of Arts, and even the University of Engineering and Technology. Amid the serious academics and the ultra-right radicals were restless pockets of would-be painters, poets, playwrights, and musicians. These kids were a collective liberal powder keg waiting to be set off by a creative spark.

I felt as if I'd met a group of long-lost comrades, and I experienced the same sort of adrenaline rush as when I'd joined the guitar club at Tappan Zee High School. But the challenges facing us here were enormous. Many Pakistanis looked down their noses at rock musicians even without help from General Zia. My father's brother-in-law, Uncle Anwar, was right. Pop and rock musicians during the eighties were considered the moral equivalent of *mirasis* or *kanjars* (low-class singers and musicians or dancers). Even stand-up comics, who were pretty low down on the food chain themselves, made musicians the butt of their jokes and got guaranteed laughs anywhere. In Pakistan, you had to be a masochist to be able to face the merciless leg-pulling, cackles, and poisoned arrows aimed at you if you dreamed of playing rock music for a living. Even if you wanted to pursue what many deemed a "wasteful hobby," you had to be prepared to hone your skills and learn your craft without the luxury of music teachers, schools, concert circuits, clubs, or even music stores.

But I was determined to try to grow some flowers out of the concrete around me. My mind went back to the bearded student who'd broken my Les Paul and the vow I'd made to fight. The time to fight had come. My dreams had been bottled up for too long, and I decided to wage my rock and roll *jihad*. My love for music had never died, and after four years of hiding in the shadows I felt strong enough to launch my musical mission. It was the only way I knew how to express the multitude of conflicting emotions I'd felt since returning to Pakistan. Despair and hope and doubt and faith all maintained an uneasy alliance inside my heart. And in a society where reminders of General Zia's cult of personality loomed large, I wanted to rise and challenge the failed and outdated ideas of jingoistic dictators. I felt empowered by the legacy of rock and roll's search for truth and sticking it to "The Man." I wanted to sing songs of peace, love, and transformation. Mine was a sort of Sex Pistols situation in reverse. While Johnny Rotten's anarchic image and abrasive punk rock were intended to punch conservative British nationalism and the First World Order in the gut, I wanted to unite and heal the divisions in the Third World. I felt that through music, I could inspire opportunities for kids like Yameen from my old neighborhood in Lahore to get jobs and nurture their own creative passions. Maybe they could even live out a "rags-to-raja" story. It was overly ambitious and megalomaniacal, I knew, and the chances of success were pretty bleak. But that's what rock and roll rebellion is supposed to be about. My passion was taking me to the front lines. And I was going to bleed if I had to.

Over the next several months, I developed a loose Lahori network of friends and acquaintances and started a traveling guitar club. We'd gather in small groups, once or twice a week, in different locales across the city. One day we'd meet at my grandmother's place on Lawrence Road or in student dorms near Gowalmandi Market. Other times we'd jam in friends' living rooms in Lahore's Gulberg and Cantt neighborhoods or in vacant office spaces above the bustling Liberty Market. We would take any place where we could make a lot of noise and mask the sweet scent of hash smoke with cigarettes and *paan*—all without attracting the morality police. I called our gatherings The Rock Club, but people brought harmonicas, Casio synths, flutes, acoustic guitars, self-composed Urdu love poems, and even *dhols*, *tablas*, and harmoniums. We'd pick out our favorite tunes and then reincarnate them into a loud, electronic cacophony of *desi* Muzak! It was an eclectic mix of people, and the song list reflected our varied tastes. There were famous Bollywood hits and eighties pop songs like "Against all Odds," "Every Breath You Take," "(I Just) Died in Your Arms," "Take My Breath Away," "Dancing in the Dark," and "Danger Zone," nestled next to guitar-heavy stuff from Zeppelin, Pink Floyd, Santana, and Jimi Hendrix. I'd oversee the musical mayhem like a mad professor and write down chords, work out bass lines, figure out vocal harmonies to the songs, and then help my musical jihadis sing or play the songs on their instruments. I was like Jack Black in a Pakistani *School of Rock*. Med student and cricketer by day, I became music teacher, A and R (artist and repertoire) man, part-time manager, PR person, and rock promoter all rolled into one by night.

I also discovered that I had a good eye for talent. Being the music scene's Jack of all trades allowed me to observe all different types of people, and before long I'd picked out a bespectacled med student named Ali who had the voice of a Bollywood "playback" singer. I had him put his harmonica aside and focus just on singing Bollywood songs and *ghazals*. My med-school classmate Omar the Limey was an all-rounder: he had a Duran Duran hairstyle, could play a little keyboard, and loved U2, so he sang English songs. Another rock aficionado called Vicky couldn't sing or play but had tons of charisma. He spoke in a deep voice that echoed Jim Morrison's, so we'd jam on "Road House Blues" while he'd just drape himself over the microphone stand and look coolly tormented. Another tall FC College kid called Asim could hold down a solid bass pattern. Plus, he owned his own bass and amplifier and also had a practice place—rarities on all counts. Asim brought in Inti, the hopeless romantic, and the handsome Jamal. Inti sang Phil Collins songs, and Jamal knew how to play the intros to "New Year's Day" and "Take on Me" on his keyboards. Others showed a penchant for percussion. And of course there was a small but determined army of future guitar players, including a Lahori Hendrix who was known simply as "*khabba*," or lefty. Khabba's real name escapes me but the rest of him was unforgettable. He had designed his own guitar in the shape of the physical map of Pakistan. Khabba perfectly illustrated the innovative and creative spirit of most Lahoris to want to be different and to stand out from the crowd. "*Lahore Lahore Aye!*" we'd say in Punjabi. "Lahore is unabashedly Lahore!" Now Lahore was rocking.

To an outside observer, this generation of Pakistanis might have seemed thoroughly obsessed with Western music and styles. But they had equally solid grounding as *desis*. They could listen to black market cassettes of Deep Purple, Scorpions, and Black Sabbath and party all night long. They saw no contradiction when, the next day, they'd accompany fathers, brothers, and cousins to Friday prayers in the mosque or a Quran recital, wearing white *shalwar kameez* and skull caps. Islam had always been a part of daily life in Pakistan, without the bearded ones having to shove it down people's throats. As in other faith-centric countries like Israel, India, Ireland, and America, religion for most Pakistanis provided an important spiritual and cultural bond between tradition and modernity. It linked generations together naturally. Unlike the fear-mongering mullahs, my generation was comfortable and happy living in the modern world—and especially with modern music, which we thought of as a rainbow bridge that linked us to the rest of the planet. We certainly didn't want to go hide in any cave or fight jihads in Afghanistan or Kashmir on behalf of some crazy fanatic's agenda. Especially since that agenda—from the time of Aurangzeb all the way up to Osama bin Laden—had nothing to do with religion and was driven solely by a greed for political power and control.

But while I was rocking with my friends, plenty of kids our age did want to go off and fight. These were the ones who already had three strikes against them, even before they were born. My musical-maniac friends and I had had the advantage of being loved, fed, clothed, and educated, all essential ingredients to having a tolerant outlook on life. We were frustrated teenagers living in a stifling environment, yes, but our form of venting was to sing "Livin' on a Prayer" and "Message in a Bottle." We weren't about to be recruited, brainwashed at madrassahs, and told to hate the infidels—though we could see the mullahs' appeal to the forgotten souls of society. All of our consciences were bothered by the war in Afghanistan and unresolved political conflicts involving Muslims in places like Kashmir and Palestine. Social justice is a core principle of Islam. But the course taken by me and my musical friends was about unity and brotherhood. We took to heart the lines in the Quran which say that saving one human life is like saving the whole of humanity, and that killing one person is like killing the whole of humanity. It was a hard message to get out, though, when radicals used Muslims' suffering in any given location to whip up sentiment and label music-loving Pakistanis as being too soft, bad Muslims, or "brown sahibs." The tolerant and nuanced voices always seemed to get drowned out when faced with noisy extremists. The environment next door didn't help, either. America's war against the Soviets in Afghanistan was being fought with the blood of young Muslims. And the U.S.

conveniently looked the other way while Pakistan and Saudi Arabia stepped on human rights at home but helped secure American interests abroad by fighting the Soviets. General Zia's jihad wasn't my jihad. In this climate of fear, I wanted to wage a cultural jihad and kick-start a revolution to take us back to our Sufi roots of coexistence, acceptance, and musical ecstasy.

Coming back to Pakistan, I'd felt like Captain Kirk beamed down to a radically transformed Earth. But meeting those like-minded kids and playing that gig in Dacca had sealed it for me. I now knew I had to get a band or two started. That meant having instruments for everyone. But getting our hands on equipment was a challenge. So we'd ask anyone who had relatives or friends going to Singapore, Hong Kong, Europe, or the U.S. to bring back anything they could: guitars, amps, keyboards, drums, drum machines, or even music magazines and books. We promised to pay them as soon as we were able. Friends who'd become enthused by our passion also wanted to be part of the action. They became enablers either in cash or in kind, helping us raise money in exchange for free performances by us. Gradually we assembled ourselves into groups with names like The Doctors League, Eastern Winds, Direct Action, String Fellows, and The Wanderers. Initially I found myself playing guitar in multiple bands due to the dearth of equipment and players. At that time everyone played covers of Western rock and pop songs and Bollywood hits, but no one played Pakistani tunes or original songs. It just wasn't considered hip to do so. That would soon change. As news of this musical guerilla movement spread, we heard of other musicians from around Islamabad and Karachi who were also forming bands. One of those bands was called the Vital Signs.

Vital Signs was for me what the Yardbirds were for Jimmy Page. The band was my vehicle to showcase my guitar talent and discover my songwriting skills. From there I also began a long road to musical and social freedom. After my graduation from King Edward, Vital Signs' founders Rohail Hyatt and Shehzad Hasan, along with the charismatic singer Junaid Jamshed, lured me away from medicine and cricket to join the band. Vital Signs became Pakistan's first and most successful pop band, and our debut album *Vital Signs 1* in 1989 included the mega-hit national anthem "Dil Dil Pakistan." The song, meaning "Heart Heart Pakistan," catapulted us into overnight teen sensations and made us the voice of a new generation.

But back in 1986 we were all just scraping by and playing gigs underground. They were mostly sponsored by hip aunts and uncles or friends with connections who invited us to play "musical evenings" in backyards, living rooms, and basements. Despite these small and discreet family audiences, the buzz was infectious. Gossip travels fast in Lahore. Overnight, it seemed, we transformed Lahore into the nerve center for Pakistan's counterculture and underground band scene.

We also got some support from unlikely quarters. Some of the medical professors found out about The Doctors League and my passion for the guitar, and word reached the highest corridors of KEMC. During my fourth annual exams, I appeared for my pathology viva (oral examination) after an all-night cramming session. My professor, Dr. Nagi, began the exam by questioning me about a lung disease called bronchiectasis. I'd memorized the names, symptoms, diagnoses, and treatments for dozens of diseases but my mind drew a complete blank on that one. I stood speechless looking at the professor like a condemned soldier. If I failed the viva I would have to repeat the entire year. Nagi looked at me hard.

"I have heard from the grapevine that you've been playing your guitar-shitar on campus. Is that true, roll number 196?" he asked.

I'm doomed for sure, I thought. He won't even use my name. But the secret was out. There was no point in hiding behind my overalls and stethoscope. Unlike Batman, I had finally been unmasked.

"Yes, sir," I replied unrepentantly.

The graying and bespectacled professor looked sternly into my eyes. Then his face softened and he broke out into a wide-toothed laugh. He leaned close to tell me that he had a confession to make. He had seen Carlos Santana playing "Samba Pa Ti" in concert in San Francisco during the seventies!

"Doctor *sahib*, it was a very, very wonderful show, you know!" he said with real happiness in his voice.

The professor's candid admission of his rock rendezvous with Carlos refreshed my medical memory, and I began singing the causes of that lung disease like a bird. By year's end I had passed the exams and was in my final year of med school. Along with Dr. Nagi, I found another ally in a pharmacology professor who similarly loved music. The sari-clad Dr. Zafar went a step further and actually helped to promote Doctors League. She put the word out on us and also helped organize a few private fundraising concerts to help poor and needy patients suffering from blood anemias. She was also being a cool mom. Two of her daughters, Saima and Ayesha, were fans of the band.

Word about our musical exploits was spreading fast. And then one summer day in 1986, one of the bands I played with, Eastern Winds, finally got a paying gig. Or, sort of a paying gig. A friend's uncle asked if we would play at his restaurant opening on Lahore's main boulevard in exchange for free ice cream. He expected about a hundred college students to show up. His estimate was way off. More than a thousand girls and boys gate-crashed that small "private" gig at the restaurant. It was crazy and anarchic. We performed half an hour of cover tunes ranging from U2 to Bruce Springsteen, but we could hardly hear ourselves play because of the screaming, shrieking, and singing of the crowd. We felt like we were at a Beatles Cavern gig in Liverpool during the early sixties—especially when the noise level alarmed everyone in the neighborhood so much that they called the police. Before long the cops raided the restaurant, sending the kids scurrying away and leaving us Eastern Winds members alone to face a different kind of music. But our friend's uncle was a smart entrepreneur. He invited the cops in for a buffet dinner, and the lure of a free meal made them forget about pressing charges for causing a public nuisance and disturbing the peace.

That "ice cream concert" really opened up possibilities. If a thousand kids could show up in a place which only held a hundred, we reckoned, why not do a bigger venue? All we needed was guaranteed security against a raid by the bearded ones or the cops. The resourceful restaurant owner came up with a plan. He had connections in the Punjab government and could get us permission to do a "cultural evening" in the best auditorium in town. Lahore's red-brick Alhamra Arts Council auditorium had a capacity of three thousand, and when I told the restaurateur about the other underground bands from the various colleges, his eyes lit up with rupee signs. For the structure of the show, I found myself once again taking inspiration from my life back at Tappan Zee High School.

"*Yaar* (Dude), let's have a 'battle of the bands,'" I said.

With most of the bands in Lahore on the bill, a sold-out show was guaranteed, and we could actually get paid in real money. Word spread fast about the "Battle of Alhamra." Among the bands were Doctors

League, The Wanderers, Eastern Winds, and a then-unknown, new band called the Vital Signs, from Rawalpindi.

The Vital Signs stood out from everyone else. They had the latest keyboards and drum machines. But, more importantly, the quartet had style and stage presence. Even before they played a note on stage they seemed to be a force to be reckoned with. The main focus of that band was the tall, good-looking lead singer named Junaid. He had attitude to match.

"Sally boy," he said to me during the sound check, "you should be playing with us rather than those amateur Eastern Winds!"

I was impressed by his confidence but laughed and said, "JJ, the Vital Signs will be wishing that they never stepped out of 'Pindi!" That healthy competition was great and would lend an edge to the evening, I thought. I wasn't wrong.

When the doors opened it looked like the whole of Lahore's student population had arrived at the gates of Alhamra. Each band had a loyal following. The security volunteers had never seen anything like this before and were clearly overwhelmed by the size and contours of this largely youthful audience. The Lahori hordes included teenagers from the premier women-only Kinnaird College. The girls were decked out in stunning *shalwar kameez*, perfumed and made up to attract all the male attention. Before the concert it seemed as if there was a parallel fashion show going on with its own subset of gawking admirers from the crowd. It was all peaceful and fun and resembled the mixed-gender merriment at cricket matches I'd gone to. Spring had come to Lahore at last.

Then the bands came up on stage and, one by one, strutted their stuff with gusto. Amazingly, finally, in this benighted country, a real auditorium was coming apart at the seams with the sounds of rock and roll! Hundreds of legitimate ticket holders had to be left outside. The demand was just too great. It was as if a whole generation starved of all youth entertainment for a decade was inside and outside the Alhamra's doors. Each band was allotted a twenty-minute set, and by the time I opened the Eastern Winds set with "Smoke on the Water," there was pandemonium in the arena. I looked out at a sea of happy faces that included Samina, as well as her younger sister Ayesha and college friends who'd come along to chaperone my fiancée at this rendezvous with me. I felt blessed. Something special was taking place, I thought, and there is a God up there who can make all things happen.

But chaos, as always, was lurking just around the corner. As we finished our set to raucous applause, we were followed up by the Vital Signs. By now the crowd had gathered close to the stage and there was an erotic frenzy in the air. The well-coiffed, well-groomed, well-dressed, tall and *goray* (fair-skinned) Vital Signs opened with a-ha's "Take on Me." All the girls started shrieking uncontrollably. These were nice boys—the kind the girls could invite to meet their parents. The sounds coming off the stage were pleasant and melodious. The Signs were Pakistan's Beatles—or at least, the cute "Love Me Do" Beatles of the 1960s. As they sang "The Lady in Red" and "Take My Breath Away," the decibel meter inside the Alhamra got even higher. Our Eastern Winds fans started getting edgy and worried. These Vital Signs were going to win the battle of the bands if something drastic didn't happen. Unbeknownst to himself, Junaid skated on to thin ice as he hammed it up on stage, singing improvised lyrics to "West End Girls."

"Vital Signs boys, just look at these girls!" he said with a wink.

Then something drastic did happen. My bass player Asim's fiancée took off her heel and winged it at the stage. Forget Cold War politics and missiles named after Islamic warriors. This projectile was launched out of pure teenaged jealousy and connected with deadly accuracy to Junaid's jaw. That was the last note of the show. A massive brawl ensued. Rival fans clashed with each other, not knowing that the offending shoe was thrown by a girl. With no rhyme and less reason they tore out the chairs and broke the glass windows, overly high on their newfound freedom. Life would never be the same after the Battle of Alhamra. The flying heel became part of Punjabi folklore. But there was a price to pay. The authorities completely banned all cultural evenings at the Alhamra despite the fact that they and the promoter made a killing through ticket sales. And there was a cultural backlash as well. There was much hand wringing in Urdu newspapers about the lack of discipline and decorum of Pakistani youth and their loss of "Islamic values." The bearded ones and their pals in the vernacular press blamed all us musicians for leading the youth astray.

That was bullshit. The truth of the matter was that the conservative media and the other self-appointed custodians of culture couldn't face up to reality. They'd been blind to the needs of the younger generation for way too long, and now a counterculture movement was growing right under their noses. Pakistanis had also become totally sick of military rule and they wanted change. That change was democracy, which would come under dramatic circumstances when Benazir Bhutto became the first woman elected as prime minister in the Islamic world in 1988. Music wasn't the only thing that the entrenched powers had to fear. Another kind of drumbeat had begun.

The Battle of Alhamra might have driven a wedge between the fiercely loyal Vital Signs and Eastern Winds fans, but it brought Junaid and me together as friends. After that show he often came over to my grandparents' house to listen to music and hang out. There was a typical Pakistani film-hero charisma about Junaid which attracted a lot of female attention. He would talk big and dress retro-cool like Waheed Murad. He'd wear dark sunglasses and sometimes a red scarf around his neck and drive around town in a borrowed car with a-ha's "Take on Me" blaring. He was intensely ambitious about wanting to become someone important and someone people would look up to for guidance. Like most Pakistanis, he had an opinion on everything from girls to cricket to music to religion. His fair complexion and good looks gave him a big advantage in a post-colonial but color-conscious society. His boy-next-door demeanor made him the object of secret fantasies for both mothers and daughters and maybe also for Pakistan's camouflaged gay community. Born and raised in Pakistan to doting and loving parents, he had grown up wanting to be an air force pilot like his father, but his bad eyesight ruled out that career path. Junaid was very impressionable and vain, but in an endearing, funny, lead-singer kind of way. As happens with so many other people, his surface bravado and confidence were really about covering his personal insecurities. We laughed a lot and got along, but there was always a certain sense of competition between us. He perhaps saw me as being a little arrogant, a little too blunt when I talked about growing up in America's cultural melting pot. Junaid had had a sheltered upbringing with a protective family and an education at Pakistan Air Force schools that emphasized respecting authority. His eyes widened when I mentioned seeing Freddie Mercury and Queen live at the Meadowlands in New Jersey. Most Pakistanis could only see live concerts on pirated videocassettes. Our other serious common interest was cricket, and my having played with Imran Khan and the Pakistan cricket team obviously strengthened my *desi* credentials to Junaid. In Junaid's tone and gestures was a combination of envy and respect. He would typically shake his head and run a vigorous hand through his hair to telegraph both his impatience with and continued interest in my endless stories. Being the front man of the Vital Signs, he wouldn't easily be outdone, though. He quizzed me on the exploits of Muslim heroes like Tariq Bin Zaid, who was so determined to stay in Europe and expand his empire that he burned the boats on which he and his men had sailed to Gibraltar. Junaid was a one-man Islamic and Pakistani-history search engine. He could preen and posture on the stage like the best Western poppers, but he also had a messianic zeal to promote Islamic history and the *hadiths*, or sayings, of the Prophet Muhammad.

That's where our paths diverged. In the late nineties Junaid was confronted by his friends in the Tableeghi Jamaat, a Muslim missionary movement, and asked to choose between his contradictory urges. The sacred and profane cannot coexist, they told him. The handsome, well-dressed kid from Karachi who fronted the country's first big pop band gave up pop music and became a nasheed- (hymn-) singing preacher who shepherds lost souls to Mecca to perform *hajj*. He was like a Pakistani Cat Stevens, trading his leather jacket for a maulana's beard.

But back in the mid-eighties, the one thing that set both of us apart from millions of other young Pakistanis was playing pop and rock music. From the time we met, Junaid and the other Signs were trying to get me into their band. Their multi-instrumentalist Nusrat Hussain, who was leaving the uncertain future of the music scene to become a PIA pilot, originally recommended me to the Signs. The band tried even harder to recruit me after witnessing me in action at the Alhamra. Up until then my reasons for not being part of Vital Signs were simple. I had to finish medical school and show my parents and my future mother-in-law, Aunty Nina, that I had kept my promise. Nina had agreed to give Samina away only when I became a licensed doctor. That would happen by the end of 1987. The second reason was that I saw no long-term future in playing American and British pop songs for a small, Westernized Pakistani elite. I had always wanted to play original music and saw in music a way of changing the world the way the Beatles had done. That wasn't going to happen by playing covers of "Heaven," by Bryan Adams. No one in the band scene was interested in writing his own songs. The conventional thinking among the musicians was: why would anyone be interested in material *we* come up with? I didn't want to be tied down to just another cover band. Besides, the Vital Signs hardly had any "guitar" songs. Their icons were bands and artists like the Pet Shop Boys, A Flock of Seagulls, George Michael, Madonna, and a-ha. Aside from top 40, band members would on rare occasions listen to Pink Floyd's *Dark Side of the Moon* album, just to expand their musical horizons. But it wasn't enough for me to become the lone rocker among these soft poppers. I was hearing a different music in my head but didn't as yet have the right vehicle to pursue my rock and roll *junoon*. All that changed one day when Junaid came over to my place, bursting with excitement, to play me a demo tape that the Signs had recorded in Islamabad on a cheap four-track cassette recorder. He also showed me a *TV Times* magazine article featuring the Signs. I popped the cassette into my car stereo. One of the three demo songs that caught my attention immediately was called "Dil Dil Pakistan."

This was fresh, original pop music, and I was intrigued. But intrigue turned to serious interest when Junaid told me the story behind the music of "Dil Dil Pakistan."

"Salman, *yaar* [dude], one day a television producer turned up at our band practice in Islamabad," Junaid began in the brash voice of his public alter ego.

"His name's Shoaib Mansoor and he's a very talented, shy, and bohemian kind of guy," Junaid explained.

The tall, soft spoken, and principled Shoaib had apparently refused to cast one of General Zia's personal family friends in his TV show. His punishment was his transfer from the prestigious Karachi TV station to the bureaucratic Islamabad TV academy to teach. Ever-restless, Shoaib had an idea to do something rebellious out of Islamabad. He told Junaid he wanted to introduce a pop band on television. Initially, said Junaid, the Vital Signs just looked at him with skepticism. The censorship on TV was so strict at the time that the authorities would have sooner hanged pop groups than given them live airtime. But Shoaib told Junaid and the other Signs that each of the five national TV stations was producing a song to be judged by audiences all over the country. Only a year after the ill-fated "Battle of Alhamra," which had earned aspiring pop musicians multiple tongue-lashings from the establishment, Shoaib told the Signs that they represented modern Pakistani youth. They blended Western tastes with very strong Eastern roots and they would be the first pop band to appear with an original song on the airwaves. Shoaib gave the Signs a set of lyrics he had written, to put chords and melody to. He told them to dress in their normal denim jackets, T-shirts, and jeans. This was such a far cry from how national songs were supposed to be produced, I thought as Junaid told me this story. I had been buried for two months studying for my final exams, and getting hit with a report of this kind of music-world action was like getting ice water dumped over me. Normally, you had a collection of twenty or thirty boys or girls, all standing at attention like zombies, their expressionless faces singing how much they loved Pakistan. Vital Signs took that love but set it to an almost unheard-of sound.

"We wrote a simple, fast-moving melody based on a rock beat," said Junaid.

"The gist of the song is 'we love Pakistan.' Somehow the video got past the censors, who probably didn't give it a look, knowing that it would be a national song," he told me.

The five videos aired on August 14, Pakistan's Independence Day, in 1987. The phone response was phenomenal. Almost 90 percent of the calls were for "Dil Dil Pakistan." "We won the song contest!" Junaid said. "Even the mullahs didn't mind us playing guitars and drums so long as it's a patriotic song!"

Listening to Junaid's story filled me with a hope I hadn't felt since my college talent show. "Dil Dil Pakistan" had seeped into the national consciousness after just a couple of airings on TV. Even with bare-bones production standards, the song worked and had created a powerful ripple that would steadily gather momentum. Vital Signs keyboard player Rohail Hyatt's home production carried the stamp of Pakistani innovation. The reverb effect on Junaid's voice came from singing in a room with bathroom tiles! The accompanying video, produced by Shoaib, was a single-song Pakistani version of "A Hard Day's Night" that captured and communicated the spirit of the times. It featured the four college-age Signs driving around in Jeeps and on motorcycles, playing guitars, singing of hope, and celebrating being alive. I was floored and shared Junaid's excitement and the Vital Signs' ambition to record an entire album. I promised to join the band in early 1988 after securing my medical degree. I shared the news with my fiancée and she was over-the-moon happy for me. She knew my heart would not rest until I gave music my best shot, and the timing of "Dil Dil Pakistan" was heaven sent. We decided that after graduation Samina would start her pediatrics residency at Services Hospital and we would start planning for our wedding to take place in January 1989. My parents and mother-in-law had no idea that I would put down the stethoscope and pick up the guitar for good as soon as I married Samina.

One spring day in 1988 I got on a Lahore-to-Rawalpindi bus with Junaid to officially join the Vital Signs. In the garrison city, I met my other new band mates Rohail Hyatt and Shehzad Hassan and our producer Shoaib Mansoor. After a raunchy, banter-filled meal of chicken tikka with naan and ice-cold sodas in Lalazar, my new companions embraced me as their own. I felt a strong kinship with all of them right from the get-go. I also thought of the meeting as a salvo of revenge against the ruling class. We were hatching our plans in the very same city where General Zia had Zulfiqar Ali Bhutto hanged in 1979. In just a few months, we would push the cultural envelope all over Pakistan together. Shoaib—serious and quiet but with a razor sharp satirical wit—became a lifelong friend and mentor.

Our first band meeting began with a bang—literally. On the morning of April 10, I woke up at Rohail's mother's house to the sound of bombs and rockets raining down on the residential neighborhoods of the sister cities of Islamabad and Rawalpindi. It felt like Armageddon had come, with whistling sounds followed by blasts and a great shuddering of earth. At first we thought India or the Russians had attacked Pakistan, but state TV had no news of any outbreak of war. The military had sealed off the sites that were bombed. All we learned was that it was an accident at an ammunition depot called the Ojhri Camp and that our heroic soldiers had the situation under control. This was pretty typical of the paltry information we'd get from state TV—except that this time the state propaganda was a total fabrication of the facts. We were there on the scene and we met people fleeing for their lives to escape the bombs. People figured that it was a case gone haywire of the military blowing up smuggled weapons, but no one really knows for sure. Anyway, the cause didn't matter. Many innocents were killed and many more injured, but most of the country didn't know it thanks to General Zia's control of TV and radio. The 9 o'clock news didn't show any of the damage wrought by the loose munitions flying around town. No one anywhere was safe. But this news blackout was typical of the mindset of successive Pakistani governments, military as well as democratic. Just pretend everything's fine, they'd reason, and no one will notice any wrongdoing. This time was different and the suppressed voices of the people spoke out powerfully.

Within a few weeks there were organized political protests on the streets. The uprising coincided with Benazir Bhutto's agitation for the restoration of democracy. Benazir had returned from exile in 1986, and she held mammoth rallies mocking General Zia's dictatorship. The tectonic plates of Pakistan were grinding again and the vital signs of change were everywhere. During that year, we found more and more young people coming out fearlessly and embracing our message of hope and freedom. All of us believed in a common, peaceful future for Pakistan. We saw ourselves in those millions of young Pakistanis who believed in our music, and in us. It was a magical but fleeting moment that comes only rarely in any country's history. We'd beaten overwhelming odds and had helped open the doors for positive transformation all around us. Change was in the air as we decided to base Vital Signs in Karachi and write new music at my parents' place. Karachi was the only city which had a real recording studio, a place owned by the idealistic son of Pitras Bokhari, a major literary and cultural figure in South Asia. Mansoor Bokhari, a Pashtun, was a dreamer who had singlehandedly carried the baton for arts and culture during the reign of General Zia. His EMI recording company had borne the biggest brunt of Zia's forced Islamization (it's pretty hard to sell music if you can't hear it on TV and radio). Mansoor was a mentor of Shoaib's and of Arshad Mahmood's, the classical composer who worked for EMI as an A and R executive. These three men conspired to put Vital Signs into the recording studio. Bokhari *sahib* loved to play bridge and dress in stylish clothes, and like Shoaib and Arshad, he was a million laughs. He saw the potential of the Vital Signs and gave us a royalty advance of 150,000 rupees and unlimited time in the studio to record a proper album. It was more money than any of us had ever seen. We got seriously busy and came up with the music for twelve catchy tunes that reflected our mindset and the signs of the times. Shoaib wrote the hopeful, yearning, and puppy-love-laced lyrics, and Pakistanis devoured them all. In a year's time, our unlikely band's cassette and CD would sell more than a million copies. Everybody—Punjabis, Sindhis, Pashtuns, Balochis, Muslims, Parsees, rich, poor, old, and especially the young—bought it. It was an easy-listening album targeted at a teenaged audience. Our three guardian angels—the boisterous Mr. Bokhari, the shy Shoaib, and the extroverted Arshad—saw in us a glimpse of the future, and they were betting that we would win against the forces of darkness at large in Pakistan.

We knew we were present at the creation of a new age in our country. With violence and carnage on the one hand and freewheeling music and the promise of democracy on the other, something had to give. And it did, under dramatic and mysterious circumstances no one could have foreseen. General Zia and his top generals died in a plane crash in Bahawalpur in August 1988 along with U.S. Ambassador Arnold Raphel. Junaid and I had just finished listening to our new song called "Do Pal Ka Jeevan" ("It's Only a Couple Moments' Lifetime") when we heard the news. There was an instant power vacuum which was filled with the first elections in eleven years. We all felt part of a historic cultural change, and we refocused our energies toward making the best music album we possibly could. Dictatorship was history and the voices of the people were back. It was a profound moment of sanity and reflection. The tectonic plates had ground once again, and I looked toward the future with a hope that finally now Pakistan could be rid of corrupt and unjust leaders.

I was twenty-four years old, a recently licensed doctor, a recording artist, and just a few months away from marrying the love of my life. Most people would have forgiven the idealism and naivete that blinded me to the hidden, cynical designs and corrupt schemes at work among the politicians. Over the next decade Benazir Bhutto and Nawaz Sharif would take turns plundering the public's money and making a mockery of the rule of law. The national tragedy and failure of leadership would continue well into the twenty-first century. But I didn't give up on my spirit of passion, which in time would create a new Junoon in Pakistan.

SEVEN

Freedom

The voice on the other end of the phone sounded official, and important.

"This is the secretary to the managing director of PTV," said the man. "Prime Minister Bhutto would like your band Vital Signs to perform for the country at the Aiwan-e-Sadr on Constitution Avenue in Islamabad."

It took me a few seconds to compute those words. Prime minister. Vital Signs. Aiwan-e-Sadr (the president's official residence). *Perform?* But that's what the secretary said. With my band mates staring at me and me staring back, I stammered out an affirmative reply to the PTV secretary and then hesitantly looked at Junaid, Rohail, and Shehzad.

"This is a joke, right?" I said.

The four of us were hanging out at my parents' house on Bahria Street in Karachi when the phone rang. Earlier that day, we'd been putting the final touches on our first album, *Vital Signs 1*, at Bokhari *sahib*'s EMI studios. I was also preparing for my long-awaited nuptials with Samina. My focus had been on looking for a medical residency and finding a way to support my wife-to-be. But with one phone call from the Ministry of Culture, I suddenly had one more entry on my short-term to-do list—one that I could hardly believe. Not only were we being invited to play before Pakistan's newly elected prime minister, Benazir Bhutto, but the gig was to be televised and shown in part on the widely seen 9 p.m. news. The idea of suddenly packing up my guitar and flying off for a performance before the leader of the nation seemed beyond preposterous. I thought someone was playing a gag on us. I was wrong.

"Please come to Islamabad on time," said the secretary.

That invitation was like a powerful gust propelling me and the Vital Signs higher into unchartered territory. Pakistan was at a crossroads, and the promise held in this phone call provided a glimpse of a possible new future. I had spent the last few years playing in secret at a variety of improbable venues, from dorm rooms to basements, hiding my music in the shadows as if it were something pornographic and shameful. And now, Pakistan had changed so rapidly that our band's music would not only be showcased before the new prime minister, a young Muslim woman, but would be broadcast before the entire nation.

I put the phone down and turned back to look at my band mates. Our hearts were rapidly beating in unison and I allowed the euphoria of the moment to course through my veins like an overdose of endorphins. The battle between the progressives and the fanatics was over. We had won.

For now.

General Zia's death in 1988 could not have been a more dramatic U-turn for Pakistan. For the previous eleven years, the country had traveled a self-destructive path of violence, hatred, and division. Despite the dictator's attempts at garroting it, democracy had always been alive in the people's hearts. Pakistani voices finally had a chance to be heard. True to their freedom-loving nature, voters rejected the religious parties that had cooperated with Zia. The nationalist Pakistan Peoples Party won a majority of seats. We had no hesitation in choosing a young, beautiful—but ultimately flawed—woman to be the country's new leader. Benazir seemed to be just the torch-bearer we needed as Pakistan entered a new age. America had forgotten about Pakistan (and Afghanistan), following the defeat of the Soviets and the fall of the Berlin Wall. After the war ended in Afghanistan, warlords ran amok and fought for the scraps of what was left of their ravaged country. An extremist student force called the Taliban—created in part by the Pakistani army and its intelligence wing—would eventually take over Kabul. In Pakistan, meanwhile, we were basically on our own. And to the shock and delight of the progressive youth of the nation, Bhutto won a handsome victory. A Harvard-educated woman who was only thirty-five years old at the time, she represented our hopes and ideals—that Pakistan could return to a centrist and democratic path that would bring freedom and prosperity to our country. I was excited about the sudden change in the political climate, but it still felt remote to me. It was something I saw on TV, that didn't really have anything to do with my day-to-day life. And then came the call from the Ministry of Culture.

During the Zia years, the airwaves were dominated by religious broadcasts and news items hailing the heroic Islamic mujahideen who were fighting the godless Soviets in Afghanistan. We were humbled by the knowledge that our performance would be the first pop music show aired from in front of the Presidency in more than a decade.

At the time I had no way of knowing how short-lived this victory for our values would be. The dark forces that had threatened Pakistan's democracy since 1947 were still out there, lurking like an undead Creature from the Black Lagoon. Those forces would have much more power over our new leader than anyone initially thought.

On the day of the concert, though, the Vital Signs were in collective heaven. We were flown first class to Islamabad and given the red carpet treatment. After being greeted enthusiastically by government officials at the airport, we were taken in a limousine to the Marriott, which in 1988 was the city's only five-star hotel. That afternoon, we were driven to the Presidency. Two gigantic black gates bearing the name "Aiwan-e-Sadr" in gold letters loomed in front of us. A fleet of black Mercedes Benzes with green MNA (member of national assembly) number plates was parked along the long, crushed-stone driveway. Miniature green and white Pakistani flags with the star and crescent fluttered from the front corner of the expensive cars' bonnets. It was a cool December afternoon and the white Presidency glinted in the sun's rays.

Driving through the pristine streets of Islamabad, with its manicured lawns and majestic, mountainous scenery, I realized how so many Pakistani politicians became detached from the needs of the people. Islamabad is an illusion. The city is a conscious effort by the ruling class to create a sanctuary of wealth and beauty far removed from the poverty and suffering of the masses. A few years of living in this environment and anyone would start thinking that Pakistan was a rich European country with few problems. One only needed to go into the neighboring villages around Islamabad to see the absence of schools, hospitals, and even electricity. There would also be thousands of out-of-work young men in those same villages, praying that God would hear them and provide sustenance.

The unreality of it all came home to me as we were shepherded inside the Presidency. The residential staff was dressed in green turbans and white vests lined with gold filigree, with the Pakistani crescent emblazoned on their chests. Dapper servants politely approached us with trays of pomegranate and mango juice. A rich variety of hors d'oeuvres were offered, including vegetable and meat *samosas*, and a delicious sweet dish called *burfi*, made of condensed milk and cooked in sugar.

Outside, kids' happy voices echoed through the air. Benazir had invited a large group of schoolchildren to attend the outdoor concert in front of the imposing backdrop of the Presidency. General Zia's sterile, joyless workplace was being transformed into a teenagers' playground. The late afternoon sun warmed the students as they sat expectantly on rows of comfortable, red-cushioned chairs. The youth were the future of Pakistan, Benazir had said, and the evening was to be dedicated to them.

Despite this talk of Pakistan's future, I felt as if I had entered a colonial European past. I looked around at the audience standing on the green lawns waiting for the show to begin and was overcome by déjà vu. It was as if I were back at the governor's mansion in Lahore where I had spent part of my childhood. The ghost of colonialism still haunted the corridors of power. The Presidency was filled with subservient staff members graciously catering to the Pakistani politicians and foreign diplomats. There was no trace of the Pakistan that I had lived in for the past seven years. As I looked at the crowd of beautiful and rich people nibbling on the food, I began to understand the isolation of someone like Marie Antoinette from the realities of the average citizen. Benazir Bhutto represented an egalitarian future to me, so I was surprised at the old-fashioned, aristocratic aura of this gathering. I felt like I was at a reception for a medieval Mughal queen rather than a modern head of government. It was a comparison that would later prove tragically apt.

And then a door opened and the prime minister herself entered. Benazir was dressed in a flowing green *kurta*, a white Hermes scarf elegantly covering her head, more fashionable than modest. She was accompanied by Aslam Azhar, the once and current managing director of PTV. With Benazir's election, Aslam had returned from the political wilderness and reclaimed the post that he had held during the 1970s, when Benazir's father was president. During the elder Bhutto's reign, Aslam had used state media as an outlet for drama, music, and poetry; and the arts had flourished on television. When Bhutto was overthrown and executed by General Zia, Aslam was unceremoniously ousted. But now his forced retirement was at an end, and tonight's performance was his opportunity to resurrect art and culture on Pakistani television.

Benazir approached us, and I was struck by how beautiful she was. Her dark hair contrasted sharply with her fair skin, and she walked with measured, regal steps. Benazir looked less like a prime minister and more like a cast member of *Dynasty* or *The Bold and the Beautiful*.

"The country is so proud of you Vital Signs," Benazir said. "We will do anything to promote you."

She then turned to Aslam.

"Aslam *sahib*, please provide these young men with everything they need." And with that, she turned and went to greet the other guests.

Junaid impetuously blurted out to me, "*Yaar*, she's so beautiful! Pakistan's prayers have been answered. She obviously loves us!"

Aslam smiled at us with great enthusiasm. He singled out Junaid and me and spoke in a perfect English accent, his voice a deep baritone.

"Salman and Junaid, congratulations to you and the Vital Signs for your meteoric rise against the forces of darkness," he said with a flourish. "You are the flag bearers of the new Pakistan."

I turned and looked at my band mates for the umpteenth time as a wave of surreality washed over me. Was this really happening?

It was, though not in the way Rohail and Shehzad liked. Junaid and I were getting all the attention.

Then it was time for the show. Benazir had invited us to open with a performance of "Dil Dil Pakistan." The audience took their seats and the PTV cameras rolled. I grabbed my guitar and pushed out the thought that tens of millions of Pakistanis were likely to be watching. I did what I always did when I performed at a gig. I went inside my heart, forgot the outside world, and played.

The cameras focused on us and didn't capture the reactions of the audience. But I felt on top of the world as they clapped and moved to the music. Even the prime minister got into it, tapping her feet to the rhythm of the future.

The moment the show was over, the PTV phone lines lit up. Young people from all over the country called to express their enthusiasm. The Vital Signs were seen as a symbol of the new Pakistan. We were young, clean-cut men with professional backgrounds singing about our love for the country. We represented education, hope, and progress. Pakistan had virtually no other pop band comparable to us up until that moment and we would start a revolution inspiring other Pakistani kids to take up music as a career. The Vital Signs had touched a nerve in urban society, and there was an immediate reaction—what would soon be called "Vitalmania."

The next day, the Vital Signs flew to Karachi to put the last of the finishing touches on our first album. We were asked to sign countless autographs on the plane. When the PIA plane landed, we stepped inside the Karachi Airport and noticed people staring and pointing at us. My parents' home was soon flooded with phone calls from young girls, many of whom would drop by the house in cars driven by brothers or chaperoned by older male cousins. The girls would wait across the street for hours to see us arriving or leaving. Some overzealous girls climbed over the fence to catch a glimpse of us. Others had their brothers ring the door bell and pose as journalists. But all the questions they asked were about our marriage plans.

Meanwhile the demand for the Vital Signs to perform grew exponentially. We started getting offers to play "Dil Dil Pakistan" in cities, towns, and villages across the country. We played to sold-out audiences all over the four provinces of Punjab, Sindh, North-West Frontier Province, and Baluchistan. "Vitalmania" had gripped Karachi, Lahore, Islamabad, Rawalpindi, Peshawar, Faisalabad, Sukkur, Multan, Dharki, Quetta, and even the former princely state of Bahawalpur, where thousands of kids came to our shows carrying Vital Signs posters and banners, singing, shouting, and screaming in unison.

The jacked-up attention was also causing fissures and tension within the band. Junaid and I flew by ourselves to the show in Bahawalpur after an all-night band argument over ego, money, and visibility. Fame had come too fast and we were grappling with it and trying to keep our sense of balance. The fight was a typically loud, no-holds-barred shouting match that only ended when my father broke it up. Shehzad and Rohail refused to go with us to Bahawalpur, in effect trying to show Junaid and me who was boss. But Vitalmania had gotten so big that the entire city turned up at the outdoor show to hear just the two of us perform a few songs with a hired local percussionist. Nobel literature laureate V. S. Naipaul's wife Nadira, then a writer for the Pakistani daily *The Nation*, was among the crowd with her teenage daughters.

"You guys are even more popular than Imran Khan!" Nadira's idealistic daughter, Anisa Mustafa, told us breathlessly after the show.

Anisa's comment was a shock to me. It was grossly exaggerated, but it underscored how rapidly Pakistan's cultural vacuum was filling up.

Even the serious newspapers and magazines and radio and TV programs began to notice the commotion. We found ourselves being interviewed by pseudo-intellectual reporters who didn't have a clue about our music but had begun to carry the banners of freedom and change as if they'd invented those concepts. Amidst the confusion and mayhem we also started getting paid in real money—although some of these early concerts were organized by fly-by-night promoters who ripped us off on more than a few occasions. After years with almost nowhere for kids to blow off steam, some of our gigs turned into primal group therapy sessions and didn't last beyond the first few songs. Young people just weren't used to this kind of freedom, and fights broke out spontaneously. We also got threatening phone calls from jealous guys, religious fanatics, and even upset university gang leaders. One guy in Karachi known as T.T. called my father at work threatening to kill me if I didn't cancel our show at the Karachi Gymkhana. Alarmed, my father decided to become the Vital Signs' temporary manager and reasoned with the impulsive gangbanger. Abu took a risk and invited T.T. to our house for tea, figuring it would defuse the situation. T.T.'s eyes were initially skeptical, angry, and confused, but he turned out to be just another kid who wanted his life to matter. To my surprise, I found out that his passion was writing, so I offhandedly said to him that Pakistan needed knowledgeable and honest journalists. A few years later, a familiar-looking guy wearing glasses would come to interview Junoon for an Urdu newspaper. It was T.T. He had nurtured his *junoon* and was making something of himself in this new environment.

Order had come to the political sphere, but in the world of pop music, a new kind of creative chaos was unleashed. During "Vitalmania," we routinely got mobbed, followed, and stalked. Once, some fans' adoration threatened to cost us our lives. In conservative Peshawar near the Afghan border, an all-girl, completely veiled audience turned up for an afternoon show at the Nishtar Hall. By the time we finished the concert, the repressed emotions of the Pashtun girls had come out in full force. They threw their veils, chadors, and burqas on the stage, revealing beautiful cheering faces, shoulder-length tresses, and stylish threads. We were being surrounded for autographs and pictures simply because we sang songs of hope. In their mad frenzy for souvenirs the Pashtun women nearly tore our clothes off. We were lapping up the attention when we were told by our worried promoter that the girls' brothers would come for us with pistols, machetes, and Kalashnikovs if we didn't get out of town right away. So we grabbed our guitars and keyboards and ran out of Peshawar leaving the Pushto-speaking mob screaming, "*Dil Dil Pakistan! Jan Jan Pakistan!*" ("My heart and my life is for Pakistan!") A screenwriter couldn't have made that day up. And yet I felt like I was in some sort of a Beatles movie, but a weirder and more dangerous one directed by Quentin Tarantino. John Lennon had spoken to everyone when he'd said all we needed to do was just imagine. And here we were. We were Pakistan's first real pop group.

I was now a national figure. More important, I was finally about to get married. Samina and I had waited patiently for over five years for our special moment. We wanted an intimate ceremony with a few close friends, but family pressures and "Vitalmania" made that impossible. Newspapers all over the country ran stories about my impending wedding. My parents were besieged by last-minute requests from famous and powerful people, including Nawaz Sharif's brother Shahbaz, to join in the festivities. Nawaz Sharif's father was an old friend of my grandfather, K. B. Rashid Ahmad. Mian Sharif was a widely respected, humble, and self-made man. But his son Nawaz was power-hungry and vainglorious. Nawaz would jump on the military establishment's shoulders to become prime minister in 1990.

Pakistani weddings last over several days, with each night featuring a special ritual and festivity to mark the occasion. One of the most important nights before the wedding itself is the *mehndi*, a ceremony where henna is applied to the hands of the bride, who is veiled in yellow and kept in seclusion from the bridegroom until the wedding day. The *mehndi* is also a time for young men and women to compete in singing and dance contests that symbolize the eternal battle of the sexes. Our planned small, private ceremony took on the trappings of a carnival when my band mates from the Vital Signs arrived to play for an audience of what had now mushroomed into hundreds of guests.

The day of the wedding felt like a dream. I dressed in a traditional white *achkan*, a groom's long jacket. I had a white turban on my head and wore a traditional *sehra*, a veil made of jasmine flowers and roses. I symbolically rode a horse for a short distance as we entered with the groom's entourage, surrounded by family, friends, and fans. The ceremony itself was held at the Avari Hotel on Mall Road. The place was overflowing with well-wishers. As is typical at Pakistani weddings, some of these people had only the remotest claim to kinship or social connection. My bride and I found ourselves getting photographed with many people we barely knew. But it was a small price to pay to be finally known as Mr. and Mrs. Ahmad.

Samina was seated on a dais, dressed in a bridal gown of scarlet and gold. I sat down next to her as a *maulvi* (cleric) asked her three times per Islamic law whether she agreed to marry me of her own free will. Each time she answered softly, "Yes."

With my family, friends, and band mates looking on, I lifted a pen and signed the marriage certificate. Then we all raised our hands and prayed the Fatiha, the opening chapter of the Holy Quran, to bring God's blessings upon the union.

Seven years earlier, I'd seen Samina singing at Uncle Fareed and Aunt Hina's wedding. I'd known even then that this day would come. Samina and I were finally husband and wife.

In the immediate aftermath, everyone in the audience crowded the stage, hoping to get a photo with the bride and groom. One of the most illustrious guests on our roster was Madame Noor Jehan—the Barbra Streisand/Aretha Franklin of Pakistan. Noor Jehan was a classic singer who had entranced audiences in Pakistan and India since her days as a child actress in Bollywood in the 1930s. She had become a towering national icon and had received the title *Mallika-e-Tarranum* ("The Queen of Melody"). Noor Jehan was now in her sixties and reigned over Pakistan as its paramount diva.

I greeted Noor Jehan with great reverence as she came to sit with us for the photographers. She smiled and blessed us both, wishing Samina and me a joyous marriage. And then she looked me over with a worldly glance and whispered to Samina: "Keep an eye on your man." With that, she assumed a regal pose for the cameras.

My Uncle Javed had been waiting patiently to get a picture with us as a variety of notables crowded the stage. Seeing Noor Jehan comfortably ensconced by our side and enjoying the attention of the paparazzi, he turned wearily to a friend and whispered: "Don't family members have any rights?"

I didn't catch my uncle's quip, but Noor Jehan apparently had bionic hearing. She got up in true diva outrage and gave Javed her famous evil eye. "I thought I came to a wedding of honorable people!"

A hush fell over the crowd at the sight of the proud queen's outburst. I gave Javed a desperate look of warning, but he decided to go for broke. Looking at Noor Jehan with steely eyes, he smirked.

"We all know how honorable *you* are."

Noor Jehan's private life had been filled with scandal and gossip for decades, and her love affairs were well known to the entire nation. But to bring it up in public was a shocking violation of etiquette.

Noor Jehan's mouth fell open. And then, with the speed of a cheetah, she rushed Javed and went for his throat with her painted fingernails.

As her daughter Tina managed to calm down the enraged melody queen, I turned to Samina, who was overwhelmed with embarrassment. I took her hand and smiled until she finally managed to laugh.

Pakistanis love drama, and there's no event more fertile than a wedding for a good, old-fashioned emotional explosion. The wedding-day soap opera was a reminder to prepare ourselves for anything and everything, and a hearty sign that the Pakistani spirit was ever-present in all of our lives.

At the time, we saw Pakistan's spirit embodied in Benazir Bhutto. But Benazir (who'd had the playful nickname "Pinkie" at Harvard) was also a savvy politician. She realized that she could use our band to promote her visions of a progressive Pakistan. She gave the go-ahead to TV producer and Vital Signs mentor Shoaib Mansoor to organize a major pop concert to be broadcast on Pakistan Television. At this historic moment, Shoaib looked at the concert as a chance to use state television resources that the military and the mullahs had hijacked for their propaganda, and to resurrect the nation's progressive values. Shoaib asked us to perform at the concert and we readily agreed.

The concert, called Music '89, was held in the basement of the PTV studios in Islamabad. Shoaib corralled three thousand young men and women to join the audience. We rocked along with several prominent Pakistani musicians, including the young and glamorous singer Nazia Hassan and her brother Zoheb. We performed "Dil Dil Pakistan" and "Do Pal Ka Jeevan." In that latter song I played the first Van Halen–style finger-tapping solo on Pakistani television, a move that would inspire many future talented guitarists.

We were surprised at the crowd's restrained response to the music. The young people clapped politely, but there was none of the wild cheering or exuberance that we'd come to expect at our shows. And then we realized that these kids were terrified. They were going to be on national television in a society that had been brainwashed for the past decade to believe that showing happiness and enthusiasm in public was sinful. They didn't dare release their feelings and risk bringing public shame on their families. But while they looked timid, we could see in their eyes that the fire of rock and roll was lighting them up inside.

The concert was taped and then broadcast a few days later. It was a massive hit. Over 70 million people watched the show. Taking advantage of the successful program, Shoaib quickly filmed us acting in a musical teleplay for PTV titled *Dhundley Rastey* (Misty paths). Following the telecast of Music '89 and our eyeball-catching acting debut, "Vitalmania" reached a new high point.

Our success was met with shock, outrage, and fear by the religious right, who saw their decade-long efforts to control the hearts and minds of the masses vanish in an instant. This national outpouring of support for our band shattered all illusions that the Pakistani people supported their backward thinking and policies. The Wahhabi-wannabes had deluded themselves thinking that their extremist values were the same as those of the general public. Now they were faced with massive public adulation for "sin" and "vulgarity" that revealed how utterly irrelevant they had become.

An event outside Pakistan further enraged the morality police.

The following week while I was at Friday prayers, I heard the name "Salman" being discussed in angry tones by everyone in the congregation. Initially I feared that someone had complained to the *maulvi* at my local mosque about my Vital Signs adventures. But a controversy involving another Salman had erupted across the Muslim world. A firestorm was swirling around Salman Rushdie, whose novel *The Satanic Verses* earned the Indian-born British writer a death sentence from Iran's Ayatollah Khomeini. Rushdie's book—which the ayatollah charged desecrated the memory of the Prophet Muhammad—added fuel to the Pakistani mullahs' fire. All Muslims completely lose their minds over any hint of desecration of the Prophet. It's like telling a Jew that the Holocaust never happened, or using the N-word for an African-American. The *fatwa* against a Western writer emboldened the holy soldiers and meant more violence at home. Pakistani pop culture was the intended target. Pakistan's mullahs were looking for a reason to clamp down on the "alarming" progressive changes following Bhutto's election.

So they reacted the only way they knew—they struck back violently. Mobs of goons from the religious parties, still angered by their recent losses at the polls, rampaged through the streets. They broke TV sets in cafes with bottles and set fire to the Lahore television studio with Molotov cocktails. I received death threats again, which in my career would have to be endured like a chronic case of heartburn. I quickly decided that it was a good idea to get Samina out of the country until things calmed down. We left for two weeks on a hastily arranged honeymoon to New York.

As Samina and I went on drives into Manhattan and took long walks around the neighborhood where I had become an American *desi*, I wondered what kind of welcome would await back in Pakistan. The future was a big question mark. But Samina answered my thoughts by saying that she would support my *junoon*, no matter the cost, death threats and all. As the heat subsided we returned to Pakistan to face the bearded ones.

We had millions of young people on our side who had publicly repudiated the tyranny of the music police. I assumed that we also had the support of Benazir Bhutto. I was wrong. Facing her first crisis as prime minister, she decided to end the unrest by caving in to the mullahs' demands. The tapes of Music '89 and the Vital Signs' *Dhundley Rastey* TV show were removed from the PTV library, never to be seen again. (Until the advent of YouTube.)

Benazir's behavior confused me. She had the backing of an entire nation that was fed up with a minority of religious fanatics dominating its culture. But she decided that it was more important to preserve her power than to put these violent idiots in their places. In the process, she emboldened them and those in the ISI who sympathized with them. The ISI soon discovered that the threat of losing power was enough to get Bhutto to agree to other demands—including nurturing the extremist Taliban next door in Afghanistan. The Creature from the Black Lagoon was stalking democracy again and Benazir's lack of foresight squandered this historic opportunity to change the future of Pakistan.

My disillusionment with Benazir coincided with a more personal crisis. Now that the Vital Signs were national figures with millions of young fans, we were in a position to have a real impact on culture and society.

That's what I thought, anyway. My band mates had other ideas.

EIGHT
Junoon

In 1990, the soul of Pakistan was up for grabs in an epic struggle.

Benazir Bhutto, celebrated in the West as a champion of democracy, was showing her true feudal colors at home. She put her progressive agenda on the back burner and was singing a different but familiar Pakistani tune called "Power Equals Corruption." The young prime minister was following her father's script, making shady deals with the military establishment and the mullahs from behind a façade of strong populism. But the *jinn* was out of Pakistan's bottle and people were ready for real change. At the Vital Signs' concerts across the country, Pakistanis were showing their true, joyful faces after years of living in the shadow of a dictator. I didn't want to see that spirit get stuffed back into any bottle by anybody. So I turned to music for ammunition.

In 1990 I wrote a bunch of songs for the Vital Signs' second album which reflected my growing awareness of the bubbling youth spirit. Young people wanted their voices to be heard, not hijacked by politicians. That year, I agitated for heavier-themed music that went beyond the Signs' "Red Red Wine"–influenced offerings. I also wanted us to drop the group's happy-go-lucky image. Young Pakistanis were ready for a band that was socially conscious and not just limited to patriotic pop platitudes and puppy-love anthems. But my band mates thought I had it all wrong.

"Sal, our popularity's going to plummet if we record your songs, *yaar*," an exasperated Rohail said to me as we rode to a show on a tour bus in July of that year.

Rohail and I happened to be going to a concert hosted by Nawaz Sharif, then the chief minister of Punjab. Traveling on that bus, I felt like a jester on his way to the king's court. We were just another prop for a politician to display his so-called progressive credentials. I'd had it. Living in Pakistan for the past eight years had awakened me to some of the ways of the world. I'd made my band mates squirm by writing finger-pointing op-eds for *Newsline* and *The Star*, challenging politicians to do something meaningful about campus violence and drug addiction. I also wanted our "leaders" to bolster kids' opportunities to express themselves through the arts. An arrow had pierced my heart and I wanted to bleed my passion into my work.

But Rohail, Shehzad, and Junaid gave me an ultimatum instead of empathy. After the "Concert for Nawaz" in the northern hill-station resort of Patriata in July, the three of them told me to quit rocking the boat with my "save-the-country complex" or leave. My obsession with social reform and writing songs that shook up the system were viewed as a direct threat to the band's pocketbooks. Quitting would mean going back to scratch. I also had to think about Samina. Only a few months after the euphoria of "Dil Dil Pakistan," I'd come to an imposing crossroads.

In the end I decided my soul wasn't for sale. I picked up my guitar and walked away from the Signs—but not before kicking and breaking a large flowerpot and getting into a shouting fight with my band mates. We had begun by arguing in Urdu and English about the band's (lack of) vision and ended up spitting curses in Punjabi against mothers and sisters.

One month later, in August 1990, Bhutto was ejected from office by President Ghulam Ishaq Khan amid allegations of corruption. She'd served less than half of her term. Nawaz Sharif was elected prime minister in November, vowing to fight corruption. He would quit in July 1993 after being accused of the same thing.

It was early morning near dawn in the winter of 1990. I had gone to sleep asking God for guidance. It came in the form of an unforgettable dream. A man dressed in a flowing white robe, with long white hair and striking kohl-lined eyes came to me and shook me hard by the shoulders. "Salman," he repeated, "you have a *junoon* for music!" I woke up, dazed. But the word junoon kept reverberating inside my head.

As I made a decision to move on from the Vital Signs, that feeling of *junoon*—that obsessive passion—became my touchstone for how I would make my music and live my life.

My independence had its price, though. As soon as I parted ways with my band mates, I found myself out in the wilderness. The media, friends, and family saw me as a crazy renegade who had left the "freak" success of an unlikely group of musicians just as they had taken off. Blinded by the massive success of "Dil Dil Pakistan," many in Pakistan thought the Vital Signs were invincible and irreplaceable. No pop group had made it so big, so fast. Meanwhile, since most of the money the band had made had been spent or been reinvested into new equipment and a recording studio, I was left with almost nothing to show for my work except public visibility. Now I was visibly alone. The media portrayed me as the forgotten Sign who'd given up his ticket to riches to stand stubbornly solo and penniless for his passion. For a while, that seemed accurate. While I struggled to find a new path, the Vital Signs signed huge endorsement deals with Pepsi-Cola, shot multimillion-rupee music videos, performed shows across the country, and seemed to be on the covers of all of the nation's newspapers and magazines. Lots of people thought I'd simply missed the magic bus. The same Vital Signs fans who'd once strained to catch a glimpse of me at concerts or on the streets now taunted and reviled me. Some in the press gleefully wrote my musical obituary even before I had a chance to come out with any new material. To make matters worse, even my parents and Samina's family just couldn't understand why I wouldn't go back to being a respectable doctor. The only two people who believed in my musical dreams were Samina and me.

I searched my heart and considered how to move forward. I developed a syllabus for a self-taught course in all aspects of show business, researching music, movies, TV, books, and magazines. An unexpected shot of encouragement came from an American writer and guitar player. When I was still in the Signs, I'd written a letter to *Guitar Player* magazine's Joe Gore, who wrote a column that covered different guitar styles from around the world. With the letter I'd included a short bio of myself and our CD. A few months later, to my surprise, I got a care package from San Francisco bearing Gore's return address. He'd featured my letter in his column and sent me new albums by Jeff Beck, Joe Satriani, Steve Vai, Steve Morse, and Andy Summers.

Along with a free subscription, Gore shared some good advice.

"Perhaps it would be wiser to go in a more Eastern direction with your music?" he wrote.

Gore and many others were anxious to hear new sounds, he wrote, and he paid me a high compliment, saying he'd heard something unique and authentic in my riffs. He also told me, bluntly, that America didn't need a Pakistani version of the Pet Shop Boys or a-ha. I knew that was right. But what kind of new sounds could I come up with?

I heard an inkling of an answer one Sunday night in Lahore watching a bootleg videotape of *The Last Temptation of Christ*. As Samina and I sat sunken in our couch watching Martin Scorsese's controversial film, I heard a familiar *desi* voice on one number from the soundtrack. It was Pakistan's *qawwali* maestro Nusrat Fateh Ali Khan singing *taans*—high, melismatic vocal flourishes—on top of a modal bed of synths. Something clicked when I heard that blissful union of sounds. During this time I was watching other movies and studying soundtracks, trying to figure out how music complemented the action on the screen. But there was nothing in *The Doors* or *Field of Dreams* like what I was hearing with Samina that night. Nusrat's voice and the synthesizers sounded natural and beautiful together. I couldn't tell where East ended or West began.

Hearing Nusrat's collaboration with Peter Gabriel was the beginning of the answer to the question I'd put to myself. Nusrat's musical influence would help pave the way for Junoon to take the risks we did when we married hard-rock guitar riffs and sitar-like phrases to *bhangra* drum and *dhol* grooves and Sufi lyrics.

Nusrat turned out to be a star guest instructor in my self-guided tour through the music world. We met later thanks to Imran Khan, who asked his friends from Pakistan's arts community to do concert tours to raise funds for his cancer hospital. On a spring day in 1991, I found myself at Lahore's Alhamra Arts Council, the very same venue where I'd battled it out with other bands in 1986. I felt a little out of place, carrying a Fender Stratocaster and a guitar amp to my first *qawwali* rehearsal with the celebrated Nusrat. He sat onstage, cross-legged on a Persian carpet, looking like a Punjabi Buddha, while his *qawwali* group brought out harmoniums, *tablas*, and cups full of Lahori chai. After the traditional greetings of *Salaam aleikum*, I nervously asked Nusrat what he wanted me to play on the first song, "Mustt, Mustt" ("Lost in You").

The South Asian musical legend and perhaps the most influential Sufi singer of the twentieth century looked at me with the innocence of a child.

"Do whatever your heart tells you to do," he said.

That turned out to be the strongest piece of career and personal advice anyone could have offered me. Nusrat's voice and the songs performed that day and later on the tour had a profound impact on my music. The devotional Sufi love poetry and the intense, trancey, *raga*-based choruses opened doors to new spaces. John Lennon, Jimmy Page, and John Lee Hooker threw a grand party inside my heart with poets like Rumi, Bulleh Shah, and Iqbal.

Nusrat broke the traditional mould of the *qawwali* singer when he collaborated with Peter Gabriel, Michael Brook, and Eddie Vedder of Pearl Jam. Nusrat's feelings about fusion music actually sprang from a deep spiritual conviction. Nusrat was a living exemplar of unity in diversity. Long before 9/11 and the subsequent war on terror and talk of a clash between Islam and the West, Nusrat sang ecstatically about the Oneness of God and love for humanity. Years later, when I met Peter Gabriel he told me that it was Pete Townshend of the Who who had turned him on to the King of Qawwali. Talking to Nusrat about his brilliant album with Michael Brook, *Night Song*, the Sufi singer told me that he loved fusion because the Quran says that God loves diversity. The most powerful way to celebrate and express diversity, Nusrat felt, was through music.

I agreed. And I never forgot his advice.

After I left Vital Signs, I felt kind of like a mad scientist. There was no such thing as an original *desi* rock band, so Pakistan actually served as an excellent lab for experimenting with a new South Asian rock sound. This kind of musical alchemy would be trial and error, but mistakes and failure didn't faze me. I loved improvising and jamming and besides, music wasn't a job. It was a *junoon*.

Apart from *qawwali*, I soaked up the nuances of *ghazal* and folk music by watching performances of open-throated Sindhi and Seraiki singers like Abida Parveen and Pathaney Khan. I felt the sounds of classical sitar, *sarod*, and *tabla* music and absorbed the effortless fluidity and emotional intensity of virtuosos like Pandit Ravi Shankar and Ustad Ali Akbar Khan and Ustad Zakir Hussain. The burbling rhythms of the *tabla* captured my imagination like no other percussion instrument. The *dayan* (right) and *bayan* (left) drums, in the hands of a maestro like my Calcutta-born friend Pandit Samir Chatterjee, can make you forget the troubles of the world and infuse you with a transcendent joy. Like two reunited soul mates, the combination of the guitar and *tabla* would give Junoon its signature sound from the get-go.

I was psyched by my new sound discoveries but I needed band mates to accompany me on my junooni journey. During the recording of Shoaib Mansoor's Music '89 concert, I had met Ali Azmat, the talented lead singer of The Jupiters. The Jupiters were a wedding band from Lahore, and the teenaged Ali looked like a misfit with them. While The Jupiters had ambitions to play filmi (melodramatic) pop anthems at weddings all over Pakistan for the rest of their lives, Ali felt more at home singing Def Leppard and Bon Jovi songs. He knew my work with the Vital Signs and was eager to work with me. Luckily he lived with his parents a few houses down from Samina and me in Lahore.

The crew-cut Ali showed up to audition as Junoon's lead vocalist wearing dark glasses, black jeans, and a blue T-shirt, looking every bit the rocker.

"*Yaar*," he said with an eager sparkle in his eye, "I can sing whatever you want me to sing."

To prove his point and impress me, he mimicked "Hysteria" and "Pour Some Sugar on Me." He also did hilarious versions of Elvis's "Blue Suede Shoes," Little Richard's "Tutti Frutti," and Michael Jackson's "The Way You Make Me Feel," complete with choreographed stage moves for each song. I was sold. Ali was a natural entertainer and a prankster. Not only did he do David Coverdale and Jon Bon Jovi impersonations, he also mimicked my guitar solos a la Wayne and Garth in the movie *Wayne's World*. But underneath his flippant persona and Teddy Boy image, I heard an authentic, soulful *desi* voice. I was driven by a fierce urgency to fix an undefined hole in my heart. Ali wanted to be a *rangeela* (colorful) rock star and wanted the world to recognize him as a *shoda* (brash) *shehzada* (prince)—preferably with his money for nothing and his chicks for free. He and I would huddle in the one-bedroom, upstairs apartment on Mumtaz Street that Samina and I had rented from my Dada and Dadi after our wedding. With rickshaws, cars, scooters, and motorbikes screeching outside in Lahore's bustling Garhi Shahu district, I strummed out chord progressions to some of the songs I'd composed while still with the Vital Signs. I had Ali sing the same melodies that the Signs had rejected as worthless and I recorded the earliest versions of those tunes on my Tascam eight-track recorder. Even in that primitive state, I felt the songs had passion. Samina, her sisters Tehmina and Ayesha, and Ali's sister "Baby" (Junoon's first "Band-Aids") agreed when they heard the rough demos. Ali was fine singing the rock songs. The more melodic ones like "Khwaab," "Jeeain," and "Jogia" would prove to be a challenge. But given time, I felt, his voice could develop into something unique and powerful.

With me on guitar and Ali on vocals, we needed one more member to complete the band. That turned out to be the nervous and eccentric—but talented—Nusrat Hussain, a.k.a. "Baba," the former member of Vital Signs whose place I'd taken.

"Baba," I said with a salesman's pitch over the phone, "if you want to be part of Pakistani rock history, this is your chance!"

Nusrat hesitated.

"Salman, I'm not sure, I have to consult my older brother," he said. "You might want to be a part of history, but I still want a successful future!"

Nusrat's older, PIA-captain brother Sarwat encouraged him to get on the Junoon rock flight. (He also told him that there was nothing to lose if Junoon crashed.) This would be a part-time gig for Nusrat anyway, since he had a big day job flying planes for PIA. To record the first Junoon album, all of us flew to Karachi, where Nusrat lived. We drove to EMI's studios in the S.I.T.E. area outside of Karachi's city limits, passing miles and miles of slums. We sped by poor people sardined together in one-room, tin-roofed houses looking out through their iron-barred windows like prisoners. Politicians promising change had come and gone, but these people's song remained the same.

As a brand new band, our humble session carried none of the hullaballoo of a Vital Signs production. We got no advance money, but Bokhari *sahib* gave us two weeks of free studio time. We had to work frenetically to record and mix the album. Nusrat and Ali sang lead vocals. I was thrust into the role of producer, tunesmith, co-lyricist with Sabir Zafar, and guitar and bass player. I also shared keyboards and backing vocals with the others. My hands were full!

There was help from outside as well, in the form of a friend named Fifi Haroon. On our twelve-song album titled *Junoon* were two songs based on the romantic folk tale of Heer and Ranjha. One was a guitar instrumental with *tablas* by Ashiq Ali called "Heer" and the other was "Jogia." "Jogia" was the first Pakistani rock song recorded by a woman.

Fifi, a writer from Karachi, had been a big support to me throughout my difficult breakup with the Signs. Fifi's voice was sweet, but the whole recording process was rough, tumbled, and hurried. Our engineer, Iqbal Asif, freaked out when he heard Guns N' Roses–like guitar feedback coming from the amplifiers, worriedly saying, "That noise is no good for recording, Salman!" I had to explain to him that distorted solos were part of rock and roll! They *needed* to be loud, I said. Even though the album sounded like a demo-quality recording, it had power and drive. It meshed mystical poetry, social commentary, and lust-laden lyrics sung by four vocalists in Urdu and English with folk and classical melodies, eighties rock guitar, drum machines, *tablas*, and *dholak*. If the Junoon lab experiment was going to be a failure, it was going to be a loud and noisy one.

For Ali and me, all this was a learning process and we were happy to make up our album as we went along. But the nervous Nusrat threw in the towel when he heard the final product.

"Salman," he said, "these songs aren't going anywhere! People will cringe listening to this album!"

He sounded just like his former Vital Signs band mates, who'd told him I was delusional and that he was better off flying planes. Nusrat quit Junoon to pursue his pilot's career. I couldn't really blame him. There was no money or respect in this venture. Not yet, at least. Junoon's first album would eventually become a classic, but at the time the abrasive guitar and raw vocals jarred Pakistani tastes. The inauspicious debut and lack of commercial gigs were a hindrance to putting out a sophomore record. But the scientist in me wasn't going to give up so easily on my rock and roll string theory.

In the meantime, I needed some money. My *junoon* had brought me this far musically, but the band I'd named after my life's guiding principle wasn't paying the bills. Samina's residency only paid 1,500 rupees a month, so I began to look around for other work. I found it in TV. Along the way, I learned how art can shape society.

I heard that PTV's famous feminist director-writer duo, Sahira Kazmi and Hasina Moin, were looking for a male actor to cast in a TV drama called *Aahat* ("Sound"). In a changed environment for television, the two women had come together after a long hiatus to do a daring and bold production about female children and family planning. Both issues were controversial in a male-dominated, developing society. Sahira needed someone to play an angry young man whose middle-class dreams of having a boy have been frustrated by his wife's giving birth to multiple girls. It's a very common Pakistani tale and I decided to audition, figuring I had nothing to lose. My only previous acting role had been with the Vital Signs, playing myself. The creative and intense Sahira, looking for a fresh face, cast me despite my inexperience and over the objections of many established PTV actors. Appearing in a Sahira Kazmi–Hasina Moin TV show meant maximum eyeballs. Even Indian viewers were hooked on their soap operas. Luckily it was a six-episode play and I could grow into my role as a tormented male chauvinist who finally learns how to respect women. I played the role opposite one of Pakistan's leading TV actresses, Sania Saeed, and even though I had jumped into the deep end I learned quickly from her about camera angles, dialogue delivery, expressions, and even PTV politics. Apparently there was a campaign to keep Sahira down because she wanted to use new artists and pop musicians (like me) in TV shows. That didn't fly with many in Karachi's cliquish TV center where we filmed the shows. Some TV people raked me over the coals behind my back. I just ignored the whispers and gossip and tried to do the best I could. Junoon also got an unexpected plug when Sahira asked me to do some of the soundtrack music for the show. I gave her a song called "Khwaab" ("Dreams"), that Nusrat had sung on the Junoon album. "Khwaab," thanks to the success of *Aahat*, became a classic for Junoon fans. In time Nusrat would fondly remember singing the "songs that weren't going anywhere."

Junoon's *desi* rock album had bombed, but *Aahat* became a runaway success. The emotional drama struck a deep chord, gripping the country for six weeks. Millions of families watched it across the nation, and my character of the weak, frustrated husband with four little girls got me recognized in circles which were streets away from rock and roll and Junoon. I met cab drivers who were so drawn to the story that they urged me to be nice to my wife and daughters! They also confessed their guilt about their own real-life roles of dealing harshly with sisters and wives. Those experiences drove home for me the powerful role of popular culture in bringing about change in society.

I was happy to get recognition as an almost accidental actor. But what I really wanted was to be known for my music and my rock band. I kept moonlighting (doing music for and producing the Imran Khan documentary *Leading from the Front*), but I dove back into writing songs. I was energized by both the success of *Aahat* and Pakistan's win against England in the 1992 World Cup. Junoon had been performing the odd gig with a rotating lineup of musicians from Karachi, including Malcolm Goveas on drums, Ashiq Ali on *tablas*, and an assortment of bass and keyboard players. At the same time I was working up music for Junoon's second album, *Talaash* (*The Search*) and itching to record. But we needed a solid, experienced musician in the studio, someone who could help me with engineering and production.

I knew just who to call.

I rang my high school buddy Brian O'Connell and asked him to come out to Pakistan to help with recording *Talaash*. It turned out to be a good time to ask. Brian was then in Buffalo, and suffering a downward spiral. His girlfriend had left him, he was battling alcoholism, was in credit card debt, and wasn't playing much. I'd sent him Junoon's album to listen to but wasn't sure he would or could make the eight-thousand-mile journey east. But one February day in 1992 I got a letter from Brian with some good news.

Dear Sal,

the Junoon album has been a 'hit' among me and my friends . . . (and) I would absolutely LOVE to join you in Pakistan . . . The U.S. is in a severe recession and my job won't be waiting for me when I come back (even) as I am hesitant to "Burn my Bridges behind Me." If I can help at all with your endeavors—I'LL BE THERE! I consider your invitation the opportunity of a lifetime. LET's DO IT! All my love, Brian.

That was a powerful sign from God.

Brian's father Tom loaned him the money to take a PIA flight and my old friend landed in Karachi in the middle of a sweltering May heat wave, wearing a corduroy jacket and pullover. He had his Fender Stratocaster in one hand and a guitar amp in the other. Driving to the airport, Ali and I decided to pull a prank on Brian. As Brian came out of immigration and customs, Ali sauntered up to him, posing as an ISI agent.

"Sir," asked the faux Officer Azmat, "are you bringing in any drugs in your guitar case?"

That scared the living daylights out of Brian and he earnestly pleaded innocent.

"Officer, I've been invited by my friend Salman Ahmad of Junoon, who should be here any moment. I am telling you the truth, sir!"

Officer Azmat made Brian stand there until I came up from behind and slapped him on the back. Brian let out a huge sigh of relief and punched me hard on my arm. The new Junoon was together and we were ready to take over Pakistan!

Brian wasn't just making a one-time trip across the oceans. He would end up staying in Pakistan for more than ten years and diving into the culture. What I did in Tappan, Brian did in Pakistan. Brian ate up the spicy cuisine and learned proper Urdu and how to curse in Punjabi. He met and married a beautiful Pakistani disc jockey, actress, and model named Ayesha. They had two lovely girls, Rachel and Allyssandra. I was best man at his church wedding in Karachi in 1994. We had come full circle from Eclipse to Junoon.

But it would be a long and difficult road ahead: 1992 to 1995 were years of constant struggle, and there was little to show in terms of musical or financial success. But having my long-time, trusted friend on board was a source of motivation. Brian just dove into *desi* culture, developing a taste for *nihari* (beef curry) and giving up alcohol. Junoon fans embraced this white, Irish-Catholic American as their own—even if they mangled his name into "Mr. Brain." Brian turned out to be as loyal as he'd been enthusiastic. *Talaash* met with mediocre success, but Brian stuck by me. I was proud of the self-produced videos we released, including "Aap Aur Hum," "Heer," "Talaash," and "Heeray." But critics and the TV establishment pounced on our lack of sophistication and polish. In a 1993 magazine survey, we were voted the worst group in Pakistan.

As time went on I felt more and more pressure from my parents and friends to go back to medicine and say goodbye to my musical dreams. Everyone except Samina thought I was crazy to continue playing guitar and writing songs that only made sense to me and a small number of fans. Ever my greatest backer, Samina supported my decision to move to Karachi so the whole band could be in one city. But money was hard to come by and I found my dream slowly slipping away.

At the beginning of 1995, I was struggling and mired in self-doubt. I was the father of three young boys, Shamyl, Sherjan, and newborn Imran. I was getting more worried all the time about how I was going to provide for them and Samina. One consolation was that Junoon's rebel vision was gradually beginning to get noticed in the national English-language press. Initially written off as "tuneless noise sounding like the shrieking of dogs and cats," Junoon's ugly duckling image began to change. Our socially conscious message, flamboyant stage performances, and hard-edged, guitar-driven sound stood out from the dozens of other bands and artists in the country. But that critical acclaim didn't translate into big concert offers or even album sales. In Pakistan's nascent pop music industry, piracy was also rampant, and cash-strapped record companies had virtually no promotion and marketing budgets. *Desi* concert promoters were shady characters who would hire you but could then disappear without paying you a single *paisa*. *Desi* cultural organizations were also wary of hiring a rock band that didn't play the usual syrupy Pakistani pop. Junoon had a small cult following in colleges and schools among the urban elite in Lahore, Karachi, and Islamabad, but getting gigs outside of the tri-city academic institutions meant dealing with red tape and resistance from conservative small town officials. They worried about the "radical" image we represented: long hair, jeans, guitars, and "*uchulna koodna*"—jumping up and down onstage. This wasn't the correct behavior for "*achey bachey*"—good kids. With little TV and radio support or multinational sponsorship we invariably had to end up forking out our own money to play.

By this time, Benazir Bhutto was back as prime minister. But the political environment was even worse than it had been before. Rock and roll concerts were more common now, and that was a good thing by itself. But nasty politicians with agendas to peddle had figured out a way to co-opt the entertainment industry.

One night, for example, we played a set at a multi-act show at the KMC Sports Complex in Karachi. A young promoter from the student wing of the Muttahida Qaumi Movement came to me with a demand. Before the next act went on, he wanted me to welcome their party leader, Azim Tariq, on to the stage.

"Sorry, *bhai*," I said, "I came here to play music, not suck up to politicians. If you can pay us our fee, we'll be leaving."

The student pulled out an AK-47 and said, "How does this payment look to you?"

My friend Mujahid Hamid dragged me away from that unwinnable fight at the KMC Complex, saying, "You can't play music or change the world if you're dead, Salman!"

Mujahid was right, but as long as I was alive I was not going to be silenced by thugs posing as politicians. That was the first of my many run-ins with the MQM, whose party workers used to threaten Karachi musicians regularly and get them to perform for free. It was like living on the set of *The Godfather*, except the bullets and blood were real.

Political violence disrupted our recording sessions. In early 1995, the whole city of Karachi was under curfew as a gang war between two rival factions of the MQM spilled onto the streets. One day I arrived to lay down guitar tracks at Amir Hasan's recording studio near Gulshan-e-Iqbal and saw the gruesome sight of a man in his twenties on his knees a few hundred yards away from the studio being shot in the back of his head by a political opponent. The pistol shot sounded like a firecracker going off. A dark red fountain of blood squirted out of the condemned man's skull, and he slumped forward into a lifeless lump as his masked assailant escaped on his motor bike into a side street of a deserted marketplace. I felt sick to my stomach and unable to breathe as I hid behind a pillar. I watched helplessly as political activists threw the corpse into the back of a car and disappeared into the sweltering heat.

Ali, Brian, and I also were practically broke. The economics of playing and recording new music was eating into our meager savings and we spent our last rupees developing Junoon's third album, *Inquilaab* (*Revolution*). We went heavily into debt. We ate *daal* and *chawal* (lentils and rice) for months in the studio because we couldn't afford anything else. I felt constantly stressed and irritable for not being able to be with Samina, who had just had a cesarean section and had gone to her mother's in Lahore to heal and recuperate.

With little money and with gangs of Karachites killing each other in daily blood baths, the futures of both Junoon and Pakistan seemed hopeless. I simultaneously fought to stave off depression and tried to keep my music alive. For most of that year we worked on the album in fits and starts. Between blackouts and curfews, we somehow managed to record an album whose music was alternatively dark and light, socially pointed and spiritual. It was guitar-heavy and carried a revolutionary message of hope and positive action against cynicism and national apathy.

Of *Inquilaab*'s twelve tracks, "Saeein" is one of my favorites. My childhood fascination with the raw yearning of the *azan* was the inspiration behind the song. "Saeein" opens with heavily distorted and slurred legato notes from my black Ibanez. The ominous tone reflects darkness before a distant dawn. The electric guitar intro leads into a trance-y Sindhi *tabla* and *dholak* groove. That groove is seamlessly wedded to Brian's hypnotic bass and my folklike, Zeppelin-esque acoustic guitars in altered D tunings. "Saeein" is a rock *qawwali* which reaches a crescendo when Ali belts out a full-throated "Allah." That musical moment opens the door for classic rock to ride the Sufi vibe. What comes next is a frenzied guitar solo over galloping percussion that sounds like a hundred Arab chargers riding over the desert plains before finding the final oasis.

"Saeein" showed me an early glimpse of the potential and depth of a future Junoon sound that people would start referring to as "Sufi rock." But "Saeein" would be alternately praised and criticized. The criticism came from the archaic and hidebound Urdu press, whose knee-jerk reaction was to fear anything new. The fear had nothing do with the song's lyrics, which are devotional. What the writers didn't like was the use of the "Western" guitar to milk the notes of the *azan* and build up an electric chord progression around the name of God. But they showed their ignorance by pigeonholing the guitar as "Western." The guitar has a long pedigree and plenty of "Eastern" relatives, including the *qitar*, *rubab*, *sarod*, and *oud* (all of which were played or, in the case of the *oud*, designed by famous Muslim musicians). History—and ill-informed critics—aside, though, the Pakistani kids had no doubts. They loved this new sound—at last. But the reaction to "Saeein" wasn't atypical. Over time, Junoon's music would be loved by the fans, hated by the critics, and banned by the government.

Having started the *Inquilaab* (*Revolution*), I felt that my perseverance and patience had finally paid off. But just a few weeks after my seventh wedding anniversary, in early 1996, I got a phone call that would open doors to a new level of fame and success and make Vitalmania a distant fading memory.

My old cricket-playing friend, Ahmad Kapadia, a creative director at the Orient McCann-Erickson advertising agency, called me up. His voice was excited—and a little bit desperate. He'd just landed a huge account, Coca-Cola's sponsorship of the cricket World Cup, which was being held in Pakistan, India, and Sri Lanka in March 1996. Coke and Pepsi were competing fiercely in the Pakistani cola market, and Coke urgently needed a jingle to give it an edge. Since Pepsi had signed the Vital Signs to a lucrative contract—making the lives of my former band mates very comfortable—my competitive nature understood immediately that this was a huge chance to show the Vital Signs and Pakistan what Junoon was really about.

Initially, I wasn't sure I had anything that would interest Ahmad, but then I remembered the song I'd just finished for *Inquilaab*. It hadn't been part of the original album lineup and was recorded after my son Imran's first birthday. Imran's birthday, falling on my own, had lifted my spirits. Driving around Karachi one calm day after gang violence had paralyzed the city for weeks, a melody came floating to me from the ether. It was a simple tune and it stuck inside my head. I didn't want to lose the moment, so I pulled over and hummed it into my small Sony cassette recorder. Sitting there in my Toyota, I put down the first notes of what would become our song "Jazba-e-Junoon"—"The Spirit of Passion."

Those few simple notes in the key of A minor would turn into an ode to joy and hope for an entire nation. "Jazba" called out to all Pakistanis: "If you have the spirit of passion, never give up / those who struggle will always reach the sky!" We recorded it in super-quick time at Nizar Lalani's studio near the busy Tariq Road. "Jazba" features a Santana-ish wall of sound of guitars, bass, Latin percussion, horn synth, *tablas*, and *dholak* by Ashiq and a soulful lead vocal from Ali. All of us, including our co-producer and engineer Nizar and our friend Shahine Sherali, sang harmony vocals, standing in a circle around the microphone, and it was done. "Jazba-e-Junoon" meant a lot to me personally since its message was one I was forcing myself to remember as I was going through some of my darkest times.

I stuck the phone up to a boom box and played Ahmad a recording of "Jazba."

For a moment I heard nothing from the other end. And then, this: "*Zabardust!*" (Awesome!), Ahmad said. "That's it!"

Thankfully for me, Ahmad wasn't the only one who liked my song. Sabir Sami, the young Coke marketing director in Lahore, shared his enthusiasm and made a deal with Junoon to feature "Jazba-e-Junoon" as the official song of the cricket World Cup. I couldn't believe the turn of events. From penniless paupers we were transformed into raja rockstars. Coke rolled out its biggest sponsorship in its history in Pakistan, throwing 30 million rupees into promoting the song on radio and TV. The lyrics struck a chord with people in Pakistan, who were so tired of violence and corrupt politics.

"Jazba" was the big break we needed as a band. All of a sudden, Junoon became a nationwide sensation after years of struggling for recognition. Junaid Jamshed came over to congratulate me and to share a secret: he was thinking of going solo because he was tired of dealing with the Vital Signs' daily childish arguments and ego struggles. The Vital Signs didn't last much longer, breaking up a year or two later. I felt vindicated by my earlier decision to leave them, and "Jazba"'s lyrics defined my own life's journey. I had struggled for my passion and Junoon was touching the skies.

Just as I was at my highest point from the success of "Jazba-e-Junoon," I met one of the men who'd inspired me to take my junooni journey in the first place: Mick Jagger.

As the World Cup drew closer, I got a call from Imran Khan. Imran had retired from the game and entered politics in an attempt to counter the corruption of both Bhutto and Sharif.

"Mick Jagger is coming to Lahore for the World Cup," Imran told me nonchalantly. "Can you show him around?"

"You're joking, right?" I said to Imran.

"No, he's a huge cricket fan," Imran replied. "Jagger always travels to see the World Cup, wherever it's held. Now he's coming with his daughter to Pakistan on my invitation."

Managing to find my voice, I quickly agreed. How could I not? Back in high school I'd reverentially played Stones cover after Stones cover with Eclipse. But this was something entirely different: never in a million years had I imagined I'd get to meet Mr. Jumping Jack Flash himself!

When Jagger arrived in Lahore, I was surprised to see that he was much smaller than I imagined. But he was wiry and fit, his body lithe and full of energy. Mick's beautiful twenty-year-old daughter Jade, from his marriage to Bianca, joined him, as did a bodyguard.

On my first meeting with Mick, I felt like a twelve-year-old fan, barely able to contain my admiration. But I tried to keep my cool and shook his hand, welcoming him to Pakistan. A chauffeured black Mercedes drove Mick and Jade to a spacious suite at the Avari Hotel, right next to the red-bricked Alhamra Arts Council on Mall Road.

That night, our cricket posse, including me, Imran and his lovely young British wife Jemima, Mick, Jade, and Mujahid, who had just arrived from Shanghai, went to the *haveli* (old-style mansion) of Yousef Salli. Yousuf the flambuoyant batchelor is a grandson of the poet Iqbal and is a legendary host in Lahore. He welcomed Jagger and Jade to his historic home, where he had arranged for an exclusive and private *qawwali* performance by Nusrat Fateh Ali Khan.

Sitting next to this rock and roll icon, I couldn't resist asking Jagger a barrage of Rolling Stones trivia questions.

"Wasn't Mick Taylor a better live guitar player than Ronnie Wood?" I asked.

Jagger raised his eyebrows at me, surprised that this young musician from Lahore knew so much about the Stones while Nusrat's *qawwali* party jammed on into the wee hours of the night.

The next afternoon, rejuvenated by the qawwali shower, we all met up at the World Cup cricket final. Australia was playing Sri Lanka, and Jagger was heavily rooting for the Aussies to win. Coke provided us with a special private enclosure with a buffet dinner and TV screens. Imran and Jemima joined us, but Samina was back in Karachi watching on TV and I was missing her tremendously. The TV cameras projected us on the giant screens in the stadium and an almighty roar went up. I smiled at Jagger and Imran, delighted that they had received such a warm welcome from the forty thousand passionate cricket fans. And then I heard what the crowd was chanting.

"Jazba!" "Jazba!"

I froze. But I kept smiling at Jagger and Imran and told myself not to make too much of the commotion. "Jazba" was the official song of the World Cup, so the crowd was just reacting to the heavy marketing around the cricket championship, nothing more.

The final turned out not to be much of a game. Sri Lanka stunned the crowd by kicking Australia's ass. By the dinner break it was clear the Aussies were down for the count and weren't getting back up. Mick got distracted from the cricket and turned to me.

"What is there to do in this city after the match?" he asked.

The Rolling Stone was clearly bored and wanted to get out of there. I thought for a second, and then a crazy idea popped into my head, mostly as a joke.

"Do you want to see the dancing girls of Lahore?" I asked, and then immediately regretted it. What was I thinking? I quickly started listing other, less-scandalous alternatives. But it was already too late. Jagger was intrigued.

"Tell me about these dancing girls," he said, a lascivious smile spreading across his weathered face.

The dancing girls of Lahore are part of an ancient tradition of courtesans going back to the days of the Mughal Empire, when young princes would be sent to learn the social graces—and the art of love—at the skilled hands of the beautiful dancing girls that lived in the red-light district near Anarkali Bazaar. The Mughal emperors had vanished into the annals of history, but the dancing girls remained. Like the geishas of Japan, they represented the last vestige of a culture that revered female grace and beauty. Even during the austere days of General Zia's rule in the 1980s, the dancing girls were left alone—partly because many of the cops were lovers of *mujra* dancing.

When Jagger heard this, he was ready to go at once. Imran gave me a pained look for suggesting the idea and tried to talk Jagger out of it. As a politician, Imran would be unable to join us inside the red light district without creating a national scandal.

"That Aravinda de Silva really stuck it to the Aussies, didn't he?" said the former Pakistan captain in an attempt to change the subject.

Jagger shrugged and gave me a wicked smile. "Let's go right after the World Cup ceremony's over!"

I glanced at Imran apologetically as Sri Lanka's captain, Arjuna Ranatunga, lifted his country's first gleaming World Cup trophy. Then I led the rock and roll entourage out of the floodlit cricket stadium and into the Lahore night.

When we arrived back at Yousuf's *haveli*, which is right next to Lahore's red light district, Jagger insisted that he wanted to walk around the area and see the city for himself.

And so it was that I found myself guiding Jagger, Jade, a couple of their British friends, and a shanghaied Mujahid through the ancient alleyways of Lahore. We walked past the Badshahi Mosque, the stunning Mughal house of worship built by Emperor Aurangzeb in 1673. Many Englishmen had walked the cobbled streets of Lahore before, but this was the first time a Midnight Rambler from London had marveled at the red sandstone walls and the white domes towering above us. We then passed the ancient white Lahore Fort, whose exact origin remains a mystery to historians.

We finally arrived in Hira Mandi, Lahore's red light district. A few hundred years ago, Hira Mandi was an elegant bazaar where silk-robed princes came to learn the joys of love at the skilled hands of the royal courtesans. But today it is little better than the sleazier sections of London's Soho, or Bangkok.

We walked past leering pimps and a colorfully dressed gang of flamboyant *hijras* (hermaphrodites). I was extremely self-conscious about bringing Mick Jagger to this seedy part of town. But he seemed to be loving it.

That's when I heard whispers of "*dheko, dheko*" ("look, look"). We were approaching the alleys where the dancers performed. I turned in surprise to see a group of young men racing toward us, and I cursed myself for not insisting that Jagger bring his bodyguard. Uh oh, I thought: he had been recognized and we were in huge trouble.

As the crowd bore down on us, I tried to push Jagger out of the way. It turned out that I didn't need to. The boisterous young men rushed right past him and crowded around me.

"Jazba!" "Jazba!" they chanted.

As I struggled to get away from the eyes and double takes, Jumping Jack Flash and his daughter looked at each other and burst out laughing.

I managed to drag our entourage into a side street where the dancing girls would be waiting. There was no chance of anonymity since we were still being followed in Hira Mandi by the Junoonis. One Junoon fan actually offered the keys to his car when he saw the rush around us. I took the keys for our getaway from the crowded streets later. The Junooni's only request was that I provide an autograph and that we return the car to his residence whenever we could.

I pummeled the first door I saw. A startled young girl opened the door and we fell inside a small, dimly lit room with the smell of incense and jasmine. The door slammed behind us, hiding us from the searching, inquisitive eyes of the public. Brits and Pakistanis all huddled into a tiny room in Hira Mandi. It was a pity that there were no video cameras.

My eyes adjusted to the light and I saw that we were inside one of the dancing girls' quarters. It was a tiny, square room with purple curtains. An old Persian carpet lined the floor, and a few colorful cushions provided the only seats.

As I caught my breath from the craziness that had just happened outside, Jagger looked at me and winked.

"OK, so let's see the show."

The dancing girl emerged, followed by her small band of *tabla* and *dholak* players. She was sixteen years old, but her eyes lacked the innocence of most Pakistani girls her age. There was sadness there, but also a defiant fire. I could tell that she knew society looked down on her and her profession, but that she'd kept her head high and her dignity in place. This was her turf, and she was both master of ceremonies and the main attraction.

She smiled at us seductively, and then she saw my face. Her practiced smile vanished, replaced by shock.

"What are *you* doing here?" she asked me in Urdu.

Good question, I thought, don't tell anyone. She was clearly worried for my reputation.

I quickly hid my own embarrassment and nodded at Jagger. Speaking in Urdu, I said: "I am here with one of the greatest musical artists in the world."

The dancing girl looked him over dubiously.

"He's really old," she said.

I smiled at Jagger quickly, hoping he had no idea what we were saying or thinking. He didn't understand the words, but he saw the look of skepticism on the girl's face.

"What's she saying?" he asked me, his eyes narrowing.

I improvised.

"She can tell that you're an amazing artist just from the look in your eye," I stammered.

Jagger looked at me closely with his iceberg-blue eyes.

"C'mon, mate. What did she really say?"

I realized that he was going to see through every lie I manufactured. So I decided to just let it all hang out.

"She thinks you're too old to sing and dance."

Jagger looked the dancer over. And then he got up. He took off his jacket, revealing a white shirt over black pants with the narrowest of waists, then nodded to the musicians.

"Tell 'em to play."

I nodded to the *tabla* and *dholak* players, who started knocking out a sinewy *desi* groove. Jagger reached over and grabbed one of the purple curtains and used it to cover a lamp, bathing the room in psychedelic mauve lightning.

"Tell 'em to go faster," he said. I complied, and the percussionists ratcheted up their rhythm, creating a rapid *bhangra* beat.

And then the Rolling Stone placed his hands on his hips and started gyrating wildly. He was in his fifties, but he shook his bootie better than any teenage girl. The one teenage girl in the room looked at him in shock. Jagger stuck out his tongue at her defiantly.

"Come on, child, show me what you got."

He leaned forward close to the stunned dancing girl and shook his chest right next to her breasts.

The girl was speechless. This fifty-something-year-old white man had just strutted onto her turf and showed her up.

So she got up and let loose, showing him the true power of *mujra*, the ancient erotic dance of Pakistan.

We watched, mouths agape, as Jagger and the Lahori dancing girl put on some of the hottest, most improvised moves I've ever seen in show business. This was East meets West in a breathless embrace of animal movement and spiritual elevation. I could see the headlines now: Jumping Jack Flash does the *mujra* while the Junooni dervish laughs in suspended disbelief. So much for the "clash of civilizations"!

Jade grinned at me as her father moved his feet while the dancing girl ground her hips to the *bhangra* beat. The girl leaned forward close to Jagger, teasing him with her body and then whirling away just before their flesh touched.

Nobody is ever going to believe this, I thought, as I looked at the blushing, bearded Mujahid. Both our faces betrayed a mixture of shock and reverence. As a high school kid in Tappan, I'd learned the riffs to "It's Only Rock 'n' Roll (But I like It)." Now I was watching the singer of that song dancing *desi*-style in a moonlit Lahore night. The whole thing was more than surreal.

Mick Jagger took out a 100-pound note and held it close to his face, daring the girl to take it from him. The girl leaned in with a seductive smile. And then she pinched Jagger's cheek and grabbed the money. He roared with laughter.

Jade turned to me with a smile.

"He was pissed about Australia losing the World Cup," she said. "But you gave him a night he's never going to forget."

Neither would I.

NINE

Banned in Pakistan

One of the poignant moments of that "Jazba"-filled 1996 was a dinner that Samina and I were invited to by Imran Khan and his twenty-one-year-old wife Jemima. That evening, we were introduced to the guest of honor: Diana, the Princess of Wales.

Diana had come to visit the Shaukat Khanum Memorial Cancer Hospital and its patients, as well as the family of her secret Pakistani lover, Dr. Hasnat Khan. Diana's private visit was also a deliberate snub to Prime Minister Benazir Bhutto and her husband. The real-life princess couldn't abide the would-be queen's corruption scandals, which had made headlines in the United Kingdom and elsewhere. Diana smiled radiantly and looked ravishing in a specially designed cream-colored *shalwar kameez* as the equally stunning Jemima introduced her to Samina and me. Diana had won many Pakistani hearts that day when she reached out with genuine empathy and warmth toward the terminally ill children at the hospital named after Imran's mother. Samina, impressed by Diana's social advocacy and natural, down-to-earth demeanor, received a treasured autograph from the princess.

It was the kite-flying season of Basant. That spring night, I gazed at this unlikely collection of post-colonial royals, healers, humanitarians, athletes, and artists all gathered in my city of Lahore. My mind wandered off, wondering what was next on my journey. My dreams had brought me close to the music I wanted to make but also given me a growing insight into the worldly definitions of success. It's easy for people to lose sight of what matters during our short time on Earth and self-destruct, chasing illusions of power, money, and fame. The things we leave behind that are truly valuable are our memories and stories of love, creativity, and kinship. Were these thoughts echoes from a time long past, signs of the present, or an omen of the things to come?

During that dinner Samina and I shared a table with Nusrat Fateh Ali Khan and his wife. From the smiling maestro I learned an interesting new detail about his youth. He told me that his father had wanted him to be a doctor as well because musicians always faced hard times! He said that he was happy with my Sufi quest through music and liked the direction of "Saeein." That night he spoke enthusiastically about collaborating with Junoon. It was a huge honor just to hear those words escape his lips.

Both Princess Diana and the King of Qawwali would die a little more than a year after our special night together in Lahore. Imran and Jemima's brand-new marriage would break up a few years later. And in 2007, Benazir Bhutto would be assassinated in a suicide bomb attack.

Nothing ever lasts except the music.

A couple of weeks after Imran's dinner, Junoon and Nusrat Fateh Ali Khan's *qawwali* party jointly headlined a concert at Karachi's huge field hockey stadium. Before us, in the steamy night, thirty thousand entranced, jumping fans sang along to "Saeein," joyfully mimicking our song back to us.

"Saeein (Lord), you are my truthful one and I am your devotee . . ."

As one of the legends of Pakistani music looked on, the fans also sang Sufi *qawwali* chants and "Jazba-e-Junoon." The concert, put together by a big-hearted television woman named Rana Sheikh, was also a rare occasion in bringing the rich and the poor together to celebrate their love of music. That evening, rock and Islamic mystical music, and modernity and tradition, were united in a tight embrace. The spirit of passion had swept across the dancing multitudes of a country which had been divided by sectarianism, dictatorship, and venal politicians. Up on that stage, beside one of my heroes and playing my songs, I felt as if a baton was being handed to me from Nusrat. "Keep the music alive" was the message I silently heard from him as the galloping *tablas* and harmonium meshed with ringing electric guitars, vocal acrobatics, and funky bass and drum grooves. I felt humbled, and elated to be on this Earth.

But something still didn't seem right. As I scanned the aisles, I saw that the most ecstatic fans were standing in the bleachers, trapped behind barbed wired fences and straining to steal a glimpse of Junoon and Nusrat. Meanwhile, right in front of us in the VIP section were the entitled rich and well-connected of Karachi society, sitting smugly on red-cushioned sofas and sipping tea and guzzling soft drinks. Here, directly before me, was blatant social apartheid. It bothered me deeply that despite the veneer of democracy and cultural openness, this gap between the haves and the have-nots had continued to grow alarmingly throughout the country. So between songs I decided to describe what I saw—to everyone.

"Looks like those behind the barbed wire fences are the real Junoonis, while you guys in the rich seats just seem passionate about eating and drinking!" I teased the VIPs.

At that, a big roar of approval came up from the great unwashed masses. Those voices echoed inside me. My band mates and I were thrilled to be in the spotlight, no question. "Jazba-e-Junoon" and our album *Inquilaab* were massive successes, and we were straddling the top of Pakistan's rock world. But I was also beginning to feel that if I wasn't careful I could easily go blind just like most of the VIPs sitting on their couches in that Karachi night.

Over the next few months, I would have ample opportunity to search my soul for what was important to me. Listening to the roaring crowds that night, I heard an answer, even before I could ask the question.

For the first time in my life, I should have been completely satisfied. I was financially secure and living a comfortable existence with Samina and our boys in a nice, decent house in a clean Karachi neighborhood. But I wasn't fulfilled, due partly to my need to keep evolving creatively as an artist. I couldn't just rest on the laurels I'd created with "Jazba." I didn't want to repeat the mistakes of the Vital Signs. They relaxed after "Dil Dil Pakistan" topped the charts and slowly faded away. History is filled with musicians and bands who have fried their brains in the bright lights when they should have focused on making new music. My *junoon* kept me restless.

I also couldn't look around Pakistan and in good conscience be happy. For the past eight years, the governments of both Benazir Bhutto and Nawaz Sharif had been swimming in a cesspool of corruption and decadence. It didn't matter that they'd been chosen by popular vote—they had made a mockery of democracy and civil rights. Benazir's husband, Asif Ali Zardari—who became president of Pakistan in September 2008—was caught up in corruption scandals that would make Al Capone blush. Zardari, who was investment minister in Bhutto's Cabinet, was known as "Mr. Ten Percent" for allegedly demanding kickbacks on government contracts. Bhutto and Zardari were accused by Pakistani investigators of embezzling as much as $1.5 billion from government accounts. Bhutto's and Zardari's shenanigans got the attention of international publications like *Newsweek* and the *New York Times*. The couple were dubbed "the princess" and "the playboy" in a BBC documentary. While most Pakistanis were barely scraping by, Zardari reportedly enjoyed an estate in England, and the couple was alleged to have hidden millions of dollars in Swiss banks.

Opposition leader Nawaz Sharif—a protégé of General Zia—was no prize either. I actually knew Sharif from my days of playing cricket at the same Lahore gymkhana. You can learn a lot about a man by the way he plays his sport. Sharif was vain and vindictive and would threaten the umpires' jobs if they ever gave him out. He would ensure a weak opposition so that he would look good and no game could start before he arrived with an army of sycophants and valets carrying his fancy Gunn & Moore and Duncan Fearnley cricket gear. The gymkhana went from being one of Lahore's best teams to the laughingstock of the city's cricketing circles.

The man who would later ban Junoon's music revealed his poor judgment and decision-making skills even before my band recorded our first album. In 1987, when the World Cup was held in Pakistan and India, I played two warm-up games for Punjab against the visiting West Indies and England teams. Sharif, then the chief minister of Punjab, had a pie-in-the-sky dream to become a national hero by beating the *farangis* (foreigners) at cricket. His audacious scheme to showcase his talents in a game with real players and real umpires would have been inspiring had it been a movie like *The Natural* or *Heaven Can Wait*. But there were no actors in this game. Sharif's "successes" in the fixed gymkhana games falsely emboldened him. Bat in hand, he strode into Gaddafi Stadium. The chief minister looked like an astronaut without an oxygen tank, decked out in a helmet, chest guard, forearm protector, thigh pad, gloves, leg guards, and an abdominal protector. A busload of hired fans took their seats in the stadium, beating *dhol* drums and chanting *"Sher-e-Punjab zindabad!"* ("Long live the Lion of Punjab!"). Inspired by the roar of the crowds and the promise of glory, Sharif decided to lead off the Lahore innings against the West Indies—one of the world's top cricket teams. But no amount of gear, cheers, or prayers could prevent the giant Jamaican fast bowler Courtney Walsh from running in and destroying Sharif's daydream with his second delivery. Sharif's hurried, swishing bat missed the ball by a mile. The entire stadium saw and heard the death rattle as the ball uprooted Sharif's stumps. But the lion refused to surrender.

We played Mike Gatting's England team in the second game, held at our Lahore gymkhana home ground. This time, Sharif batted at number three and joined me at the fall of our first wicket. Even before facing a ball, he walked gingerly toward me from the striker's end and whispered nervously, "What is the ball doing?"

"*Mian sahib,*" I told him, using his formal family title, "stay on the front foot and watch out for Phil DeFreitas's away swinger!"

Sharif took his guard, this time totally determined to succeed. He dug into his crease. But in cricket when your luck has gone, nothing can save you. DeFreitas had been bowling outswingers to a menacing cluster of fielders waiting for a catch in the slip cordon. The English bowler charged in and pitched the ball way outside the off stump. Sharif lifted his bat high like an experienced professional but forgot to cover his castle. The ball unexpectedly swung back like a boomerang, completely bamboozling the startled Sharif. It shattered both his stumps and his ego. Two ducks in a row for the Lion of Punjab. Sharif looked up, mystified.

"Look what you made me do, Salman!" the future prime minister screamed down the wicket in Urdu. "You told me to watch out for his outswinger!"

"*Ji, Mian sahib,*" I replied, "but you should've also been ready for the one that comes back!" As Sharif reluctantly left the middle, I thought to myself, What if one day this guy becomes a prime minister? Heaven help Pakistan!

That hot October day I genuinely felt sorry for him as he made his long and lonely walk back to the pavilion.

My thought was a bad omen. I lost my sympathy for Sharif after he actually took the reins of Pakistan's government. Sharif was prime minister of Pakistan twice in the 1990s. He behaved like a modern-day pharaoh, as if above the law. During his term, honest and respected journalists like Najam Sethi were beaten up and thrown in jail. Chief Justice of Pakistan Syed Sajjad Ali Shah was dismissed and replaced with a crony of Sharif's. In a show of total contempt for justice, goons stormed the Supreme Court. Both President Farooq Leghari and General Jehangir Karamat, the chief of staff of the Pakistan Army, were unceremoniously removed. In a decision that would later bite him, Sharif replaced Karamat with General Pervez Musharraf. (Musharraf ousted Sharif in October 1999.) Both Benazir and Sharif came from wealthy families. But their greed for even more was just staggering. In a country where the majority of people lived on less than a dollar a day, these shameless leaders took turns plundering Pakistan's poor.

During the nineties the people of Pakistan could be forgiven for forgetting their one weapon against rulers like these: the country's much-abused constitution. It was time for us to exercise our constitutional right of protest and speak up. I was inspired by national voices calling for political reform, writers of conscience like Ardeshir Cowasjee, Najam Sethi and his wife Jugnu Mohsin, and intellectuals like Eqbal Ahmad. Even my cricketing hero Imran Khan launched a political movement for social justice.

The best way I knew how to speak out was with a song.

I found a willing ally in my friend and mentor Shoaib Mansoor, who helped me put together a song and music video titled "Ehtesaab," or "Accountability." I chanted the chorus and twisted the arms of other well-known artists like Ali Azmat, Najam Shiraz, and Nizar Lalani to sing along to the refrain: "How many eyes must sleep before they see their dreams unfold? The answer to all questions is accountability. Now!"

It was a Woody Guthrie/Bob Dylan kind of protest song, asking people to stand up for their rights and hold accountable fat-cat politicians, generals, and bureaucrats—and also people like the dirty cops who'd thrown me into jail when I tried to defend my grandmother's land. The blunt, hard-hitting "Ehtesaab" video shows Pakistani children working backbreaking menial jobs, juxtaposed with fictional politicians gorging themselves at five-star hotels. It also includes a scene in which a horse is dining at a luxury hotel—a deliberate reference to polo ponies kept by Asif Zardari. Those mares ate better than many of Pakistan's poor. In air-conditioned stables, no less.

Having gone through medical school, Samina and I had seen Pakistan's privilege gap at hospitals. The rich seemed to get treated right away while the poor were left to the mercy and compassion of overworked and underpaid doctors. Samina joined me enthusiastically as I played the song and video at colleges all over the country. Scores of students, men, women, and children joined us on an accountability march on Mall Road in Lahore in early December 1996. The climax of the accountability campaign was a free concert in Karachi's Nishtar Park on December 21. Junaid Jamshed joined Junoon onstage as ten thousand Karachites came out to protest governmental corruption. Rumors actually started flying that I was going into politics, and even my band had questions about my intentions. But I didn't have any such designs. I was just following my heart. I hadn't asked anybody to sponsor my social activism. Except I did actually have an unwitting corporate sponsor of sorts. In addition to the money we'd made from Junoon concerts, I used my share of the cash from Coke's World Cup sponsorship of "Jazba"! The song had urged people to never to give up. So I was taking the lyrics to heart and using the money for a populist cause. By this time many writers on the left were criticizing me for supposedly "selling out" to corporations. Maybe they were just plain jealous or incapable of seeing beyond their inflexible ideologies. Whatever their reasons, I ignored the "progressive" press and used Coca-Cola's money to skewer corrupt Pakistani politicians.

In America, musicians like Green Day or Kanye West can criticize politicians all day long, and most people usually just shrug. Not in Pakistan. The Nishtar Park show almost didn't happen. When we arrived at the venue, local officials had cut off the electricity to try to disrupt the concert. The politicians had sent their spies to check the pulse of the audience and found angry, flag-waving youths screaming out for accountability. But help and power came from an unlikely source. As the crowd raised slogans against the politicians and got restless, I went to a nearby madrassah out of desperation, to ask if we could run a power cable to our stage. The young bearded cleric eyed me closely and recognized me from Junoon's spiritual hit "Saeein."

"You mentioned Allah in the lyrics," said the young man. "For the love of God, we will give you a line!"

But there was a condition. We had to stop playing during the call to prayer.

"*Inshallah*!" I promised him, running out to launch the concert.

The song and video and that night's show were all a hit with our intended audience: the people. But the caretaker government overseeing Pakistan's upcoming elections thought otherwise. The "Accountability" video was banned from state television, on the grounds it would destabilize the country.

Not only did the video get banned. I also got threatened.

One night, an angry former aide to the dismissed Prime Minister Bhutto called me at home.

"Salman," the aide said, "you're committing suicide. You're biting the hand that feeds you."

That was rich. After all the fervor I'd seen in people's eyes all over the country for accountability, I wasn't going to put up with that. I told him to go fuck himself.

This was war. The national and international media lapped it up. The accountability campaign and Junoon's music and the "Ehtesaab" video were featured in the BBC film *The Princess and the Playboy*, an exposé on Benazir's and her husband's reign. In *Newsweek*, Carla Power dedicated a full-page story to Junoon and included my campaign, with the headline "For God and Country." The politicians hated us, but what did they expect? Art disturbs.

The chickens soon came home to roost for Benazir. Her government was voted out of power in 1997 and she was replaced by Nawaz Sharif. In time, Sharif would ban Junoon from state TV and radio and even public performances. That meant we could play almost nowhere in our own country—a ban we flaunted as best we could by playing private and secret gigs. According to Sharif, our long hair, guitars, and "jeans and jacket" culture was "anti-Pakistan." Despite—or maybe because of—the bans, I was inspired to write new music. I was elated by the gradual evolution and success of our music and the ripples it was beginning to make in society. For our next album, I pushed for a radical change in Junoon's music and image.

We would have had smoother sailing from a business standpoint without the bans. But I couldn't complain. I knew that making art in Pakistan was never going to be easy. But I also knew that the music would find a way.

For much of 1996, I'd been obsessed with domestic political life in Pakistan. But soon the country the globe forgot after the Cold War was flooded with foreign products and new technologies. "Globalization" had come to Pakistan, bringing with it both the temptations of modern materialism and the power of a new digital order.

Pakistan was then deeply indebted to the International Monetary Fund, and millions of people still lived in crushing poverty. Yet tempting images of McDonald's, Nestle, BMWs, Nokia phones, De Beers diamonds, Coke, Pepsi, and YSL couture were hypnotizing Pakistani souls. These seductive symbols overshadowed priorities like health care, education, and a clean environment. Joining the "goods" race with the rest of the world, Pakistanis were addicted to material comforts whether they could afford them or not.

But along with the dangers of unchecked greed came opportunities. The appearance of the Internet and satellite television meant that everything local was now also global. Junoon decided to make the most of these new media tools. My younger brother Sherry, who had graduated from UCLA and had worked at JPMorgan in New York, decided to help by moonlighting as Junoon's international promoter. We flew to MTV Asia in Hong Kong and found VJs who liked our sound and videos. They were hungry for fresh regional programming and started running our music videos "Talaash" ("The Search") and "Aap aur Hum" ("You and I") from our second album *Talaash*, in regular rotation. Junoon's music up till then was mostly limited to Pakistan. But thanks to the communications revolution, fans began to share it virally throughout the international *desi* diaspora. It was Sherry's idea, too, to set up what's commonplace now but was unusual at the time: a Junoon web site. The site, www.junoon.com, was the first Pakistani band site and still serves up band news, merchandise, music, and videos and has a discussion forum, which began attracting all kinds of comments. It was like having our own talk radio station. Fans would discuss music, Bollywood, cricket, Islam, Pakistani politics, and Muslim dating and even offered each other (and us) marriage proposals. Some couples actually tied the knot after meeting on Junoon.com. Khurram Abbas, a Pakistani-American kid from Kalamazoo, Michigan, nicknamed "Spock," became the web site's most recognizable and loyal blogger and now runs the site, along with a Junooni from Karachi called Talha, a.k.a. "Zerocool." It seemed the music was uniting everyone, no matter where they were. Even when we were banned at home, anyone with an Internet connection in Pakistan or elsewhere could listen to our songs, buy our souvenirs, or browse news about us. So much for Sharif's attempt to drop a curtain of night around what he thought was his own Gotham City.

One of the best parts of our newly internationalizing fan base was a

"Just another brick in the wall" (third from the right, back row), *M. Bhatti (Junoon Archives)*

Young Salman at the mosque, Lahore. *Ejaz Ahmad (Junoon Archives)*

Parents: Shahine and Ejaz just after the wedding, January 1963. *M. Bhatti (Junoon Archives)*

Samina: friend, soulmate, and muse. *Arif Mehmood (Junoon Archives)*

Salman and The King of Qawwali, onstage with Nusrat Fateh Ali Khan (extreme right), Karachi's field hockey stadium, 1996, our last performance together. *Arif Mehmood (Junoon Archives)*

A guitar player with twice the passion (at John Alec's house in Grandview, New York). *John Alec Raubeson (Junoon Archives)*

Vital Signs, Sal with Junaid, Rohail, Shehzad, and a friend backstage, in Islamabad, 1988. *Fuad Khan (Junoon Archives)*

Grandparents Aba and Ami Aziza in Patiala, India after their wedding, 1940. *Unknown (Junoon Archives)*

Making up after the wedding fiasco with Madam Nur Jehan, the Melody Queen of Pakistan, 1989. *Ayesha Muawaz Khan (Junoon Archives)*

My three sons (left to right: Sherjan, Shamyl, and Imraan) getting ready to go for Eid prayers in Karachi. *Samina Ahmad (Junoon Archives)*

School's out for the summer! (right to left: Sal, Brian, and Paul with Eclipse and Tappan Zee high school musicians and friends, 1981. *Chul McGuire, Halfmoon 1981*

A Nobel galaxy of stars: Oslo, Norway, December 2007, where I met the amazing Melissa Etheridge. *Courtesy of Nobel committee*

In the zone of *fana* (mystical ecstasy), live in Karachi. *Arif Mehmood (Junoon Archives)*

Trading Sufi licks with Brian. *Arif Mehmood (Junoon Archives)*

The cricketer and the newlywed couple. Imran Khan shares a joke with Samina after my *Nikah* (marriage) ceremony at Samina's place at 39-Ata Turk block in Garden Town. Aunt Nosheen looks happy as well. *Shehryar Ahmad (Junoon Archives)*

Searching for the lost chord, live at the Pragati Maidan in New Delhi. *Vikrant Tunious (Teens Today)*

A bad hair day in the Bahawalpur desert, shooting the "Bulleya" music video. *Khawar Riaz (Junoon Archives)*

Junoon, "Three Yet Only One," live at the Channel V Awards at Nehru Stadium, New Delhi. *Athar Shahzad (Junoon Archives)*

Samina and me with a bald Ali, Brian, our friend and producer John Alec (in the dark glasses), and drummer Jay Dittamo and the New York sky line on location for the "No More" video shoot. *Humera Afridi (Junoon Archives)*

Feeling good after Junoon won the Channel V Best International Group Award in India. *Athar Shehzad*

Mother and son, London, summer 1967. *Tasnim Ashiq (Junoon Archives)*

Jumping Jack Flash and the Sufirocker in Lahore, 1996. *Mujahid Hamid (Junoon Archives)*

"So what kind of shampoo do you girls use to keep that shine?" *Arif Mehmood (Junoon Archives)*

At the UN General Assembly concert hall with former UN secretary general Kofi Annan, Shashi Tharoor, and my brother Sherry. *Richard Murphy (Junoon Archives)*

Lost in their *junoon*. Junoonis at the Karachi hockey stadium concert. *Arif Mehmood (Junoon Archives)*

constant cultural osmosis. A girl from Norway wrote through the web site saying that she had been born in Scandinavia of Pakistani and Indian parents and spoke fluent Norwegian, Punjabi, and Hindi. Our newest Junooni had embraced our universal message and loved Oslo, Mumbai, and Gujranwala. The circle of light was glowing brighter.

New opportunity came with this new digital world. *Desi* students at U.S. and British universities invited us to perform in their music halls or university centers. In the spring of 1997 we toured America for the first time. My brother set up the entire tour after interfacing with the digitally-savvy Junoonis online. Brian and I returned to American shores, playing to *desi* audiences in far-flung cities like Birmingham, Alabama; Houston; San Jose; Los Angeles; Boston; Washington, D.C.; and the city that gave me my musical dream, New York. We played America for six weeks, exploring and rediscovering the country I'd left so many years before. And what a head trip it was. While Pakistanis were being screwed over by corrupt leaders and eking out their livings, one of the biggest recent films in America was *Jerry Maguire*. Over and over, we kept hearing the catch phrase "Show me the money!" from that hit movie. It was a constant refrain from promoters, fans, and the media, and seemed to define the American zeitgeist. Money was God to everyone in the U.S. entertainment industry. But having once played for ice cream, I found the movie's line to be a joke.

Our final concert of the tour, at Manhattan's Roosevelt Hotel ballroom, provided a Rockland County reunion with my high school buddy John Alec and Brian's entire Irish-American O'Connell clan. John had come to mix the sound at our show and get his first peek at Junoon's live act. Both *desis* and *goras* were blown away by the music and the positive vibe of the sold-out show. That night, twelve hundred *desis* did the *bhangra* in the ballroom, and John Alec, like Brian before him, got hooked on our sound.

But even as we were playing shows on that tour to enthusiastic audiences, I was still questioning what my life's purpose really was. The material monkey was chasing my back from Pakistan to America. I had to keep a balance, so on that tour I started composing new tunes while passing through airports and in and out of hotel rooms and concert venues.

I found myself in deeply meditative moods as the noises and sights of the tour bombarded me. From beyond the electric wall of sound we'd build each night, I began to hear new, quieter acoustic melodies. Back in my hotel at the end of the day, or on the plane, I was reading the poetry of Muhammad Iqbal, Bulleh Shah, and Rumi. I was going back to the source. I'd always collaborated on lyrics with Pakistani poets like Sabir Zafar and others, but now I took inspiration from the powerful spiritual verses of the historical masters. In their centuries-old poems, I sought new answers to old questions about faith, love, and life.

Two of Iqbal's poems, in particular, spoke to me powerfully. The first is "Khudi," or "Self"—the poem that inspired my mother's name, Shahine:

Khudi ko kar buland itna
Kay har takdeer sey pehlay
Khuda bandey sey khud poochay
Bata terey raza kya hai
Sitaron sey agey jahaan aur bhi hain
Abhi ishq kai imtihaan aur bhi haain
Tu shahine hai parvaaz hai kaam tera
Terey saamney aasman aur bhi hain
Tu shahine hai basera kar
Paharon ki chatanon par.

Raise yourself so high that God has to ask you:
"What destiny do you desire?"
There are worlds beyond the stars
And many challenges of desire and faith still to overcome
You are the falcon
Your goal is to fly
You are the falcon
Make your home on the edge of mountain peaks.

Iqbal's poem "Saqinama" ("The Wine Pourer") also resonated inside me. I borrowed part of it for our song "Zamane ke Andaaz," or "The Ways of the World."

Zamaney kay andaaz badley gaye
Nya raag hai saaz badley gaye
Khirad ko ghulami sey azaad kar
Jawanon ko peeron ka ustaad kar.

The way of the world has changed.
The tune is new, the instruments have changed.
Free the intellect from mental slavery,
Make the young teachers of the old,
Pour me the wine which burns the veil
For the season of the rose won't last forever
That wine which wakes the conscience
That wine which intoxicates the entire universe.

Being on tour in America gave me time to try out some of the sounds that were echoing inside my head. I jammed with our *tabla* player, Ashiq Ali, experimenting with the basic folk rhythms of all four Pakistani provinces. Over the centuries, troubadours have told their stories and sung their songs in time to these regional grooves. These Sindhi, Punjabi, Balochi, and Pushto sounds give Pakistanis a sense of unity in diversity. The grooves transcend sect and tribe, and I could identify with all of them. All the rhythms were hypnotic, uplifting, and somehow relaxing at the same time. Inside my head they melded into a bigger sound, one populated not just by *desi* tradition but also by funk, rock, reggae, and blues. Stripped down, all music has two basic elements: melody and rhythm. And so on stage we married the music of Bob Marley or Howlin' Wolf with galloping six-, seven-, and eight-beat *tabla* and *dholak* grooves. Jamming with Ashiq, I found that these traditional grooves made the rock, blues, or reggae riffs and melodies come freshly alive. They spoke to me in a completely new and exciting language. And they worked! I could see the positive results of our mad alchemy just by watching the audience move and grind to songs like "Meri Awaz Suno" ("Hear my Voice"), a Marley-inspired social justice anthem.

The band decided that the best way to use the energy of the concert tour was to go straight into Nizar Lalani's studio in Karachi and record the songs we'd been trying out at our shows. John Alec had been so moved by our Roosevelt Hotel show that he flew to Pakistan from Tappan to co-produce, mix, and engineer the new album, *Azadi* (*Freedom*). The music and the lyrics fused the trancelike rhythms of *qawwali* with the power of Zeppelin-esque guitar riffs. Ali's voice had matured and could now carry the soaring message of Iqbal, and Brian found a unique pocket to place his groovy, funky bass lines.

The music also led to changes in our looks. Ali grew long, curly locks.

I had a goatee with shoulder-length hair. Brian sported a moustache. Embroidered multicolored *kurtas*, Jinnah-style jackets, jeans, Pashtun sandals, earrings, and rosary beads replaced our AC/DC T-shirts, motorcycle boots, and leather pants.

We also took our visual art to a new level by hiring Asim Reza, a young and dynamic director, to film the video of our song "Sayonee" (Soul Mate). Asim suggested Multan, the city of saints, for the video shoot. Multan lies on the border of Punjab and Sindh provinces and is a bustling city filled with Sufi shrines. The domed shrines are beautifully ornamented with geometric designs, tapering walls and glazed tiles, and intricate Islamic motifs and calligraphy. Asim did a brilliant job in taking a snapshot of a *desi* rock band straddling faith and desire, and the past and the future.

Azadi was released on the fiftieth anniversary of Pakistan's independence from colonial rule. The reception wasn't quite what we were expecting. No one knew what to make of Junoon's U-turn from head-banging rebels to Sufi rockers. Trend-worshipping music critics tore us apart and some fans wanted the old Junoon back. But others were intrigued with the transformation. Meanwhile, by singing lines from one of Pakistan's greatest poets in our song "Khudi," we pissed off the government yet again. Hearing the national poet's verses being sung by a rock musician through a Peavey 5150 amplifier was more than Nawaz Sharif could take. In a ludicrous move, Sharif decided to kick us off radio and TV for allegedly desecrating the memory of Muhammad Iqbal. The "Lion of Punjab" was still smarting from my "accountability" campaign and ranted about "long hair and guitars" pop culture. Sharif banned not just our mystical love-inspired songs but, incredibly, all pop music from the airwaves. We were promoting Pakistan's authentic Sufi heritage—the antithesis of the Wahabbism that had been grafted onto the country by Sharif's mentor, General Zia. But to the lion we were just lepers with too much hair.

Unfortunately for Nawaz Sharif, times had changed since the days of the dictator. The government couldn't control satellite television, where Junoon's music and videos were played regularly. Sharif now believed pop musicians were a threat to Pakistan's religious values. Unable to do anything meaningful for health, education, or the poor, Sharif took a page out of Zia's playbook and targeted arts and culture. In a desperate action that was so stupid it was funny, he ordered state-controlled PTV to censor all male musicians who had long hair. That was the best that he could do in this new media environment. We just shook our heads in disgust. This was the same guy who'd invited the Vital Signs to perform at one of his events in 1990. But Sharif's campaign against us was just a diversion from his failures of governance and the culture of cronyism and corruption he'd helped to create. Maybe it was really our long locks that drove the bald politician around the bend.

Idiotic as it was, the ban still hurt us. We depended on TV and radio to air our videos and songs. Both were also a source of income. Junoon's videos were "brought to you by Coca-Cola" and other companies. Sharif attacked our wallets as well as our growing identity as the rebellious voice of the youth. In years past this tradition of civil protest through art had been largely confined to poets like Faiz Ahmed Faiz, Habib Jalib, and Ahmed Faraz. But the mid-1990s saw a new era in which pop culture drove politics. After "Ehtesaab" we had become a thorn in the politicians' sides. The Junoon-Sharif grudge match sparked a debate in the media about what Pakistani culture is. We'd said our piece in song. And for good measure, I wrote an op-ed titled "Pariahs of Pakistani Culture" in the national newspaper *Dawn*, saying the government had no business interfering in the nation's cultural evolution.

New technology had let us win a partial victory. Our music was getting out over private channels, and Junoon's popularity continued to grow. But, officially, we were still banned in Pakistan. And with the region on the brink of yet another seismic change, it wouldn't be the last time.

TEN
Fusion

For as long as I can remember, God has shown me signs. Over the years they've been by turns small and large, subtle and dramatic. God works mysteriously through multiple parallel universes. If one door closes, He can easily open up many others.

Fed up with the Pakistani government banning our music from TV and radio, I decided in 1998 to chart a new course: legal action. One day in Lahore, I went to see Raza Kazim, a legal mind par excellence and one of Pakistan's leading human rights attorneys. Raza, a music lover, advised me to send a legal notice to government officials asking them to identify their objections to Junoon's music in writing. To take the action up a notch, Raza also began preparing a writ petition that he would file on my behalf at the high court. Our case would challenge the government's views about "proper" music, culture, and public morality. I'd reached a crossroads in my life and had to take this kind of step to keep my music alive. Had the petition reached the court, it would have been the first instance of any artist challenging the state's policies on culture and music.

But God had other ideas.

Not long before I was to go to court, I got a phone call from my agent, Sajjad. I could hear the excitement in his voice even before the receiver reached my ear.

"Salman!" exclaimed Sajjad, known to me as "Boris." "You've won your case against the government without even going to court!"

"What are you talking about, Boris?" I asked, puzzled.

"Junoon's been invited by India's Zee TV to perform in Mumbai for a live telecast of a film awards ceremony on March 14! This is just the news we need to hear, brother!"

I quickly called up the rest of the band, who were as blown away as I was. This would be the first time that a Pakistani rock band would perform in India. We'd play our songs in front of both a star-studded studio audience and hundreds of millions of viewers from across India, Pakistan, Bangladesh, and the *desi* diaspora. At home, the government had barred us from the airwaves. But God had conspired to expose us to the biggest audience of our careers! Sharif's ban on Junoon was as good as dead.

In the days leading up to our performance, Pakistanis and Indians both switched on Zee TV and saw us advertised multiple times a day as "Sufi rock band Junoon." We'd be sharing the same stage with Bollywood megastars, including Shahrukh Khan, Aishwarya Rai, Salman Khan, Karisma Kapoor, Kajol, and Juhi Chawla. Anxious Pakistanis who looked to India as the Mecca of South Asian film and music couldn't wait to see how their compatriots Junoon would fare in the world of manufactured dreams that is Bollywood.

More than fifty years after the subcontinent gained its independence from Britain, Junoon actually had an Englishman to thank for getting us known in India in the first place. Adrian Cheesely, EMI Music Arabia's marketing man, had seen us perform in Dubai in 1997. A fan of bands like Radiohead, Oasis, and Blur, he was intrigued by Junoon's sound and impressed enough to sign us to a three-album contract. He immediately began promoting our album *Azadi* in India and got MTV to play our "Sayonee" video in heavy rotation. We were battling bans at home, but the international airwaves were ours. "Sayonee" made waves in India, and I soon found myself being interviewed by Vatsala Kaul, an Indian journalist with *Teens Today* magazine. Indian media had had very little access to Pakistani musicians and artists, at least until the Internet appeared. Vatsala was intrigued about this rock band from the "enemy country" and wanted to tell our story to Indian kids. Junoon had begun to cross a virtual line of control.

And then, one day, we were there in the flesh. Brian, Ali, and I landed in Mumbai on PIA Flight 274 on a humid sunny afternoon, just in time to watch the colors rain down in the streets as Hindus celebrated the festival of Holi. We were received by Shahnaab Alam of Platform Entertainment and Wizcraft, the companies hired by Zee TV to look after us. During the twenty-minute drive from the airport to our hotel in the city's Juhu section, I opened my eyes to a strange but oddly familiar world. This was the country I had seen through a glass window all my life. It was the land my four-year-old mother fled with her family to escape the religious violence that had erupted after the partition of British India. It was the source of movies starring the objects of my childhood affection, like Sharmila Tagore and Helen. But I wasn't watching India on my grandparents' Philips TV in Lahore. I was in India.

Since Partition, in 1947, India and Pakistan had fought three wars against each other, and politicians on both sides had ritually demonized the other's people. But now, for the first time, a rock band from Pakistan had "invaded" India with a message of peace, love, and tolerance. When we arrived the whole of India was singing along to the chorus. As we went to dinner on our first night there, we heard "Sayonee" blasting out of Mumbaikers' CD players and FM radios. The visit was off to a good start.

It just got better. The "Sayonee" video was running on the music channels, and FM radio stations were calling up to interview us on the hour, every hour. Junoon had become a household name in India and even Vatsala's sixty-year-old mother knew each of the band members' names. "Sayonee" was racing up the charts and *Azadi* was the fastest-selling album in the country, beating out *desi* music as well as Madonna's *Ray of Light* and albums by The Prodigy and Backstreet Boys. It even eclipsed "My Heart Will Go On," Celine Dione's love theme from the movie *Titanic*. Taking all this in, Pakistanis had developed impossible expectations for us to conquer Bollywood. As the awards show approached, I thought about how the Beatles must've felt before appearing on *The Ed Sullivan Show* for the first time. We were overnight successes in a new and foreign country. The difference for us was that Britain and America had buried the hatchet long before John, Paul, George, and Ringo appeared on American TV. India and Pakistan were still sworn enemies.

With that rivalry in mind, we took the stage at the Andheri Sports Complex and greeted the glittering audience with "Salaam aleikum," "Namaste," and "Good evening." We never looked back. By the end of our three-song set—"Yaar Bina," "Khudi," and "Sayonee"—everyone in the venue (and watching on TV) was electrified. Film actresses, actors, and directors queued up to meet us. My namesake Salman Khan told me that his sister had a crush on us. Bollywood sirens Aishwarya Rai and Karisma Kapoor had been moving to the beat and were watched by millions of Pakistanis who collectively went breathless, as if to say, "They like Junoon too!" More than a decade had passed since General Zia tried to strangle arts and culture in Pakistan. That night, we were experiencing sweet justice. Now it was Indians who were looking up to Pakistanis as cultural icons. The old dictator must have been rolling in his grave.

Over the next few months, we traveled back and forth to India, playing shows in Mumbai, Chennai, Bangalore, Lucknow, Kanpur, Chandigarh, and Delhi. Traveling the length and breadth of the country, I came to recognize the thickness of the fog of propaganda that both the Indian and Pakistani governments and their media had spread about each other's citizens. It was unbelievable how much ignorance and division had been stoked by hysterical, misdirected nationalism. On our first visit to Mumbai, our hosts were surprised to see that the women in our entourage (including Samina and her two sisters, Brian's wife Ayesha, and Ali's girlfriend Vaneeza) were educated, confident, and hip to issues of the world. Our new Indian friends weren't expecting Pakistani women to be so fashionably dressed or so informed about India. An Indian music executive confessed that they were expecting our wives and female relatives to be clad in burqas and *hijabs*. But not all Indians believed the stereotypes. Many were majorly curious about Pakistanis. And in Junoon they saw a friendly embodiment of a shared cultural past and present, as well as an unknown future.

Parts of our India visits were just pure craziness, though. Young, hip Indian urban professionals partied with us and our youthful fans in Mumbai clubs like 1900s at the Taj Mahal Hotel, Copa Cabana, J49, and Raspberry Rhinoceros. The whole scene was an out-of-hand mix of adulation, adrenaline, and killer chemicals. "Sayonee" and songs by Ricky Martin and Madonna provided the dance-floor soundtrack. Women just came up and sat in our laps, ignoring the death stares of our wives or girlfriends. Mumbai is the "maximum" city and if you're not careful you can lose yourself pretty quickly. Our fame went to our friend Boris's head and he lived on the edge for as long as he could. His out-of-control behavior eventually killed him, in addition to nearly sucking the life blood out of the band. Boris died in 2001 after going through a living hell of drug addiction and psychotic depression.

Many Indians and Pakistanis had allowed themselves to believe the myths of hatred and hostility sold to us by the warmongers and fanatics. Spy agencies on both sides relied on this specter of fear to stay in control of the people. But I never felt a need to negate any part of my identity to prove my loyalty to one individual or government. I didn't need to hate India or America to show my love for Pakistan, and vice versa. I was glad to find others who felt the same way. As Junoon took its traveling Sufi rock odyssey across India, I saw some of the imposed divisions explode. And in fact, what I mostly saw was people getting on with their lives. Poverty, lack of health care, and getting a good education and a steady job seemed to worry Indians more than the hostility coming out of Islamabad. Happily for us, the music was proving to be a binding force between the two countries. Young musicians in India found inspiration in Junoon's message and got India's nascent rock scene off the ground, forming bands like Silk Route and Euphoria. Indian rock musicians had a hard current to swim against if they wanted airplay. Many just did covers of Western hits or got swallowed up into Bollywood as composers. For some, this worked well. My contemporary and friend, Academy Award–winning composer A. R. Rahman, was a struggling South Indian rock musician and jingle composer before he was asked to create tunes for Bollywood soundtracks. But most rock musicians didn't stand a chance against the stardust-covered song and dance numbers. I was overjoyed that these new bands were looking up to us and challenging the Bollywood juggernaut.

Going to India was like a quantum leap into the future. Anything seemed possible. In city after city, we were welcomed and garlanded by hordes of smiling Hindus, Muslims, Sikhs, Parsees, Christians, and Buddhists, all of whom displayed the generosity of spirit common to most South Asians. Unlike Pakistan, India seemed to be many countries in one. It was at once rich and desperately poor. Its diversity of peoples, religions, languages, and cultures was stunning. But no matter where we went, no matter what the native tongue was, Indian souls were singing along to our music. It was as if the so-called enemy country had ingested the Sufi maxim, "When you see with the heart, all the masks fall down." Good will bred good will on those India trips. After waiting for hours with hundreds of other fans to get a glimpse of us at Mumbai's Rhythm House music store, a wide-eyed Junooni named Suniti wrote me a message which seemed to encompass all I had believed in: "You have endless possibilities, listen to your heart, embrace your own passions." Big-hearted souls like her were living proof that fear-mongers and hawks on both sides were wrong: in two countries divided over issues like Kashmir, kindred spirits could come together. To reverse a U2 lyric, India and Pakistan may not have been one. But we were the same.

The crowning moment of Junoon's attempt at rhythm-based Indo-Pak reconciliation must have been at the Taj Mahal Hotel in Mumbai, where we dined as guests of society queen and style icon Parmeshwar Godrej. At dinner with Parmeshwar and her husband Adi, we met Indian screen legend Amitabh Bachchan and his wife Jaya and son Abhishek. As Samina got up to ask Amitabh for his autograph, he turned around and sang the chorus to "Sayonee." There isn't a *desi* alive who doesn't know Amitabh Bachchan's face and voice, and I watched in awe as he sang my band's song to my wife. It was a magical moment.

But nothing—not fame, not peace, nor one's life—is permanent. Fame had opened new doors for me on the subcontinent and beyond, but it had also raised old questions about purpose and direction and meaning. Soon, two events—one personal, one political—would scream those questions at me louder than ever.

On April 25, 1998, I was riding a personal high from Junoon's first concert on Indian soil. I was back in Pakistan and happy, though a certain queasiness about the trappings of fame had crept into my head. On that day, my friend Zakir Khan, the Pashtun-Pakistani cricketer, had offered to drive me to Kharian, a city about a hundred miles northwest of Lahore where Junoon was going to perform that evening. It had been a heady few weeks for me and Zak. A month earlier, he'd come to Mumbai with me to see Junoon play at the Zee TV awards. Sitting there in the passenger seat, watching the scenery zip by, I felt like so much in my life had fallen into place. At peace with myself, I leaned over and popped in a CD of Pink Floyd's *Wish You Were Here* album. I settled back into the seat and sank into "Shine on You Crazy Diamond," the opening track, as David Gilmour's bluesy, ethereal guitar licks set the musical tone for our journey to Kharian.

Zak pulled over at a gas station on the main boulevard in Gulberg, a busy thoroughfare, to fill up his white Toyota Corolla. The car was weather-beaten and, from the looks of its well-worn tires, had been on many a road trip like this one. We had a decent drive ahead of us on the Grand Trunk Road. Built by the sixteenth century Pashtun King Sher Shah Suri, the road threads its way from its origin in the eastern Indian city of Calcutta and arcs northwest through Delhi, Lahore, and Islamabad, and up to the Afghan capital of Kabul.

Zak and I were in top spirits as we zoomed along the GTR at about 80 miles per hour. Like me, he was still high from the India trip, and he spent the early part of the ride talking animatedly about the seductive beauty of Indian actresses. He was also psyched by how many Mumbaikers had noticed his blue eyes, fair skin, and wavy brown hair. I decided to tell him that one of the top film producers in India thought he was Hollywood actor Tom Selleck.

"*Jhoot bol rahey ho?*" he said incredulously. "You're lying?"

"*Bilkul,*" I said, joshing him. "You're absolutely right."

"*Yaar*, you're a lunatic, I was thinking maybe Aishwarya Rai and I could make a movie together!" Zak said half-jokingly.

"Now who's the lunatic!" I shot back. "And besides, I don't think she does Pushto films!" I said as Floyd played on and we rolled toward Kharian.

As we neared the city of Gujranwala, about halfway to Kharian, the weather started changing. It got very dark with thick, low clouds, and the wind picked up dramatically. In the distance I could see lightning flashes followed by deafeningly-loud, staccato thunderclaps that began to compete with the music on the car stereo. Ali and Brian were already in Kharian, having gone on the tour bus early that morning. Our concert that evening was to be an outdoor show for the Pakistani army officers and their families who live in and around the twin cities of Mangla and Kharian.

Defying the politicians, the corps commander—a soon-to-be-famous general by the name of Pervez Musharraf—had invited Junoon to play after taking note of our successful tour of India. Our passage through India probably wasn't the only reason, though: Musharraf's son-in-law is the ad-film director Asim Reza, whom I'd hired to produce the award-winning music video for "Sayonee." I was going from one mind-blowing experience to another. Fresh from a tour of India, Junoon would be playing our peace-mongering music for the Pakistani army.

But with the weather changing and rain looking imminent, I was getting worried that the concert wasn't going to happen at all. Heavy rain would spoil the evening's entertainment, and I wondered if there was a plan B that the generals had thought of. As the best-funded institution in Pakistan, the military had to have a contingency plan for the show. So I decided to call Brian to find out what was going on.

It was then that I saw the truck.

As I reached for my cell phone, I looked over the horizon and saw a multicolored Bedford doing a quick U-turn on the other side of the highway. Truck drivers in Pakistan are notorious for driving recklessly and are sometimes high on hash, and this truck was appropriately painted psychedelic purple, yellow, and blue. It looked a lot like a love truck from the sixties—but this love truck was carrying heavy metal and was muscling onto the highway directly in front of us.

Zak honked the horn loud. But there was no reaction. We were already going too fast and were speeding right toward the vehicle's open bed, out of which were jutting long steel and iron rods.

We panicked and Zak jammed down on the brakes. The tires squealed loudly but got no traction on the slippery road, and instead of slowing us down pitched the Corolla even faster toward the truck. We were now about 120 yards away and gaining fast.

"I can't steer the wheel, it's jammed," Zak whispered as we quickly closed the awful distance with the steel-laden truck. Acting on instinct, I put both my hands on the wheel and tried to pull us off the collision course we were on. Nothing happened. The wheel wouldn't budge.

With the steering wheel motionless and the car hurtling toward the back of the truck, I realized with a sudden, sickening clarity that we were going to be badly hurt, or even die. An odd heaviness descended, and time actually stood still for those moments. I could think of nothing but Samina and my three young sons. Earlier that morning, I'd spoken to them from Lahore, promising them I'd be with them on Sunday. But Sunday now seemed a long way away.

For the past decade, I'd struggled to realize my dreams of becoming a musician. At thirty-four years old, I could finally say that my rebellious decision to follow my heart and leave medicine to play music was beginning to pay off. But now, in some kind of cruel cosmic joke, I was being confronted with death.

The car sped toward the truck. With us closing the distance at 100 feet, then 75 feet, I realized there was just no way out. We were going to crash. I had to surrender to the outcome and, as if watching from above, I visualized my body in some kind of tragic movie. With 10 feet between us and the truck, I stared into the long, wet iron rods and then closed my eyes to embrace the unknown.

We hit the Bedford with a loud crash. I heard glass shattering along with the grating sound of steel and the shredding of aluminum and plastic, the sound of a surreal industrial-music sample. I felt my body jerk forward and then back like a crash test dummy, and then there was a silence that seemed to last forever. All that I could hear was my own breathing. My eyes were still shut. But we were alive.

The odd part was that, despite the chaos and near-death event I'd just been through, I was in a state of peace and near-bliss. As I came back to my senses, I felt an all-encompassing presence around me, and then I opened my eyes. Sound came rushing in as I saw the scenery outside the car. Traffic stood still and the truck was blocking the road, the driver having fled, thinking he'd killed us. People had gathered around the car, and someone was shouting to call an ambulance. The rods in the back of the truck had shot like spears right through the Corolla's front bonnet, pushing the axle back in the shape of a "V." The windshield had shattered, the radiator was cut in half and leaking and the doors were crumpled up like pieces of tissue paper. I looked at my hands and feet and turned my head left and then right. Zak was sitting there unhurt, his expression frozen. The feeling of deep awe and disbelief we both shared was all over his face, and mine. We had experienced the inexplicable.

There was no reason on earth that we shouldn't have been killed or at the very least critically injured. We weren't even wearing seatbelts—as is the norm in Pakistan—so how could we be surveying this scene with just a small scratch on my right hand? The car was totalled, but the steel rods had cut through more than the machine's metal and glass. They'd sliced through my consciousness. How did the other rods miss us both and yet cut perfectly through the middle of the car as if they were guided by a laser? People had begun to help us out of the Toyota. Others were looking on in amazement. But my mind was already elsewhere, beyond the accident. Fame, Junoon, making money—I didn't think of any of these things as I extricated myself from the mangled metal and shook off the glass shards. But as my identity and my newfound, self-absorbed life in pop culture came back to me, I began to realize anew that Iqbal had been right. There were many challenges of desire and faith to overcome.

God was asking me, "What destiny do you desire?"

A couple of weeks later, in New Delhi, I got an answer. Or, an anti-answer.

Junoon had just played a show in Chandigarh for thirty thousand screaming fans. It was another night of the kind that had so lifted me during our prior appearances in India. The show had transcended boundaries and shown that Indians and Pakistanis could cheer each other's artists and exist harmoniously. At least in concert halls.

But when I walked into my hotel room that evening, the television was blaring a news development that had literally shaken the subcontinent. Without a word of warning to the international community, the Indian government had carried out a series of underground nuclear tests. They were India's first such tests since 1974, and there was immediate, widespread outrage in Pakistan over the move. But there would be more than just protest from Pakistan. On May 28, Nawaz Sharif announced that Pakistan had exploded five nuclear devices. A sixth followed on May 30. This was a mini-atomic arms race, and condemnation from foreign governments was swift.

In addition to being about 90 miles away from the Pakistani border, India's test site in the desert state of Rajasthan was close to the city of Ajmer Sharif. As I sat on my hotel bed watching the news, the irony flashed through my mind. Ajmer Sharif is home to the *dargah* (shrine) of the famous thirteenth century Sufi saint Khwaja Moinuddin Chisty. Throughout the year, hundreds of thousands of Muslim devotees—As well as many Sikhs and and Hindus who believe in the healing powers of the Khwaja—flock to Ajmer to offer prayers of peace, harmony, and redemption. The highest form of devotion, according to the saint, was "to redress the misery of those in distress [and] to fulfill the needs of the helpless and to feed the hungry." The Khwaja would have been shocked to see how his descendants had chosen to define progress and modernity. The Sufi had spoken about achieving a state of *fana*, or union with God through annihilation of the self. But I'm sure he wouldn't have wanted an atomic bomb to be the vehicle for enlightenment.

In India, the press swarmed around us in search of soundbites. As

Pakistanis we were seen as part of the story, and the BBC, CNN, and every Indian news channel asked for interviews. In them, I repeated the clever and admirable words I'd seen on a banner held by audience members at our show in Delhi.

"We want cultural fusion," I told the reporters, "not nuclear fusion."

That was even before Pakistan carried out its own tests. I couldn't have known at the time how much trouble those words would get me and Junoon in later. But the bombs were just more signs from God. I didn't believe the subcontinent's destiny should be mutually assured destruction. And I realized that the tests were giving me a partial answer to some of my own questions. No matter how big a star I'd become and no matter what the consequences might be, I had to speak out. I was taking the famous verses of Faiz Ahmed Faiz literally. Truth is free, and I was going to speak from the heart.

And kids, at least, thought we were right. We played to a sold-out crowd at Delhi's Pragati Maidan and repeated our criticisms of the tests and called for our preferred brand of fusion. The show was covered by Daniel Lak of the BBC, which is widely seen in Pakistan. It was inevitable that some kind of response would come from our statements. At first, it was almost whimsical. "Junoon: "Hindustan hai hamara!" ("Junoon: India is our country!") ran a headline in the Pakistani daily *The News*.

But the ultimate response was deadly serious.

Upon our return to Pakistan, we got a memo from the Ministry of Culture.

The letter accused us of being traitors. We were, the ministry charged, a part of India's "subversive propaganda." The ministry asked us to answer the following charges in person:

1. Belittling the concept of the ideology of Pakistan
2. Disagreeing with national opinion regarding Pakistan's nuclear test
3. Hoping for the reunification of India and Pakistan
4. Citing "cultural similarities" between the two countries

It was tempting to laugh at the charges. Except the government was out for blood. Treason carries a life sentence in Pakistan. Sharif's government also instituted a total public ban on Junoon. With no public performances, no TV and radio airplay, it meant that we were just as well dead. The atmosphere was so charged that one ministry official told me to "leave the country or else."

My response was this: I told him that the government should run all our Indian interviews on national television and let the people of Pakistan decide our fate. Ali and I were asked about our patriotism. I said that I didn't need to hate India to love Pakistan. And I wasn't going to be intimidated in a country whose constitution entitled me to my own damned opinion. We told our side of the story to the press, and the controversy in the media made us even bigger counterculture figures than we already were. We found ourselves getting supportive letters and e-mails from Pakistani and Indian kids alike. Just as satisfying, we continued to tour the world and saw diaspora kids from both countries waving dual Pakistan-India flags. We toured the Middle East and the U.K. and played an unforgettable concert in New York's Central Park in August. Thousands of *desis* and New Yorkers came out that hot summer day to show solidarity with us and groove to the sounds of *Azadi*.

Meanwhile, our album *Azadi* had gone double platinum in India and we won Channel V's "best international group" award in Delhi in November. Under an open sky at Nehru Stadium, in front of tens of thousands of cheering people and millions watching live on TV, we shared the stage with a galaxy of stars, including A. R. Rahman, Sting, and Def Leppard. The music had inspired the young people of two hostile nations to look at each other's countries with a common humanity. Two of the people who came together in Delhi that evening were my mother and father. They'd been separated since 1995, but both wanted to watch their son claim an award he'd earned by following his passion. "Music is its own reward," Sting told me backstage in Delhi. "Share it and enjoy it." At that moment, that's just what I was doing. "We always knew you had it in you, *beta*," my parents told me. "You've made us very proud." Seeing them together and happy—if only for a few hours—was a sweeter reward for me still. I couldn't help announcing my parents' temporary reconciliation to the audience in my acceptance speech.

But in May 1999, Pakistan-backed militants and India's army went to war in the hills of Kargil. It would become too much for the Indian government to have us playing on Indian soil, despite our popularity. Junoon's visits to India were soon curtailed. In Pakistan, the ban against us was finally lifted in October 1999, following the military coup by General Pervez Musharraf (whose kids were big fans of Junoon). Nawaz Sharif was now gone, and so were the charges of treason against us. India and Pakistan both had nukes and the subcontinent was a more dangerous place than at any time in its history.

Politics were out of my control. But even as Pakistan and India rattled their sabers at one another, that cool November night in Delhi brought me one sweet satisfaction. My music had been the magnet to bring my parents back together. No longer was I seen as the son who had wasted his life playing guitar and had disrespected his parents' wishes. God had chosen the precise moment and stage to shine His Light. Both my parents were celebrating and basking in the recognition of their son's musical achievement. I too owed a deep debt of gratitude to both of them. If they had not insisted on sending me to study medicine in Lahore, none of this would have been possible and my story never would have turned out as it did. In hindsight, all the twists and turns are guided by a Unity of purpose.

ELEVEN

The Flight

On a hot spring day in 1999, I found myself on a strange road trip with an old friend.

Junaid Jamshed, my old Vital Signs band mate, had turned up at my front door that morning to congratulate me on the success of Junoon's album *Azadi.* But this was no longer the Junaid I recognized, and his visit wasn't just a friendly call. The young man with whom I'd once rocked the Alhamra Arts Council had changed dramatically. Where he'd previously looked to a-ha and the Pet Shop Boys for fashion inspiration, Junaid now dressed like an Arab from the seventh century. The leather jacket and jeans were gone. In a conscious effort to mimic the Prophet Muhammad and his followers, Junaid now sported a full beard and a *shalwar kameez*. Incredibly, one of Pakistan's foremost pop stars had done a 180 and was now a proselytizing Muslim. Together with a similarly "uniformed" comrade, Junaid cryptically invited me to a place he'd only describe as outside of Karachi.

"Salman," he said when I asked him where we were going to go, "just know that you'll thank me for taking you to this place."

In the several months since I'd seen him, Junaid had become increasingly dogmatic about Islam and had been recruited by the missionary movement Tableeghi Jamaat. The organization had come up with a clever, evangelical Christian–like branding strategy in its quest for God's marketing share. Aping a modern-day ad campaign, the Tableeghis sought out prominent celebrities who were searching for meaning in their lives and made them religious ambassadors of sorts. Many of the top members of the Pakistani cricket team had been conscripted to promote Islam and lead the "misguided" youth away from music, films, and video games. Junaid, like his clerical boosters, now saw the hand of Satan in the very songs he'd sung a little more than ten years before. He'd gone from being a pop idol to a pied piper for a return-to-Arab-roots Islam.

Junaid wasn't the only one who'd grown uncomfortable with the spread of rock and pop music in Pakistan—especially music that quoted or invoked storied Muslim poets. After winning the Channel V award, and following the treason charges, Junoon's music was the subject of much parsing and discussion in the media and on our own web site. When I was out at night with Samina in restaurants, people would come to our table and interrogate me. "Do you consider yourself to be a good Muslim?" they would ask. During "Vitalmania" or the early, rebel-rocker days of Junoon, the questions would have been about music and fashion. But as our music became more and more influenced by Sufi poems and spiritual themes, the questions turned into a pop quiz about the five pillars of the Islamic faith.

"Salman," the questioners would ask, "Do you pray five times a day?"

"Do you fast?"

"Do you give charity?"

"Have you gone on the *hajj*?"

"Do you believe that there's no god but Allah and that Muhammad is his prophet"?

This wasn't what I wanted to talk about as I was trying to eat my *biryani* with my wife. I lost my appetite entirely when less-friendly kids and adults insisted to me that Islam outright forbids music. That accusation has been ignorantly lobbed at Muslim musicians all over the world. Confronted by questions and accusations like these, I felt my privacy intruded upon and didn't feel I had to answer at all. Every Pakistani grows up with Allah and Rasool (the messenger), and religion is a part of daily life, present at breakfast, lunch, and dinner. My own life is no different.

But when Junoon was banned in Pakistan, I had a lot of time to think over just how my faith fit into my life and music. Pakistanis still bought our music, even if they couldn't hear it on the radio or TV, and we continued to tour abroad. But in between trips to India or the Persian Gulf or the U.K., I withdrew into the safety of my home and family and mulled over the charges against us: that we were anti-Pakistan and un-Islamic. With mystified fans, irate clergy, and the uptight government each bearing down on us in their own ways, I realized anew that I needed to assert my place within my faith. A polarizing cultural war was going on. I needed to prove to the doubters that there was a place for music—rock and otherwise—in an Islamic country.

Junaid drove me southwest of the Karachi city limits, passing the busy port. Rolling toward the desert near the Sind-Balochistan border, we listened to *naats*, the hymns in praise of the Prophet. George Michael and A Flock of Seagulls were now dead to Junaid; he'd erased his memory and rebooted the disc drive of his consciousness with new sounds. As we drove, Junaid looked and talked just like a televangelist. He delivered a soliloquy for the length of the car ride about the spiritual emptiness of Pakistani youth. He'd gone from singing "Dil Dil Pakistan" to uttering *dawahs* (invitations to the Tableeghi organization) like a robot. Life was now black and white for Junaid; people and things were either sacred or profane. It was agonizing to listen to such a simple zero-sum worldview, and had his friend not been in the car, I would have called him out for being a hypocrite. Having lived a full and colorful life as a pop star, Junaid was on a part self-induced, part Tableeghi-indoctrinated guilt trip. To break free from his supposedly misguided musical past he had decided to reinvent himself as a Muslim savior. There was a perfect Urdu expression for the occasion, about a cat that decides to go on the *hajj* after eating nine hundred mice. But I restrained myself and nodded. I still had no idea where we were going.

After about an hour, I saw large colored *shamianas* (tents) with red, blue, yellow, orange, and green geometric patterns. Even at a distance I could hear dozens of loudspeakers relaying a chorus of impassioned voices unequal in pitch, tempo, and tone. As we got closer, I heard the vocal crescendo of a whole desert full of battle rappers. We parked, and were escorted by a dozen eager young Tableeghi youth who looked at Junaid and me with pride and admiration. They took us to the main tent and asked us to sit cross-legged on the floor with hundreds of other congregants wearing skull caps, *shalwar kameez*, and *tasbeehs* (prayer beads). The group puts great emphasis on obedience and promotes spiritual renewal through following the *hadith* (the sayings and the traditions of Prophet Muhammad). The congregation was crying out in great emotion. But all I could hear was discord.

For the next half hour I was treated to an assorted menu of fear-mongering, guilt, and the promise of pain and suffering in the grave for all those who didn't heed the Tableeghi preachers' calls to wash away sins. The sermons were the eerie flipside of the Sufi message of love, self-discovery, and compassion we'd been promoting in Junoon's songs. Wearied by the whole scene, I turned to Junaid.

"OK, so why am I here, JJ?" I asked.

My former lead singer looked at me as if he was about to reveal a great secret.

"Brother, get up and follow me," he said.

We walked toward the main dais, where he kissed the grand *amir* (leader of the faithful) who was presiding over the *ijtima* (religious congregation). Then Junaid told the *amir* that he had fulfilled his promise of bringing me into the *jamaat*, or gathering.

That's when my friendly restraint ended. This charade had gone as far it could.

"*Amir sahib*," I said, "I don't have any idea of what he's promised you, but I don't need any further affirmation of my faith, *shukriya* [thank you]."

The sunglasses-clad *amir* looked at me from head to toe with a smile on his face. For a moment I thought of John Lennon's meeting with the Maharishi. But this guy was no love guru.

"*Beta*," he said, "now that you're here amongst us, I'm fully confident that with you and Junaid leading our youth, Islam will make a powerful resurgence!"

I was stunned. The *amir* and Junaid were smiling to themselves in self-congratulation. But the show was over for me then and there. If they wanted to find God through a fog of fear, well, fine. I wasn't about to become a robot for anyone. The Sufi spirit in me wasn't going to judge them for taking their path, but by the same token I needed to be left alone to follow mine. All the same, though, I ruined Junaid's special moment by rejecting the *amir*'s invitation.

After hurried goodbyes and Junaid's apologies for my less-than-perfect behavior, we drove back. On the ride home Junaid tried to convince me that this was the true Islam and that if I wanted to be forgiven, I needed to give up rock music. I was still angry even though I was used to this kind of thing. In Pakistan, there's almost no such thing as "personal space" when friends and family are involved. Everyone's in your business. But Junaid took it too far. My trip to the desert inspired me more than ever to seek out the truth about music's place in Islam. I even put out a media statement inviting any religious scholar to prove to me that music was forbidden in our religion. Junaid had traded in his music for his version of Islam. But he got one key thing wrong: music and Islam are no either-or equation.

Junaid hadn't been the first challenger of me and my music and its relation to Islam. After the release of *Azadi*, some people weirdly assumed I'd founded a new Sufi sect since I was quoting Iqbal in our songs. Some fans went with the vibe and grasped the meanings of our songs where they counted: in their hearts. But others—even after President Pervez Musharraf took power and provided a platform for artists—saw Junoon as going places where proper Muslims shouldn't go. I was constantly being pressured by both supporters and skeptics into speaking on religious issues and Sufism. My best answers will always come through my music and my social work. But I felt more and more backed into a place from which I had to speak out, especially when I got angry phone calls telling me I was leading the youth astray.

One cloudy winter day in 1999, for example, my road manager Hasnain Alam walked into the music room of my house on Hospital Street in Karachi. I'd been noodling on my guitar, lost in my own world and trying out some chords for a new song.

"Salman *bhai*, there's a phone call from a Karachi schoolteacher," he said with a touch of exasperation. "She's insisting on speaking with you directly. I told her you're busy, but she won't listen." His voice was so urgent that I figured I needed to take the call.

"I'm very angry with you and Junoon," said the teacher, an instructor of Urdu. When I asked why, she replied:

"I've been teaching Iqbal's poetry to my kids for years. They never got it, but now since Junoon's version of 'Khudi,' they know all the verses by heart!"

So what was there to be mad about?

"Iqbal is a serious national poet!" she seethed through the phone. "These kids are singing his verses and jumping up and down like *mirasis*! They're being disrespectful to our traditions!"

Disrespectful? It was exactly the opposite. But she was just displaying an attitude typical of many conservative Pakistanis: don't question convention. Accept the party line. Put ritual-worship above true understanding and knowledge. In her mind it was okay for the students not to get Iqbal's message as long as they were obedient. It was the scholastic equivalent of the scripture-chanting kids in *madrassahs*, parroting Arabic verses they didn't understand at all. The teacher saw a funeral for our traditions. I saw a new and beautiful celebration of them.

Attacks came from other directions. Just as I was recovering from the misadventure in the desert with Junaid, Samina walked into the house and told me of a confrontation she had just had at the supermarket with two women from Al-Huda. Al-Huda, an Islamic educational institute for women, is run by Farhat Hashmi. Samina and the two representatives from Al-Huda had had a half-hour "discussion" about my music at the grocery store. The *burqa*-clad women had also had a request for my wife: to cover her head and arms in public. But it got worse. From her bag, Samina whipped out a letter addressed to me from Farhat Hashmi herself, given to her by the two women to give to me. The letter read:

Respected Brother Salman Ahmad,

Peace be upon you,

We read your statement in a newspaper challenging any religious scholar to prove that music is disallowed in Islam. People like you have been further endowed with a good voice and talent. To use all this merely for worldly gains, patriotism, romance, and fiction is not doing justice to yourself. Not using your voice for the One who gave it to you, IN THE WAY HE LIKES IT, is sad. Cat Stevens took this step years ago when he renounced not only his musical career but also his religion. When people like you or him choose (the right) path, it is an announcement of faith to the hundreds who adore you, and if anyone follows you, your rewards are multiplied. Allah is ever watching and ever aware of intentions and sacrifices.

With regards,
Farhat Hashmi

What planet was this woman living on? I felt like tearing up the letter and throwing it away. But then I took a deep breath and re-read it. Then I got it. It wasn't just me that Farhat Hashmi and her organization were after. They wanted to clone everybody. Unless I conformed to their reality I was going to be labeled guilty for even thinking differently. Their message was clear: Good Muslims don't think, don't do, don't ask, just obey.

There was no need to answer her directly. But I did need to speak out against this onslaught of ignorance and cosmetic piety. The key was to do it in a creative way.

I began to study and probe deeper matters of belonging and belief. And in my head, I heard the stirrings of a new sound for Junoon.

Having a wife who knew the Quran inside and out and who had been on the *hajj* was a tremendous help as I contemplated the various accusations against me and Junoon. As we discussed our faith together, Samina helpfully reminded me of figures from our history. Over time there have been plenty of Pakistanis and Muslims who have tried to challenge the status quo and faced tremendous opposition. The result was often the same: they were labeled anti-Muslim and unpatriotic by the vested interests around them. The examples were many: the eighteenth century poet and mystic Baba Bulleh Shah; the nineteenth century educationalist Syed Ahmed Khan, who had built the famous Aligarh University (from which my Ami Aziza had graduated); the now-deified twentieth century poets and scholars Muhammad Iqbal and Faiz Ahmed Faiz; and the scientist and Nobel laureate Abdus Salam. These men and even Pakistan's founder Muhammad Ali Jinnah had been opposed, harassed, and threatened by radical extremists, insecure politicians, dictators, and disgruntled ideologues. "Beware," said the rigid traditionalists or mullahs, "Islam is in danger. Our culture is in danger." And thus they'd rally the mobs.

All these men were essentially reformers who wanted to bring Muslims out of the darkness of ignorance and into the light of reason. Despite their diverse backgrounds and views, they all had one thing in common: they sacrificed themselves for future generations by giving time, devotion, and life energy to their work and missions. I was curious to dig deeper and learn from their personal stories. I dove into reading their biographies, as well as Karen Armstrong's insightful book on the life of Prophet Muhammad. I also found an excellent English translation of the Holy Quran by Muhammad Asad. All these books underscored a crucial point: from the seventh century to the twenty-first century, Muslims of all hues and colors have been inspired by the core message of Islam. Our religion is about seeking knowledge, truth, and justice in the world. Islam's message is exemplified by the life of Muhammad and the book that was revealed to him. But where some mullahs and put-out Urdu teachers saw the requirement to obey blindly, I saw an emphasis on inquiry and spiritual searching.

There's no better Quranic story that highlights the importance of learning than that of the Prophet's first revelation from the Angel Gabriel. Muhammad Asad relates this story brilliantly in his English translation of and commentary on the Quran in *The Message of the Quran*.

According to Asad's commentary on the Quranic chapter "The Germ Cell," Muhammad was deep in meditation one night in a cave on Mount Hira, outside the city of Mecca. Suddenly, Gabriel appeared and said to Muhammad, "Read!"

The unlettered Muhammad shook his head and said, "I can't read." In Muhammad's own words the angel "seized me and pressed me to himself until all strength went out of me; then he released me and said, 'Read!' I answered, 'I cannot read. . . .'"

Angel and Prophet went through the same ritual three times until finally Gabriel released Muhammad. The Angel then recited the verses:

> "Read in the name of your Sustainer who has created—created man out of a germ cell. Read, your Sustainer is the Most Bountiful One, who has taught (man) the use of the pen, taught man what he did not know."

I love this story of the first revelation of the Quran. Gabriel isn't saying, "Obey!" Or, "Don't question me!" He's urging the Prophet to think, reflect, reason, and inquire. It's the literary wellspring of the Sufi search for meaning. It's the basis of the transport that comes with a spiritual quest. It's the opposite of anger and fear in the desert.

The Prophet Muhammad affirmed this in his saying, "The ink of the scholar is more sacred than the blood of the martyr." Amen to that. Muhammad taught Muslims that ignorance is humanity's greatest poverty. As my mother told me when I was a boy, the Prophet urged Muslims to go to China, if necessary, to seek knowledge. A mind without education is like a brave man without arms, the Prophet believed. He also stressed that knowledge brings people—irrespective of gender, age, race, or religion—into the highest rank of human accomplishment. I couldn't have dreamed of enduring a ban on my music or making new songs without Allah and Rasool by my side.

I also didn't have to go far from my own birthplace for inspiration. Close to Lahore lies Kasur, the city of the eighteenth century Sufi poet

Bulleh Shah. While still a student at a *madrassah*, Bulleh Shah asked his religious teacher a profound question: what was the point of washing one's hands and feet before prayers if the heart wasn't clean? The cleric frowned at Bulleh Shah and refused to answer. In the teacher's mind the young Bulleh was treading very close to blasphemy. But the future poet wanted a reply. Instead of waiting for one, he found his own answer. He grew his hair long, started dressing in flamboyant garb, picked up the *iktara* (a one-stringed folk instrument), and began singing poetry. One of his most powerful poems is "*Ki janan mein Kaun*," or "Who am I?"

Bulleya, Who am I?
I'm no believer in a mosque
And I have no pagan ways
I am not pure, I am not vile
I am no Moses, I am no Pharaoh
Bulleya, Who am I?
First and last I see the self
I recognized no second to it
No one is knowing more than me
But, Bulleh, who is it that's me
Bulleya, Who am I?
(Translation by Andy McCord)

I remember reading this poem and immediately letting out a loud "Wow!" Shah had hit on one of my deepest convictions. Without inner struggle and self-knowledge, joy and enlightenment would always remain elusive. And as an added bonus for a musician, Shah's Punjabi verses naturally suggested a melody and a groove.

"Bulleya," a song inspired by Shah's poem, became the first track on what would be Junoon's next album, entitled *Parvaaz*, or *The Flight*. Discovered during a period of spiritual questioning, and set to music, that one poem was the key to the whole *Parvaaz* album. Shah's poetry of self-discovery, love, freedom, and tolerance gave a voice to Muslims chained by blind ritualism and a fear-mongering clergy. It also created a cultural and spiritual bridge among Muslims, Hindus, and Sikhs living in the subcontinent. The poet had done in spirit and lyric what Junoon was trying to do by traveling in India. Shah's message of oneness and cultural harmony had brought him directly into conflict with the self-appointed custodians of public morality, the mullahs—who labeled him a heretic. In his lifetime, Shah was constantly harassed, and when he died in 1758 the mullahs even denied him a proper burial in Kasur. Yet such was his impact on the people that today his shrine is visited by thousands of ecstatic followers from diverse backgrounds, to pray and celebrate his universal message of love.

Parvaaz was my answer to the accusing doomsayers of my own time. The words and music set my innermost beliefs to melody and rhythm. My life's experiences had confirmed what I had felt since childhood—that one can't divide people, places, or God into boxes and categories. All are one in the eyes of God.

The mystic wheel of *Parvaaz* rocked heavier than anything Junoon had done before. This was a deep Sufi river of creativity that I was swimming in, and on the eight songs that I contributed, I let go of all insecurities and allowed the Spirit to guide the music.

Parvaaz contains one of my all-time favorite Junoon songs, "Ghoom" ("Spin"). The music and lyrics take inspiration from Shah Hussain's immortal Sufi poem of the infinite revolutions of the spinning wheel. Here are some of the words, translated by my friend Andy McCord:

Spin wheel, spin
The girl spinning, reeling the thread
Long may she live, while you spin

Speak His name, breathe His name
And nothing can shake you
From a flood of five rivers choose one
Live where it takes you
Spin wheel, spin

Life keeps revolving and evolving, the verses suggest, as we go through the cycle of conception, birth, growth, decline, death, and resurrection. And choosing one river from five is an allegory about divine unity. All rivers eventually lead to the ocean of love.

Parvaaz is my favorite Junoon album. But making it wasn't all a rocking celebration.

Ali and I increasingly had been growing apart. He was my younger brother's age and had started to feel a sort of sibling-rivalry-type jealousy toward me. As Junoon got more attention, the dynamics of the band changed. Ali wanted to rebel and chart his own course but he felt trapped. He'd come a long way from being a wedding singer in the Jupiters but he was unhappy with the musical direction I wanted to take Junoon in. He couldn't understand my search for meaning. Ali's dream of being a rock star had come true but not in the David Lee Roth/Bon Scott mold he had wanted. He was now getting recognized as the "Sayonee" guy and that deeply upset him. His limelight-chasing, celebrity-loving friends filled his head up with notions of "going solo" and getting away from Junoon's electric-folk spirituality. The deep Sufi terrain got under his skin. But he presumably went along with it on *Azadi* and *Parvaaz* because it paid the bills and I assume he was afraid of losing the high-profile life that he loved. The one song he contributed to *Parvaaz*, "Sajna," was an upside-down love song in which he promises his girl the moon and then snatches it away. Ali was going through a break-up with a woman who wanted to marry him and would have made him happy. But his desires blinded him. Maybe the pressures of fame were too much to handle, or maybe we were just tuned to different frequencies. We were polar opposites from the beginning. But as often happens in music, the creative friction helped the intensity of our recording sessions.

Parvaaz was a watershed for me. We recorded the album in Lahore at a new and better-equipped twenty-four-track studio owned by our friend, the guitar player Mekaal Hasan. In the spring of 1999, John Alec took a month off from teaching music in Westchester and flew to Pakistan to help us record and produce the album. It was Junoon's best recording to date, capturing the improvisational feel of our live shows. The frenetic pace of the *Parvaaz* sessions lent an urgency and a breathlessness to the whole recording process. We would start in the morning and keep going till exhaustion or the irritating power outages forced us to take breaks. In the end we came out with a ten-track album whose unique sound was positively noticed when we later performed it in the West. Jon Pareles of the *New York Times* described Junoon as an Asian answer to Santana and compared our songs to those of U2. Others dubbed Junoon "the U2 of the Muslim world," and Hannah Bloch of *Time* magazine described *Parvaaz* as "rock with Sufi rapture." Fans mined the tracks for hidden mystical messages, and it sold well in Pakistan and throughout the *desi* diaspora. We couldn't distribute it in India thanks to the conflict in Kashmir. But for me, *Parvaaz* was a musical soundtrack for flying into a new twenty-first century.

While the differences between Ali and me grew, Brian and John and I grew closer. After the rest of the band finished putting down the basic tracks, Brian, John, and I spent a lot more time together in the studio. In between listening to the songs taking shape, we reflected on our days growing up in Tappan, going to band practices at John's grandmother's house or Brian's parents' basement, sitting and dissecting each and every lick and riff on Queen's "Bohemian Rhapsody" or Led Zep's "Kashmir." After all this time, we were still kindred spirits, connected through our musical passions. (John formed some new passions of his own in Pakistan, including Rumi's poetry, playing the sitar, and learning Urdu.) But who would have thought that so many years later we'd be sitting in my city of Lahore and paying tribute to the spirit of Bulleh Shah! All three of us were brutally honest with each other, and sometimes our creative ideas would boil over into heated disagreements. But there was a deep underlying respect that made *Parvaaz* special. We had grown as individuals as well and all our diverse cultural experiences were poured into the whole process.

After that album I felt newly confident in my abilities. I also felt free to pursue my own creative vision. And I wanted to go into the new millennium with a greater purpose.

A few months later, a greater purpose found me.

Up to and during the recording of *Parvaaz*, I'd explored the lives of a prophet and a poet: the Prophet Muhammad and Bulleh Shah. After recording *Parvaaz*, I got the opportunity to delve into the life of a politician: Muhammad Ali Jinnah, the great leader and founder of Pakistan.

Ahmad Kapadia, the same ad man who'd commissioned "Jazba-e-Junoon" for the cricket World Cup, asked me to compose the theme song to the film *Jinnah*. It had an international cast, starring the British actor Christopher Lee and India's Shashi Kapoor. Every Pakistani knows the life story of the *quaid-e-azam*, or "great leader" of the country. But by reading Stanley Wolpert's excellent *Jinnah of Pakistan* and other books in preparation for my work on the film, I fully grasped Jinnah's significance. He showed that real change—individual, societal, and political—can only come through making repeated sacrifices for your passion and beliefs.

I was happy that Ahmad and his colleague Imran Awan agreed to let me follow my instincts in making the song. I heard a bigger cinematic sound. For inspiration, I looked to my family's experiences during Partition. My mother's family had left their home and belongings in Patiala and started from scratch in a new nation state with abundant natural beauty and resources. They had a vision to rebuild their lives and to live freely in the service of others. It's not often that you get a chance to start all over again. I wanted the melody and the words to symbolize the freedom movement and capture the essence of the sacrifice made by millions to achieve a free Pakistan. I heard the orchestration and the arrangement in both dark and light shades—a stark reminder of a lingering colonial and feudal shadow, but also the fragile promise of a more hopeful, enlightened Pakistani future. To try to achieve this, I flew to New York to record the orchestration with John Alec's friend Paul Schwartz, a Piermont-based arranger. I penned the words of the chorus at my parents house in Tappan.

> *Junoon sey aur ishq sey miltey hai Azadi, qurbani ki bahon mein miltey hai Azadi.*
>
> It takes passion and love to achieve freedom, freedom lies in the arms of sacrifice.

John and I flew back together to Karachi to record vocals, *tablas*, and guitars and then mixed the results in Lahore at Mekaal Hasan's studio. Since Jinnah's freedom struggle was about unshackling Muslim men and women, and his most loyal companion was his sister Fatima, I decided to have Ali and Samina sing alternate verses and a unison chorus. I had fond memories of Samina singing at Uncle Fareed's wedding and now was our chance to showcase her talent. Samina's voice lent innocence and a light, which contrasted with Ali's darker-shaded emotions. Once the song was done, Asim Reza married powerful images from the movie to make a memorable, award-winning music video titled "Azadi."

The movie was controversial. It celebrates Jinnah as a believer in the separation of mosque and state, who stood up to the mullahs. The challenges I'd been experiencing were quintessentially Pakistani. The clergy couldn't deal with Jinnah's liberal lifestyle or his struggle for gender, religious, or class equality. While the movie was still being filmed, I met Christopher Lee, Shashi Kapoor, and the film's producer, Dr. Akbar Ahmed. The Pakistani media and the religious fanatics were heaping abuse on all of them for allegedly distorting the legacy of Jinnah. But the detractors hadn't even seen the completed film! I asked the silver-haired Lee if he was put off by the criticism, and he looked at me with his piercing eyes, from under a Jinnah cap.

"It will take a lot more than words to scare me off this film set, young man!" he replied in a deep, booming voice. Lee was the spitting image of Jinnah in his black *sherwani* and did justice to the challenging role of a misunderstood leader of a complex country. Richard Attenborough's *Gandhi* biopic had made a caricature of Jinnah, and the Jinnah movie set the record straight for most Pakistanis. It was an honor to be asked to contribute a song for a film about the founding father of my nation—the same man the mullahs had once called "the great infidel."

Artists in Pakistan have always had to wrestle with uptight clergy and politicians. Junoon's music had irked both, but with General Musharraf's appearance on the scene, a paradigm shift took place. At least for a while.

The general took power a few months after the launch of the *Jinnah* movie and his government championed both the movie and the music video as a vital sign of a new era. Junoon went from being banned in Pakistan to honored guests of the state. Having been through the eras of Bhutto and Sharif and the bans, I was used to the tenuous, anything-can-happen existence of a musician. But I was impressed with Musharraf from the get-go. Politics in Pakistan is anything but consistent. And yet I saw a leader who vowed to combat corruption, illiteracy, and extremism. In 2001, as Indian and Pakistani forces were facing each other eyeball to eyeball across the border, Musharraf would join us on stage on Christmas Day in Karachi at Jinnah's mausoleum for our founding father's birth anniversary. The president stood clapping his hands right next to me as we sang "Azadi" and "Jazba," and moved to the beat with us. It was such a relief to have a cool leader in office.

When I was invited to meet Musharraf at the President's House by his son Bilal, the general turned out to be refreshingly humorous, easygoing, and unburdened by the usual sycophants that surround Pakistani leaders. In the beginning, Musharraf committed himself to media freedom and introduced a healthy culture of national debate. He also pledged to work toward normalization of relations with India. Tragically for Pakistan, that would all change by 2007. In his quest for more power Musharraf would pull a Nawaz Sharif and fire the chief justice of Pakistan. I stopped supporting the general after he made a deal with Benazir and joined the same corrupt politicians he had pledged to purge from the country.

The Musharraf era of politics would start off well but end in tears. Meanwhile, the religious debate that had followed me just got hotter.

After the release of *Parvaaz*, it suddenly seemed as if those kids who had interrogated me about my devotion to Islam had more and louder voices. Any personal doubts I'd had about the compatibility of music and Islam were now nonexistent, thanks to my studies. There is nothing in the Quran that prohibits music or musical instruments. But some of our "fans" were turning against us, taking sides with the likes of the pissed-off Urdu teacher from Karachi.

A typical complaint on our web site went like this: "Islam never was and never will be spread with Sufi poems being sung by a rock band!"

"That's the limit!" wrote another enraged parrot on our site. "Junoon is humiliating Islam and the great poets. First they ruined 'Khudi' and now other Sufi poems are on their hit list! This could be attractive for some teenagers but not for the people who know what the real Islam and Sufism is about. Junoon should just take a bath regularly and stop with this Sufi stuff!" It was as if we were latter-day, Pakistani versions of Ray Charles, freaking fans out by mixing sacred and popular music.

But many more true Junoonis were jamming along with us.

A Pakistani fan wrote:

> I believe that Junoon did a fascinating job of not just presenting Bulleh Shah to a new audience, but in the process Junoon invented a way for a whole generation of young people to be able to peer into Sufi music, and the mysticism that it represented, that simply did not exist.

Our presentation of the song had allowed him to ask himself some of the most important questions in life, he said.

> In a small way, the realization that for me to be anything, I had to know myself first, and that nobody else was supposed to know me better than myself, was amazingly empowering.

And I knew I was doing something right when Indian fans also wrote to say what the song "Bulleya" and the *Parvaaz* album meant to them.

"This is one of the most famous of Bulleh Shah's *kafis*," or folk poems, wrote one. "In his quest for the nature of his self, it has a special place. Our philosophers and poets have often asked, 'As a man, where have I come from, and where am I going?' But, it has rarely been asked, 'Who is this "I" who comes and goes?'"

Now this was inquiry of the type that I believe Prophet Muhammad inspired us Muslims to practice! But the claims about rock's incompatibility with Islam were just dead wrong. Besides, rock music was just the latest genre in fourteen hundred years of phenomenal contributions to music and poetry by Muslims. Muslim artists—men and women—have shared their love for life, God, and prophet in music, poetry, and dance. Whether our critics (including Farhat Hashmi) were willfully ignorant or just stupid, I don't know. Whatever else they were, they were completely mistaken.

I could have debated all day, but I decided rhythm and melody would do my work for me. Junoon carried on its music-making ways by touring all over Pakistan, India, Bangladesh, the Middle East, China, and our annual concert tours to America and Europe. In September 2001 we flew to play a headlining concert at the Oslo Spectrum in Norway, where I met an old inspiration of the Vital Signs. Morten Harket, the forever-young, studious lead singer of a-ha, shared the bill with us. Morten had been introduced to us by two Norwegian Junoonis. The engaged couple had gathered the huge Nordic Pakistani community and put together the concert to build solidarity between second-generation Muslims and Norwegians. I had written a song called "Piya/The Ocean of Love" which Morten sang with us. It was a hugely appreciated concert, and Junoon was steadily making its mark among Western fans and critics. Fifteen years earlier, Junaid Jamshed and others like him would have given anything to play a show like this. But the new Junaid could have his cold desert theology and whispering phantoms of fear. At that bridge-building Norwegian concert, God was showing me what an oasis of His love looked like.

The concert was a Pakistani-American reunion of sorts as well. My friend Richard Murphy had flown in from New York, along with John Alec and our new drummer Jay Dittamo, to shoot the concert for his documentary on Junoon's cross-cultural music and message.

It was a message that, a few short days later, would need to be heard louder than ever.

TWELVE
"Speak"

On September 10, 2001, Samina and I took a boat ride with Morten Harket of a-ha and his girlfriend, Annemette.

Laughing and relaxing after our successful show at the Spectrum, we watched the calm, peaceful sights of Oslo as we drifted along on the serene blue waters. Later that day we went to see an art exhibition where painters, poets, and musicians had gathered, to look at small and large portraits of people from various cultures wearing smiling, sad, happy, and seductive expressions. We wound the lazy day down by going to a *desi* restaurant in the heart of Oslo frequented by tall, blue-eyed, and blonde Norwegians as well as *shalwar kameez*–clad Pakistanis and Indians. Morten's a shy guy and I wanted to see him blush, so I surreptitiously went over to the juke box and played ah-a's "Take on Me." The whole restaurant turned toward the Norwegian pop star and started applauding. It was then that my phone rang.

It was Shashi Tharoor, calling from New York. Shashi, currently India's junior foreign minister and an acclaimed Indian author of novels and nonfiction books, was then the high-profile undersecretary general of communication and information for the United Nations.

"Salman, I've got some wonderful news for you!" Shashi said excitedly. My ears perked up as the chorus of "Take on Me" receded.

"Your request has been accepted by Secretary General Kofi Annan!" he said. "On October 24, U.N. Day, Junoon will be the first-ever rock band in the world to perform at the U.N. General Assembly hall in New York!"

A huge smile spread over my face as I sat down next to Samina and Morten. We were going to new heights. Junoon had played a concert near K2, the second highest mountain in the world, in 1997, but being on stage at the U.N. would transcend anything on Earth.

The new millennium had begun well for me. Earlier that year, the U.N. had appointed me as a goodwill ambassador for HIV/AIDS, making me the first musician from South Asia chosen for the position. Kristan Schoultz, a bright and purpose-driven Arkansas native who headed UNAIDS in Islamabad, had nominated me. In June 2001, Kristan also set up a meeting for me with Annan and the S.G.'s staff during a UNAIDS conference in New York. At that meeting in Manhattan, I half-jokingly mentioned that it was about time the hallowed hall of the U.N. reverberated with some passionate songs of peace and activism instead of just dull speeches from politicians and diplomats. The secretary general promised to "look into it." Months later, as the energetic beat of a Norwegian pop band provided the sound track, I graciously accepted the invitation from Shashi. October in New York was going to be great, I thought. The phone call was a sign that the interrogations about culture and religion brought on by the Junoon bans were finally behind me. Maybe now I could be free to play some music. The thought energized me. I was ready to embrace the future, as we flew back home early the next morning.

Samina and I landed in Karachi on the afternoon of September 11. We proceeded to pick up the boys, who had been staying with my sister Sania. It was still a bright, sunny evening when I drove out into the Karachi traffic. I looked out at the cloudless blue skies and felt that after two decades of living in Pakistan, I had metamorphosed back into a full-fledged Pakistani and had mostly shed my American *desi* identity. The thought lingered in my head as I drove toward my friend's hair styling salon in the bustling Khadda market.

I entered through the salon's glass door and stopped dead in my tracks. Everyone in the shop was staring at the TV screens. As I followed their gaze I saw both my worlds colliding live on CNN. It was about six in the evening local time, and the first plane had already crashed into the north tower of the World Trade Center. CNN was relaying the images from eight thousand miles away but the shock I experienced was as if my own neighborhood was on fire. In fact, it was.

I stared at the TV and thought, *this is New York City*.

All my memories of growing up as an American *desi* came flooding back: everything from playing ping-pong with Frank Bianco to buying records at Bleecker Bob's in the Village to having my first crush on Joy Schloss. As I watched the towers burn, I instinctively thought of the day John Lennon had been shot. I remembered how devastated I had been then but also how the music had been a healing force. 9/11 took that feeling of loss to a whole new level. In one dark day the terrorists had ripped up the Kennedyian vision that had so lifted my mom nearly forty years ago. As I sat there motionless, "Yesterday" started playing in my head. No matter the physical distance between Pakistan and America, I could no more shake or discard my American *desi* memories than I could forget my city of Lahore or my Islamic faith. They were an indivisible part of my being and consciousness.

The first plane could have been an accident, but as I saw the second one crash, I knew there was nothing random about that moment, that day, that month, or that year. As I sat glued to the TV, the normality of life went up in the thick columns of black smoke billowing out of both towers.

"God," I prayed, "please don't let it be a Muslim who did this. Please."

But of course, it was Muslims who carried out the terrible acts in New York and Washington. Fifteen of the nineteen hijackers were from Saudi Arabia. And immediately, it seemed as if a hate virus had been released and threatened to affect the whole planet. The religion of Islam and each of its followers became the new enemy in just seconds. The global media simplified this terrorist attack into a natural clash between Islam and the West. It didn't matter that the vast majority of the world's 1.5 billion Muslims were genuinely shocked, bewildered, and saddened by the loss of innocent life. The terrorists didn't discriminate between Muslim, Christian, Jew, or Hindu, believer or non-believer. Among the victims, who represented more than ninety nationalities, was my Aunt Tahira's handsome twenty-eight-year-old son Taimur. Another Pakistani-American from Queens, Salman Hamdani, twenty-three years old, sacrificed his life as a volunteer paramedic trying to save people from the burning towers. These two Muslims and many others died at the hands of those who had hijacked Islam—a faith that prohibits suicide and the killing of innocents. The terrorists had convinced themselves they were martyrs.

But in the eyes of Islam they had forever condemned their souls to darkness.

The world had turned upside down. As I headed back home, I tried to make sense of what role God wanted me to play. I put my feelings in an e-mail to Shashi Tharoor:

The need for Peace . . .

Dear Shashi,

I arrived in Karachi yesterday only to be jolted by the horrific news of the terrorist attacks in America. I've been trying to gain some sort of perspective on the possible motives of this evil and barbaric crime, but after having soul-searched for twenty-four hours, I'm still dumbfounded.

My heart goes out to the thousands of people who lost their lives and to the countless others who have been left behind to pick up the pieces from this tragedy. As a global community we need to be careful in not pointing the blame against any one religion, race, or ethnic group. Fanning the flames of hatred at a sensitive time like this is not only foolish but could be potentially catastrophic. It is important that the Western media discriminate between peace-loving Muslims and terrorists like Osama bin Laden, who only bow to gods of hate, bigotry, and fanaticism. The sentiment in Pakistan is of shocked disbelief. The majority of the people feel genuine empathy toward the victims and share the grief of the American people. At the same time there are some who are deeply disturbed by unconfirmed reports of a possible backlash against Muslims living in the United States.

As artists I feel we have a greater responsibility to help create an atmosphere of calm and brotherhood in this emotionally charged environment. In light of the recent tragic events, the U.N. peace concert assumes a far greater importance for me. There is a great need to project a united, strong, and clear message of Peace in the twenty-first century.

I hope too that all of you at the U.N. are in agreement that terrorism should not be allowed to stain all that is good in this world.

I pray to God that you and the rest of the staff at the U.N. are safe and I look forward to your reply when things have settled down in New York.

Stay safe,
Warm regards,
Salman

Shashi responded immediately.

> *Thank you, Salman, for these moving and thoughtful words.*
>
> *You can be sure that I strongly share your sentiments and we will work to ensure that your concert proceeds in exactly that spirit.*

I was encouraged and heartened by Shashi's response. Indians and Pakistanis working together to do a peace concert in New York City to condemn the terror attacks was a good start. But a lot more had to be done, especially in Pakistan. There was a crisis looming. An understandably angry American public wanted justice. According to General Musharraf his intelligence director was told by Deputy Secretary of State Richard Armitage that Pakistan had to cooperate with the U.S. or be prepared to be bombed back to the Stone Age. Secretary of State Colin Powell flew into Islamabad and met with General Musharraf. Before 9/11, President George W. Bush hadn't even known Musharraf's name but now fate and destiny had put America and Pakistan onto a possible collision course. Bush's cowboy "you're-with-us-or-against-us" rhetoric disturbed many Pakistanis who had sympathy for America's tragedy but serious disagreements with American foreign policy. In this charged atmosphere their self-respect was being challenged by an American president who seemed to want revenge, not justice. Many people thought that America's wrath would fall upon Pakistan, which had maintained diplomatic ties with the Taliban.

It seemed that all the lights had been turned on. The al-Qaeda robots who crashed into the twin towers had been programmed with the same *jihadi* thinking that had defeated the Soviets in Afghanistan. More than twenty years later, Afghanistan was a ruin and Pakistan had suffered through General Zia's dictatorship and the incompetence of corrupt politicians. Just as things were starting to look better, 9/11 had put Pakistan into the eye of a gathering storm. There was a golden opportunity for Bush to show real leadership. He could have united the Muslim world against the terrorists. Instead, he alienated a vast majority of people with his unilateral, fear-mongering, neo-con vision of the world.

Meanwhile, the world's media descended on Islamabad, turning the city's Marriott into a broadcasting headquarters. My U.N. friend Kristan Schoultz had to flee the country she'd lived in for years as the clouds of war hung low and Pakistan was deemed unsafe for Americans. Familiar anchors like CNN's Christiane Amanpour were daily relaying footage of bearded zealots screaming "Death to America" and women covered from head to toe. Only extreme images made it on to the news, while the moderate and "boring" side of Pakistani society was largely ignored. I felt Pakistan was being unfairly portrayed as an evil twin of the Taliban. So much for "fair and balanced" reporting.

Music was the only way I could try to make sense of this tragedy. In Islamabad, I went to see Eric Falt, the head of U.N. communications. Eric, a suave Frenchman, had joined Kristan in supporting me for the goodwill ambassador post. He was now the face of all the U.N. press briefings going out to the world. Over tea I shared my idea of doing a fundraising concert for the Afghan refugees who would be displaced in the ensuing violence between the terrorists and the U.S.-led coalition. I knew that there were very few hospital facilities or properly equipped trauma centers in Afghanistan outside of Kabul. With winter fast approaching, there would be a humanitarian crisis. We needed to send out warm clothes, medical supplies, tents, and food. Eric appreciated the idea but was skeptical of how I would get permission to hold a rock concert while there was a state of emergency in Pakistan. We didn't even have a venue.

"Leave that to me, Eric," I said confidently. I didn't have a clear idea, but I hoped that God would help me find a way. As I was leaving, I said to Eric that once I got the venue sorted out I would need a favor from him.

"What favor, Salman?"

He would find out shortly.

The concert would serve multiple purposes. My idea was to bring together the arts and culture community in Pakistan so that at least someone would speak for Pakistan's moderate majority. It would also raise funds for Afghan refugees and send out a strong message to the world that Pakistanis condemn terror and violence. I sensed that a cycle of violence not seen since the 1980s was going to start all over again. We as artists had a moral responsibility to do something about it.

We had fought overwhelming odds to revitalize arts and culture in Pakistan, and we weren't going to remain silent while the bombs rained down in our backyard. But the atmosphere was charged. Airports were closed. Indian talking heads on television urged for Pakistan to be declared a terrorist state. Pakistani state media responded just as ferociously, calling the Indians "shameless opportunists." The terrorists had successfully reignited the Indo-Pak family feud. Instead of uniting against terrorism, the nuclear neighbors started their utterly predictable saber-rattling. If only they could have taken a page of diplomacy out of Shashi's book.

Samina and I worked the phones and managed to get as many musicians, actors, cricketers, poets, and dancers—men and women—as we could who were willing and available to come to Islamabad. God was smiling and helpful. Our lineup was a who's who of the film, music, TV, sports, and theatre industries. Imran Khan; our old friend Arshad Mahmood, who had signed the Vital Signs to EMI; Sania Saeed (my co-star in the TV show *Aahat*); Ali's ex-girlfriend Vaneeza Ahmed; Brian's actress-wife Ayesha; the *kathak* dancer Nighat Chaudry; and other top Pakistani figures, including Waqar Younis, the captain of the Pakistan cricket team, all responded to my SOS. Another star attraction on the bill was a newly clean-shaven Junaid Jamshed, who'd come out of his self-imposed Tableeghi exile to support my cause. It was a measure of the underlying bond Junaid and I share. That bond transcends bickering about religion and politics. When push comes to shove we've been there for each other. To paraphrase Pastor Rick Warren, Junaid and I might not see eye to eye, but we could work hand in hand. The artists descended in cars, trains, buses, and the one flight per day allowed to land in Islamabad. Just as in the movie *Field of Dreams*, a voice it seemed had whispered, "If you build it, they will come." The event management firm BBCL was willing to do a guerilla film shoot, joining us in defiance of the ban imposed on public events because of the imminent strikes in Afghanistan. There was only one problem. We still had no venue.

After all our calling and running around Islamabad to find a stage where we could hold our fundraiser, a Junooni principal came forward. Mrs. Ansari was a hip middle-aged principal of the Islamabad College for Girls. Junoon had performed in the school's intimate auditorium many times during our early rocker days. I explained the emergency situation to the administrator, emphasizing that we were doing this show clandestinely because of the emergency ban on public congregations. Our mission was to raise funds for the Afghan refugees, I told her.

"*Beta*, don't you worry, we won't let you down. *Shabash*! [Bravo!]" she said. I also asked her not to breathe a word of this concert to anyone. That was like asking CNN not to broadcast breaking news. Word got out that there was a rock concert at Islamabad College for Girls. Before long, some city officials turned up and told us to stop the show.

"Salman, don't you know we are in a state of emergency?!" said a city inspector. "You are endangering the lives of the artists and the girls. This show cannot go on."

We had come too far for this to happen. But I took a deep breath and told the city inspector we'd stop and he could go home. Mercifully the guy left the college building. I looked at Mrs. Ansari and she understood what I was thinking. The show had to go on. But how?

And it was then that God sent an angel down to clear the path for the music. A blue sari-clad woman by the name of Mrs. Rashid Qureshi walked out of nowhere and provided the answer to my prayer. Her kids had heard about the Junoon show, and so Mrs. Qureshi, the wife of a top-ranking army officer, had convinced her husband to overrule the city official. She was my guardian angel for that night of October 9. After spending most of my career as a rock guerilla fighting the establishment, the irony of having support from an army man's wife and family wasn't lost on me. I had been forced to pick that day because of the chaos surrounding the event, but I knew of its significance beyond time and space. It was John Lennon's birthday. How perfect was it to do a concert denouncing violence and terrorism in harmony with the spirit of a Beatle who had asked America to Give Peace a Chance? Two days before the show, coalition forces started bombing al-Qaeda training camps in Afghanistan. Nobody knew if our concert was going to happen.

I drove back to Eric Falt to ask my favor. I said to him that I needed him to announce our concert to the global media in his afternoon briefing of October 9. Eric looked up and gave me a look as if to say, "You're turning me into a publicist." Instead he smiled and said, "The U.N. supports all worthy endeavors of its goodwill ambassadors." He quickly added, "but only if I can come to the show!" He then announced the concert to all the networks and media people gathered there, who looked on in disbelief.

And so it was. On that balmy October night, CNN, the BBC, NBC, CBS, ABC . . . you name it, they were there to see the improbable sight of a Pakistani girls' college packed to capacity with beautiful, hopeful, and screaming young women. Some of the shell-shocked reporters and cameramen accustomed to hearing "Death to America" slogans plugged their ears with cotton when the girls opened up their powerful lungs and shouted for their favorite stars and songs. The decibels reached Jonas Brothers–show levels. I didn't have time to think about it at the moment, but that night was a summation of all that I had hoped Pakistani culture would come to represent: music, poetry, dance, sporting passion, and a higher purpose to heal society.

I looked over at Junaid, who'd shed his *shalwar kameez* for jeans and a shirt. I asked him if it was for my sake or the beautiful girls' that he'd come.

"These are my people, too, Sally boy!" he said. We both laughed at the tragic-comedic moment. It felt like Al-Hamra all over again.

Imran Khan, who had transformed from a superstar-cricketer-turned-philanthropist to the leader of a fledgling political party, Tehreek-e-Insaf (Movement for Justice), accepted my invitation to be keynote speaker, along with Eric Falt. Imran showed solidarity with the victims of 9/11 but also echoed the thoughts of the majority of Muslims and Pakistanis: that the West needed to examine the causes of terrorism, not just the symptoms.

The famous *ghazal* singer Tina Sani, one of our star performers, sang Faiz's immortal poem "Speak":

Speak, for your two lips are free
Speak, your tongue is still your own
This straight body still is yours
Speak, your life is still your own
Time enough is this brief hour
Until body and tongue lie dead
Speak, for truth is living yet
Speak whatever must be said
Speak
(English translation Salima Hashmi)

The spinning wheel of life, so beautifully described in Shah Hussain's poem, was completing another of its never-ending circles. Listening to Tina, my mind went back to that November night in 1982 at the International Hotel when I had heard the verses spoken by a medical student in defiance of the tyranny and oppression of that time. I saw the same hope and aspirations in the eyes of our young audience just as I had as an eighteen-year-old so many years before. While our performance went on, the forces of light and darkness were sizing each other up for another decisive battle. The whole planet seemed to have been put at risk.

The evening had a talent show–like atmosphere. We were making it up as we went along. Samina, looking gorgeous in a stunning red *shalwar kameez*, helped manage the concert, edited scripts, and came onstage for the first time to sing with Junoon on "Azadi." The night was a giddy celebration as well. Brian, Ayesha, Ali, and his estranged Vaneeza were all alive on stage and united for peace.

The Western media brought an army of cameras and were bewildered to see the hidden other side of Pakistan. A rock and roll *desi* circus, complete with overjoyed, idealistic girls, was happening while bombs were exploding next door in Afghanistan. It felt like heaven and hell were dancing cheek to cheek. Junaid, who was vacillating between his missionary movement and a return to the pop life, whispered that the attacks and the conflict to come were signs of the Day of Judgment. Who knew? Maybe the end of the world was near and this was just a dress rehearsal. I was going to play my role till the curtain finally dropped.

After much cheering of all who graced the stage that special night, Junoon closed the show in a dramatic finale before the raucous, hyper, adrenaline-charged college crowd. We sang "Khudi," "Bulleya," "Azadi," and Lennon's "Give Peace a Chance" in both English and Urdu, turning the show into a *desi* vocal debut for Brian.

My old friend was the only American present that night who truly understood the hearts and minds of the Pakistani people. Since he'd arrived in 1992, Brian had been loved and embraced by Pakistanis as one of their own. He had two girls who were Pakistani and American, and with his family and Junoon he had seen the highs and lows Pakistan had experienced in the past decade. Brian also knew of the resilient spirit of the Pakistani people, and it was that spirit he spoke of so powerfully when he addressed the inspired college girls who had come out to support the fundraiser.

"You are all beautiful and talented and I wish I could tell all my fellow Americans how much love I have received from Pakistan," he said.

Brian's story of his decade-long cultural ambassadorship to Pakistan brought tears to the eyes of the students, teachers, and cast and production crew. For the finale, the entire cast, including Imran Khan, joined Junoon to close an unforgettable night with "Jazba," the Spirit of Passion.

A few weeks later, a recording of the show, called "United for Peace," was telecast on Pakistani satellite channels. With the commercial support the show got, we were able to raise a profit of close to a million rupees, which I handed to a grateful Eric Falt. Equally important was the media coup we managed to pull off. All the major worldwide networks ran stories about the concert. Watching in Manhattan, Richard Murphy saw a CNN anchor tell the improbable story of a rock concert at a girls' college in Islamabad. He hopped on the next plane to finish shooting his VH1 documentary, *Islamabad: Rock City*. Thanks to the exposure of our show, people perhaps saw that this neocon-defined conflict was not a black and white, politically simplified and media-amplified case of "us" versus "them."

The reality is far more complex. To combat terrorism in our world, you need to attack its roots: extreme poverty, extreme despair, and extreme injustice. Waging violence on violence only begets violence. You can't wash blood stains with blood. Our concert on October 9, 2001, was a small but important gesture, yet the larger campaign for peace must continue. Two great lessons I learned in school growing up in America were to support the underdog and work for equality and justice. To modify the Pledge of Allegiance: "One Earth, under God, with music, peace, liberty, and justice for all."

A couple of weeks later, Junoon traveled to New York. At immigration at JFK, all of us who had Muslim names were met with icy stares from angry-looking officials. Despite having been a U.S. citizen since I was a teenager, I had to wait with all the other Muslim passengers, due to the increased scrutiny at airports. It seemed that I was being asked to prove my loyalty to the United States of America all over again. The cold vibe in New York saddened me. And it was hard to get e-mails from old high school friends who were just as confused, angry, and hurt as I about the terrorist attacks—and also to see how the Bush Administration was portraying Muslims as "hating our freedoms." One of the many e-mails I received was from Joy Schloss. It was the first time I'd heard from her in three years. In August 1998 I had invited her to come with her family to attend Junoon's concert in Central Park. Now, in this crazy time, she was reaching out again to her old friend. She wrote that she had driven from Manhattan to her parents' place in Tappan and had passed my father's house on Lester Drive. She said she stopped, looked at the house, and cried for the very first time since the attacks. In those dark times, Joy's unconditional friendship was a sign from God telling me that the powerful bond of humanity I believed in was real.

The media storm after 9/11 had created an artificial divide, but I was determined to fight it. My publicist Tracy Mann booked me on radio and television to speak about our U.N. concert and help dispel some common stereotypes about Islam and Muslims. Some of the talking points I used were my own understanding of jihad and suicide.

Prophet Muhammad described armed struggle against tyranny and oppression as a lesser jihad. He also warned against the dark whisperings of the *nafs* (ego) and called the fight against the lower self the greater jihad.

The Quran says, "Man was created weak," and it's true. The inner jihad is a struggle for self-discovery and is about uncovering our hidden, infinite potentials. It's about raising oneself up high (as in Iqbal's poem "Khudi") and never bringing others down. What the terrorists got wrong was that jihad is about overcoming our human impulses of greed, jealousy, injustice, violence, and inhumanity toward our fellow human beings.

The actions of the hijackers baffled me on a theological level. My advice to anyone who contemplates suicide is simple. You're denying God His greatest blessing to you: life. At the same time you're condemning your soul to darkness till eternity. There is no Islamic justification for suicide bombing. In seventh century Arabia, Prophet Muhammad's people were humiliated and persecuted mercilessly by the pagan Quraysh, yet never did he ask his followers to kill innocent men, women, and children or to commit suicide in the name of Islam.

With my talking points ready, I went off to meet the reporters and anchor people. Some appearances went well, like on National Public Radio's *All Things Considered*, and on CNN and in an interview with *Newsweek*.

But nothing could have prepared me for my next appearance, on Bill Maher's *Politically Incorrect* in Los Angeles on November 1. I was the only Muslim among the guests, which included Kiss's Gene Simmons, conservative talk-radio show host Laura Ingraham, and CNN's Michele Mitchell. I flew to LA with John Alec, and we rehearsed a mock show at our hotel. But our rehearsal was nothing like the real thing. I soon realized I had come to a gun fight with a white flag.

In the green room at CBS Television City, I greeted Gene Simmons warmly and told him that Kiss has many fans in Pakistan. But the fire-breathing Gene just sneered at me. He couldn't have cared less. He had a preconceived notion of Muslims, and when I repeated the friendly comment on air, he responded by saying that that those Pakistanis probably wanted to cut off his famous long tongue.

I tried to give a global context to the terrorist attacks and explain fundamentalism, but no one wanted to listen. I carried on as the cameras captured the zeitgeist frame by frame. There was a communication breakdown between the West and the Muslim community, which the fanatics were exploiting. I couldn't put years of war and conflict into a short sound bite. But that didn't stop me from trying. I told Maher that prayer, charity, fasting, and the pilgrimage to Mecca are what constitute "fundamentalism" to Muslims.

"I'm using it in the sense that we here in America think of Islamic fundamentalism, which is the portion of that religion which says, 'fly planes into buildings,' OK?" Maher said testily. "So you call it what you want."

It was a relentless onslaught from all sides. Simmons called me "delusional" and clumped together all Muslims as terrorists. Ingraham pounced on me as if to say I was insane for drawing a comparison between the ideologies of hatred of Osama bin Laden and Charlie Manson. Michele Mitchell was the only one who didn't try to muzzle me every time I tried to speak. I was in a shooting gallery. Gene Simmons had the last word and gave his expert diplomatic advice: "The U.S. should do what Israel does. You slap me and I take out your country."

Bombing the world to pieces won't get us to peace, I thought. The drama wasn't just on television; it continued after we walked off the set. In the hallway at Television City, Gene Simmons was still goading me on and said, "Sal, all those people who speak with names like 'agh-mad' are like cockroaches." That's when I stopped.

"Dude, I actually had respect for you," I said. "You're the one who discovered Eddie Van Halen! I thought you were about music."

Simmons, unable to take lip from a Sufi rocker, had this pearl of rock and roll wisdom to share: "Sal, it's never about the message, it's about the messenger. David Lee Roth WAS Van Halen, not Eddie!"

I totally disagreed, but the high priest of Kiss hadn't finished.

"Besides, Paul Stanley and me were the smart ones," he said. "We just did it for the money and the sex, man; live and learn!"

John Alec, realizing that I was being baited by Simmons, started pulling me away, but a small crowd had gathered at the studios. In its midst was Jerry Springer. Springer said he saw the recording of the show and quickly added, "Hey man, I'd ask you on my show, but that would be even worse than what I just saw you go through."

Simmons seemed like a dinosaur in a TV reality show. His parting shot at me before he left in his black limousine was, "If you want to live in America, forget about where you came from." I felt like I had just had a conversation with a mullah. (Apparently Gene had been a theology major before he started spitting fake blood at his fans.) Not all was lost, though. The previous night in my hotel room, I'd watched on TV as "Mr. November" Derek Jeter hit a homerun in the tenth inning, to help the Yankees tie the World Series 2–2 against the Arizona Diamondbacks. The Yankees weren't giving up and there was hope yet! I had kept it together on Maher's show, but I realized that words would not be enough to heal the chasm of hate and ignorance. So I flew back to New York to do what I do best: play music.

Politics and cable TV thrive on division and bad news. But that didn't mean I had to follow the same trends. I sent invitations to all my friends in New York to attend Junoon's historic concert at the U.N. General Assembly hall on October 24, as well as the couple of other New York gigs we were going to do to condemn terrorism. It was the best way of showing that there was more to the Muslim world than women in veils, Osama bin Laden, and suicide bombers.

Joy Schloss and her whole family came to the U.N. concert, as did Richard Murphy's VH1 documentary director Lucas Traub, Bilal Musharraf and his wife, my parents, my brother Sherry and his wife, John Alec, and a host of other friends as well as media. They joined a packed audience of *desis*, diplomats, and New Yorkers to take part in a collective catharsis. Keeping on message for U.N. day, I had suggested that Shashi invite the Indian rock band Euphoria to share the stage with us. The fanatics fear the power of arts and culture, as it can unite people and soothe human pain. The concert was introduced by Kofi Annan, who welcomed everyone to U.N. Day. "We are blessed in what we are about to see and hear this evening," Annan said. So began an unforgettable evening of drama and emotion. Euphoria opened up for us after the mime Marcel Marceau performed to pin-drop silence.

There, in front of our peers on the world's only truly neutral stage, Junoon—Ali, Brian, Ashiq Ali, Jay Dittamo, and I—paid tribute to the victims of the September 11 tragedy and rocked the visibly moved crowd. Over at Madison Square Garden, where U2 was playing, there might have been more people, but the intensity of emotion and the symbolism of a Pakistani-American rock band singing songs of spiritual unity would've made Bono proud.

I teased the audience by saying Kofi Annan had told me that the hippest audience is at the U.N. "You have to loosen up your ties!" I said. It was a signal for all the men, women, and children to get up and start dancing. Just as at a *qawwali* recital, we managed to destroy the wall between us and them, literally. Audience members—from suited, booted, bespectacled diplomats to a young kid with a Harry Potter T-shirt—were doing the rock *bhangra* and jiving to songs from our albums *Inquilaab*, *Azadi*, and *Parvaaz*.

For the finale I invited Euphoria to join us in singing Lennon's "Imagine," in what was certainly the first time the words "imagine there's no countries" had been uttered at the United Nations! We segued into the "nanana nanana" chorus from The Beatles' "Hey Jude," which had the mystical effect of Amir Khusro *tarana* syllables of unity. The entire hall sang along and reverberated with the spirit of coexistence.

The Quran says, "To God we belong and to Him we shall return." Those words are commonly used as a condolence for when someone passes away. For me that verse also symbolizes the ephemeral nature of our world. The few, truly golden moments of truth that emerge from our travels need to be treasured, shared, and celebrated. The music has a way of ennobling those moments and smoothing out their rough edges. Rumi was right. If you follow the music it will show you the way.

THIRTEEN

"Ghoom Tana"

Not long after the terrorist attacks of September 11, 2001, I found myself being stared down by an immigration officer at New York's John F. Kennedy Airport.

"You've got a lot of stamps in your passport, Mr. Ahmad," said the blue-shirted man. "What do you do?"

Moments before, after I'd waited in a long line to enter the country for a Junoon tour, the same man had given me a skeptical look. He'd seen my face. He read my name on my passport—my U.S. passport. And he saw the stamps in it—from Saudi Arabia, from Pakistan, from other countries in the Muslim world and beyond.

This was the spring of 2002. I was used to this line of questioning. After 9/11, I was furious that the terrorists had hijacked my religion. Seeing al-Qaeda speak for Muslims and Islam was something like having the KKK be the voice of Christianity. But to people like the officer, I was potentially one of those same murderous thugs, ready to plot war on America. The terrorists had perpetrated a sinister case of identity theft. And for me it resulted in suspicious glances, extra questions, body searches, and finger-printing.

"I'm a guitar player," I replied simply, exhausted by the sixteen-hour flight from Lahore. Just let this be over soon, I thought silently. But my reply had gotten the official's attention. His eyes widened.

"Really?" he said in a smart-alecky voice. "Would you mind holding out your hands?"

I thought I was going to be finger-printed again, so I did what I was asked. But instead of pulling out an ink pad, he felt the tips of my fingers on my right hand and then on the left. He then looked me in the eye and asked a trick question.

"So, Mr. Ahmad, are you a righty or a lefty?"

I wanted to say "neither." I wanted to tell him that real musicians play only from the heart. But that would have only complicated things further.

"You just felt the callouses on my left hand, Officer," I said instead. "That would make me a righty, wouldn't it?"

"Okay," said the officer, disappointed at not blowing the cover of a sleeper cell agent. "You're a guitar player. You're free to go," he said with a patronizing smile.

"You're a guitar player," the officer had said to me.

Was that all I was? For almost as long as I could remember, I'd tried to grow into that title, that definition, that reality. Being a guitar player was the only thing I'd wanted to be. But after 9/11, like so many other people, I asked myself new questions about meaning and identity. Of course I was happy to be a guitar player. I feel sometimes like I had been born with one in my hand. But the guitar has always been a means to an end, not an end in itself. There were other layers to me. I was also a husband, a father, a son, and a believer. When I was a kid in Tappan strumming a tennis racket and singing in front of my mirror, I projected myself into a rock and roll future. Now I'd become the person I'd always hoped I'd be. Or so I thought. 9/11 was like a huge and deadly version of the car crash I'd been through in 1998. For me the attacks and the aftermath were my collision with the Bedford multiplied by a million.

I knew I could never go back and change the past. But I could try to help shape a more hopeful future.

I began with a song. When I finished that 2002 U.S. tour, I wrote an English-language song called "No More." I collaborated on lyrics with a New York beat poet named Polar Levine. The song took its inspiration from a poem called "Pulverized / I'm Breathing" that Polar wrote after he lived through the destruction of his Tribeca neighborhood that awful September day. As the twin towers collapsed, dust collected in Polar's apartment ten blocks away. Cut off from home, he choked on the realization that along with charred plastic and crushed concrete, he was "inhaling firefighters, police officers, cafeteria workers, secretaries, and executives. Muslims, Jews, Christians, atheists, heterosexuals, and homosexuals." "No More" appeared on *The Best of Junoon* and is an anthem—like Junoon-meets-Radiohead-meets-the-Beatles-at-a-*ghazal*-evening type of song. In it, we're all discussing the crazy post-9/11 world we'd come to live in.

> God and money take the blame / suicidal video games / Stormy winds seduce the night over New York and Karachi skies / if all that lives is born to die / love remains I wonder why / No More, I'm breathing you No More . . .

But the events called for more than a song. In July 2002, Samina and I decided to slow everything down. We packed two suitcases and took the kids on a long Amtrak train ride from New York through Pennsylvania, Washington D.C, and the Carolinas, ending up in Orlando. We needed a laugh amid all the heaviness. And so to shake off the nonstop chatter about Code Orange alerts and possible new terrorist attacks, we went on a pilgrimage to the land of Mickey Mouse and Snow White and the Seven Dwarfs. There was no better place for a family of five Pakistani Muslims than Disney World. Sometimes you need to go crazy to find your sanity.

At that most American of theme parks, Samina, Imran, Sherjan, Shamyl, and I dissolved into a colorful mass of people old and young, large and small. We transformed into children and screamed our hearts out on the magical rides and roller coasters. Watching my young boys, their eyes hopeful and their spirits uplifted, I made a promise to myself to try to dedicate my life to breaking the wall of fear and mistrust between the Muslim world and America.

I also made another vow. As a Pakistani-American whose mother had been born in India, I wanted to do what I could to heal the still-open wounds between South Asia's two nuclear neighbors. In 2002, we made Tappan our home base. Most Muslims were recoiling from George W. Bush's America. But where Bush's fight was expanding, so was mine. It was time to fight a new jihad for peace on our wounded planet.

I didn't have to wait long for the struggle to begin.

In 2004, I went on a trip to a place I'd only known through my grandfather's stories. Before he died in 1991, Aba had urged me to visit his birthplace in Patiala, located in what's now the Indian state of Punjab. In late February of that year, Junoon and I were there for a concert, and Aba and Ami Aziza and my mother were there with me in soul if not in body.

When I was a young boy in Lahore, Aba told me many tales about the partition of the subcontinent and about our family's life near what's now the city of Patiala. Aba—whose given name Habib means "beloved" in Arabic—himself seemed like a character right out of a story. He was a tall, proud family man with an infectious laugh and a fondness for Tolstoy's *War and Peace*. He had piercing brown eyes and a wide forehead, and was always clean-shaven. He also had the best collection of headgear I'd ever seen: one day he'd wear a faded gray safari hat, another day it would be a red fez, and on other days he'd sport a Peshawari *topi*. Sometimes he wore sunglasses, and with his dark, handsome features he could have easily passed for a movie star.

As we approached Patiala on the tour bus from Delhi, I saw golden wheat fields and green, leafy pipal and mango trees. I breathed in the cool air and stared at all the scenery, trying to imagine my mother as a child riding with Aba and Ami Aziza from their nearby village into Patiala.

As we got into the city, I remembered to take snapshots for my mother. Through my camera's lens I saw a young kid in a blue *patka*, the traditional Sikh headgear, holding his mother's hand crossing the road. There were women wearing yellow, green, and red *chunnies* (scarves) and *parandas* (hair ribbons), coming out of small bakeries and dry fruit markets. I could smell fresh fruit and flowers near the ancient Sikh *gurdwaras* and Hindu temples and stopped to explore the imposing Qila Mubarak, a beautiful 240-year-old fort with intricate rust-colored arches and square wood-framed windows. The atmosphere was serene and peaceful, and I could smell *chambeli* flowers and sweet *agarbati* (incense). It was hard to believe that this easy-going place was the same one that my mother had had to flee as a four-year-old when the chaos of Partition ruled and peace was an elusive dream for the people of the just-created countries of India and Pakistan.

Patiala had been my maternal ancestors' home for more than three centuries. Like many other places in India, it had been touched by dark fate and tragedy after the British re-drew India's borders in 1947. After almost a century of soul-crushing colonial rule, the Raj could no longer sustain its power to deny 350 million Hindus, Sikhs, and Muslims their right to freedom and self-governance. The British left in August 1947. But instead of experiencing a peaceful transfer of power from the ruler to the ruled, India was engulfed in a bloody religious turf battle that resulted in a predominantly Hindu and Sikh India and a Muslim-majority West and East Pakistan. My Muslim family was just one forced to leave majority-Sikh and -Hindu Patiala.

I'm lucky to have heard Aba's stories at all. Having fled Patiala and sent his family off from the train station in Delhi toward Lahore, my mother's father got caught in the middle of a mob fight in Delhi and had to lie among the corpses pretending to be dead. All around were tell-tale signs of extinguished lives: children's toys, a broken mirror, a turban, an overturned solitary *chappal* (sandal), and bodies of men, women, and even children, marinated in blood. Lying helplessly among the decaying bodies on that awful night deeply affected his perception of life. All at once, Aba understood the fragility of human existence and the destructiveness of the ego. Sprawled there amid the carnage, he silently repeated a verse from the Quran.

"Y'Allah ya Salamo," Aba said to himself over and over. "God, let peace and harmony prevail."

On the February day of our concert in Patiala, I thanked God that my family had survived the tragedy of 1947 and was able to start life all over again in Lahore. I was also experiencing harmony in my mom's old hometown. Onstage with Junoon, I felt kissed by the soul of the city as the boisterous Punjabi crowd lost themselves in the accelerating *bhangra*/rock rhythms and roared with approval as we sang the Sufi classic "Dum Mustt Qalandar." More than ten thousand people came out to see Junoon perform at the outdoor concert held at the Yadavindra Public School that cool winter night. We were welcomed like long-lost friends and embraced by the entire music-loving city.

Junoon had come to perform at the closing ceremony of the Patiala heritage festival, and the audience included the then-chief minister of Indian Punjab, the former Army captain Amarinder Singh and his family. At the time of our arrival, everyone knew Junoon and its music but no one in Patiala knew my family's connection to the city. It went way back: my great-great-great-great grandfather had been Namdar Khan, a member of the Council of Regents of the princely state of Patiala when Amarinder's grandfather Bhupinder Singh was enthroned as maharaja at the age of nine in 1900. Namdar Khan had also been a guardian of the maharaja's in the ruler's teenage-firebrand years. The young maharaja was very fond of Namdar Khan and his family, and in recognition of his services to the state named a city road after him following Namdar's death. This was just one example of the kind of religious and cultural harmony that existed before Partition, Aba had told me. A Sikh maharaja had gone so far as to name a road after his Muslim guardian.

At first I didn't feel the need to share my ancestor's story with anyone in town. Why would anyone in Patiala remember an old Muslim man from a bygone era?

But my brother Sherry and I had an idea. Sherry had come to Patiala as Junoon's manager, and it dawned on us that telling Patiala about Namdar Khan could be a way of bringing back a lost time for many Indian and Pakistani families who had similar stories of shared friendships. There was a lot of pain to heal. So many Indian and Pakistani soldiers had died fighting against each other in the wars since Partition. Captain Amarinder's own book *Lest We Forget* chronicles his experiences in the bloody battles that he fought for India, including those against Pakistan. Many of my own family members skirmished with Indian forces. My mother's younger brother Farooq—also born in Patiala—died at the young age of forty in the line of duty for the Pakistan Air Force. He had fought in the 1965 and 1971 wars against India. Like Captain Amarinder Singh, Wing Commander Farooq H. Khan was a proud soldier who defended his country till his last breath. Farooq *mamun* once told me that he wanted to live to see the day when he could visit his birthplace. Now Sherry and I were fulfilling the dream of our departed loved one. We wanted to share that bridge-building spirit with everyone.

But Sherry and I also had other, more immediate reasons for wanting to tell Namdar Khan's story. It was Sherry who decided that the best way to find out where our mother was born was to tell the story of Namdar Khan to the press. The next day, the resulting story in *The Times of India* started a chain reaction. "Junoon has Patiala ancestry!" read one headline. Shortly after everybody got their morning papers, we got a message at our hotel from Maharani Preneet Kaur, saying that her husband, Captain Amarinder, would like to see us for tea that afternoon at the Moti Bagh Palace.

Captain Amarinder pulled out all the stops and gave us a royal welcome, having learned that our mother was a native Patialan and we were descendants of Namdar Khan. As soon as I entered the palace, I saw a giant-sized portrait of Maharaja Bhupinder Singh on the left above the spiraling marble staircase with mahogany railings. In the portrait he cut an imposing figure on a royal charger, with a sword in his hand, wearing a white *patka* and a sparkling white pearl necklace on his white *kameez* and *shalwar*. The maharaja's eyes seemed to be staring directly at me, as if he'd been waiting to meet the descendant of Namdar Khan who had made this journey of discovery fifty-seven years after his family fled.

Sherry and I had tea with Captain Amarinder's son, the Yuvraj (crown prince) Raninder Singh and his gracious wife Yuvrani Rishma Kaur and their beautiful girls. The conversation veered naturally to my family's roots and to cricket. During the courtesy visit I asked the burly Captain Amarinder if it was possible to locate my ancestors' homes. He let out a hearty laugh.

"The city house of your great-great-great-great grandfather is still standing on Namdar Khan Road!" he said.

"Your trip has all been arranged," the chief minister said proudly.

Amazingly, the road had retained my ancestor's name even after the wars and violence of the past half century. Captain Amarinder had also given instructions to Tejveer Singh, the deputy commissioner of Patiala, to locate my mother's family's house. Called Ashraf Manzil, it stands in what is now the town of Bassi Pathanan.

There in the Moti Bagh Palace I was transported back to another time. The big-hearted grandson of Maharaja Bhupinder Singh took us on a tour of his family estate, which was loaded with priceless art, a Raj-era palace full of historical photographs, swords, and paintings, and a room with a huge collection of medals from world wars I and II. Outside the tastefully decorated interiors were vast lawns lined with acacia, mango, guava, and banana trees. Beyond the horses' stables lay a courtyard where a *bara-dari*—a houselike structure with twelve doors—glistened in the late afternoon sunlight. Close to the Moti Bagh Palace was a beautiful cricket ground. I had stepped into a dream.

The sight of the cricket ground brought back my favorite of Aba's Patiala stories.

"Once upon a time, Guploo [my childhood nickname]," my grandfather told me with a twinkle in his eye, "the Patiala cricket team beat the Marylebone Cricket Club in an unforgettable match!" Captain Maharaja Bhupinder Singh's team of Sikh, Muslim, and Hindu amateurs took on the formidable touring MCC (England team) when it was captained by one of England's most famous cricketers, Douglas Jardine. As Aba told it, Maharaja Bhupinder Singh was a colorful giant of a man and had fathered eighty-eight children from ten wives and assorted concubines. The maharaja had been good to my family, but he was a fierce and uncompromising competitor against his enemies on the field and off. He was a passionate cricketer and well aware of the psychological advantages that could come from beating the British—for his people and for his own pride and royal standing.

He had a pit-bull mentality and was determined not to let Jardine's team intimidate him or the eleven members of Patiala's talented team. To give off an air of confidence and relaxation, the maharaja even invited the enemy to his palace. The tall, aquiline-nosed Jardine was of Scottish stock but had been born in Mumbai. Jardine arrived with his merry men all immaculately turned out, wearing blue English blazers, white shirts, flannels, and caps embossed with the imposing MCC insignia. Jardine himself was decked out in a harlequin cap to show off his upper-class Oxbridge pedigree. The Brits' swagger and outfits said it all: they wanted to trounce Patiala. And in their arrogance they figured this game would be a walkover.

During net practice at the Patiala cricket ground, the British sized up the opposition and decided that they weren't up to international standards. So the Brits decided to relax and enjoy the sights and the food and drink instead.

The maharaja offered the British a sample of his royal hospitality, suggesting a partridge hunt and inviting them to experience rich Punjabi cuisine in luxurious surroundings. Jardine and his men were in for a surprise, though, the night before the big game.

That evening, there was a special banquet at the palace where the unsuspecting MCC cricketers were invited to taste delicious *ladoos* from the royal kitchen, which the maharaja's *khaansama* (chef) had prepared especially for the Brits. *Ladoos* are made of flour, raisins, almonds, and cardamom. Formed into balls, they are dipped in sugar syrup and are a food for festive occasions.

"Mun meetha kariye," (enjoy a sweet mouthful), said the maharaja, and the MCC cricketers tore into the *ladoos*, not knowing that the loyal *khaansama* had also mixed the ceremonial sweets with *bhang*—a hemp plant. *Bhang* was known to be a holy drug and could scare away demons but wasn't as effective at enhancing hand-eye coordination.

"*Aba, phir kya hua?*" (and then what happened?), I'd ask as my grandfather weaved his tale.

Aba would throw his head back, shut his eyes, furrow his bushy eyebrows, and let out a huge laugh. And then for dramatic effect he would lean forward into the *paan daan* (betel leaf tray), spit out some red betel juice and *chaalia* (areca nut), and declare: "*Bus beta hona kya tha?*" (Son, what else could've happened?!) The "*bewaqoof gorey*" (stupid white men) "*teen din London ghoom aye*" (were transported back to London). They didn't know what hit them and were so deliriously high they were hardly able to stand the next day, much less play.

During the match, the MCC players couldn't quite figure out which of the three cricket balls they imagined hurtling their way was the real one. And so the mighty MCC were all bundled out for a very low score, much to the delight of the large crowd. The Patiala batsmen, energized by their bowlers' *ladoo*-inspired domination and the MCC's lack of foot (and brain) work, just had a ball in the field. For the coup de grace, the maharaja strode out to bat in his royal blue *patka* and whites and winked at the befuddled Jardine as he passed him by, while the Patiala fans in their colorful *patkas*, *topis*, *burqas*, *parandas*, and *chunnies* cheered his every step to the wicket. To add to the drama, there was a yellow and green *dhoti-* and turban-clad *bhangra dhol* band performing in sync to every pull, cut, and drive that the maharaja played to the listless MCC bowlers. Their line and length had been stolen from their senses and replaced with the sweet smell of *bhang*! Patiala's "victory" was wildly applauded by Hindus, Muslims, and Sikhs alike. In Aba's telling, it was a special year when Patiala trounced Douglas Jardine's MCC good and proper, thanks to an unknown *khaansama* and his unique spirit of Patiala freedom.

My head was filled with those stories throughout my visit. I also kept singing "Ghoom Tana," a song I had composed for Junoon's album *Deewar (Wall)*. As I thought about the song's message of the circle of life continuing, a light bulb went on. I had to re-record the song and make a video in light of my journey to Patiala. Doing so would also pay tribute to the rich musical vibe of the Patiala *gharana* (stylistic schools of artists linked by lineage or apprenticeship), from which many great classical Pakistani singers and musicians like Ustad Amanat Ali Khan and Ustad Fateh Ali Khan had their roots. A music video would be an audio-visual memento of the story I yearned to tell of the two cities of Lahore and Patiala, and two countries and two peoples. "Ghoom Tana" is on my 2005 solo album *Infiniti*.

On my visit I became determined to film the music video in Patiala. But I couldn't just bring a cast and crew into the city without permission. So I floated the "Ghoom Tana" idea to Captain Amarinder.

He jumped at the proposal.

"The doors of the city will be open to you and your camera crew whenever you decide to shoot!" he told me.

The shooting would come several weeks later. First, we had to visit Namdar Khan's house in the heart of Patiala city, which we did with protocol normally accorded to foreign dignitaries—complete with a police escort and a press junket on our tails. The quaint colonial-era house was well-maintained despite its age; and the current occupants, Sandeep Singh Sandha and his family, embraced us and took us in as if we were their own kin. They were living examples of a famous Patiala motto "*Mera Ghar Tera Saya*" (My House is Your Shelter). All of this local warmth was completely enchanting.

Seeing Namdar Khan's house was wonderful. But the emotional effect was nothing compared to visiting the house where my mother was born. I couldn't just casually wander into it, though. There was so much history, joyous and painful, that surrounded my visit. Aba had told me everything.

Before Partition, Aba and Ami Aziza lived in what was then a family village called Bassi Pathanan in the Fatehgarh Sahib district of the princely state of Patiala. My mother's Khan clan had originally come from Afghanistan. Most of them were either landowning farmers or worked for the state government in the judiciary or law enforcement agencies, alongside their Hindu and Sikh counterparts. During the Raj, Patiala was ruled by a Sikh maharaja. Although it was still a part of British India, Patiala had a great deal of autonomy and managed to avoid the racist and humiliating experience of direct colonial rule.

But Partition uprooted my family and flung it across the subcontinent. For Aba, my mother, and the rest of their family, the roughly 150-mile journey from Patiala to Lahore meant crossing the line between life and death as well as stepping blindly from the old, familiar colonial past into a new and uncertain Pakistani future. In all, more than 12 million people were rendered homeless by Partition and pitched into a forced exodus to seek out new homes—new lives—anywhere they could find them. As many as one million people died.

Before they got to Pakistan, my relatives were spared the tragic fate of many others by a combination of things. First, perhaps, was their will to survive, but they were also aided by *farishtas* (angels), including the Sikh maharaja's wife, who forbade the angry mobs from harming the residents of my family's village. Once my family left Patiala and the maharani's protection, however, they were on their own, and vulnerable to attack. Some of my family members rode on the backs of trucks, crammed into square wooden boxes, barely able to breathe and carrying nothing but the clothes on their backs. Some were luckier and got onto trains with a few suitcases of clothes, a little money, and a lot of memories. But there was danger even then: on one of these trains, my mother's uncles found themselves with a large number of Hindus and Sikhs going to Delhi. They overheard some of them boasting that they'd just sliced to death a whole Muslim family fleeing the Punjab.

"That's cold-blooded murder!" Uncle Latafat blurted out.

"Don't worry yourself, brother," one of the men said to him, mistaking him for a Hindu. "All is fair in love and war."

Uncle Latafat said he felt death circling close to him and mentally prepared himself to suffer the same fate as other unlucky Muslims. During Partition, one's name alone could be a death sentence. Everyone knew that Khan was a Muslim surname and that Singh and Sharma respectively denoted Sikhs and Hindus. But Latafat and my mother's other uncle Taufiq, escaped death, thanks to a kindly Sikh railway porter who saved them by hiding their luggage—which bore their obviously Muslim names. The porter was cruelly repaid for his humanity to my family, though: after news of his deed leaked, he was severely beaten by other passengers.

Members of my family also did what they could to help friends and neighbors, my father told me. A phone call to Abu's father, Rashid Ahmad, saved the lives of a Hindu man named Mr. Dwarkadas, and his family, who owned a chemist-and-general store in Anarkali Bazaar in Lahore. A raging Muslim mob had surrounded the place and was ready to burn the family alive, but after getting the call, my grandfather—then working as a secretary and advisor to the British governor of Punjab—arrived with the military police just in time to save the Hindu family and their property from going up in flames. Mr. Dwarkadas later wrote my grandfather a letter bidding both him and Lahore goodbye and leaving his family's valuables, including a necklace, in Rashid Ahmad's safe keeping. I remembered that letter as I walked around the streets of Patiala.

We visited what was left of Aba and Ami Aziza's house after seeing Namdar Khan's house. To get there, we drove for about twenty minutes on the Grand Trunk Road. Our police escorts then bid us adieu, since we were passing out of their jurisdiction and into Bassi Pathanan. From then on, local journalists, who'd done their homework, led us to Ashraf Manzil. We walked through winding streets and finally came across a broken-down shell of a Franco-Persian style property. As Sherry and I walked into the courtyard a flock of doves flew skyward as if to celebrate our homecoming. As we explored the house I'd only known previously through Aba's stories, an old-timer named Shyamlal Singh stopped by. Mr. Singh was a childhood friend of Aba's. Mr. Singh shared a story about Aba, who was the first to get wheels in Bassi and rode his bike throughout the village. Sometimes, recounted Shyamlal, he'd ride "pillion" on the back of Aba's bike and sing a song by the famous Indian singer K. L. Saigol.

"*Jab dil hi toot gya*" went the song.

"After the heart is broken, what is there to live for?"

Shyamlal's eyes welled up with tears when he found out that Aba was no longer with us, having passed on thirteen years earlier. It brought back for my grandfather's old friend, in sharp focus, the memory of those shared times and the pain of separation caused by the twists of history.

As soon as I left Patiala, I went on a search for the right voices, faces, and talent that would form the video complement to "Ghoom Tana"'s message of harmony. The story of the video (shot in Lahore and Patiala) involves a Pakistani man (played by me) crossing the "Line of Control" at the Wagah village that separates Pakistan and India to return a family necklace. The necklace was left in Lahore for safekeeping with my character's grandfather by his Hindu neighbor, who had to flee to Patiala after Partition. The idea was inspired by Mr. Dwarkadas's leaving his valuables with my family. Making the journey across the physical and psychological divide that separates Pakistan from India, the Pakistani learns that there are no demons lurking on the other side of the line, just people like him. He also discovers the generous spirit of Patiala's residents and finds himself attracted to a beautiful but heartbroken Indian woman. My character becomes pals with her young son, who has lost his soldier-father. The visuals show the emotional arc of the woman and the man overcoming history and going beyond the tragedy of loss and division into a deeper consciousness of compassion and acceptance of each other.

Having imagined the video, I'd decided on a duet and needed a woman's voice to contrast with mine. I shared my vision of the song and video with my close friends from Karachi, Delhi, Lahore, and Mumbai and was instantly awash in a tidal wave of support and good ideas. My Indian-journalist friend from Delhi, Vatsala Kaul, suggested that Indian classical singer Shubha Mudgal provide the female voice. Returning to Delhi from Patiala, I turned up at Shubha's house with Vatsala with an audio demo of "Ghoom Tana" in my hand. Before she could say anything, I popped the demo CD into her player. After only one listening and a cup of Indian *chai*, she said, "So when are we recording?" Shubha's enthusiasm and her brilliant, flourishing classical vocals ignited everyone's *junoon*.

Inspired by Aba's stories of courageous human deeds during Partition, I wanted Indo-Pak collaboration to be the creative foundation of the project. The universe conspired to give me what I wanted. My director, Karachi-based Saqib Malik, came onboard with his production team, the cinematographer Sanjay Kapoor and Bollywood film producer Shahnaab Alam. Sanjay's the son of an Indian father and Pakistani mother who live in America. I also managed a coup by getting the Indian movie star and a good friend, Naseer ud din Shah, to do a voice-over. I wanted to use the words of Mr. Dwarkadas's letter to my grandfather at the beginning of the video, and Naseer's powerfully expressive voice was perfect for the job. The exceptionally gifted Naseer—a star of Mira Nair's *Monsoon Wedding*—is an instantly recognized film and theater actor who commands megabucks for his roles and is perpetually booked. Yet he set aside everything to do this labor of love for me. "Music is the speech of angels and can make people come together," Naseer told me. Besides, he said, he'd always wanted to be part of a rock music album.

The "Ghoom Tana" team was quickly assembling, but we still had no leading lady. That was critical. And it was critical to the project that she be Indian. There are tons of Pakistani "experts" on Indian actresses with well-researched tabloid knowledge and strong likes and dislikes, and I started getting advice from everyone and his uncle. The Pakistani brigade spiritedly advised: if you want the video to be a big hit in Pakistan, get someone with big boobs! Friends, Junoonis, and their conservative cousins all started offering comments and quips about Indian actresses: Aishwarya Rai ("she's beautiful but too skinny to be a Punjabi woman"), Preity Zinta ("she looks British!"), Sushmita Sen ("she's too brainy and too tall"), Bipasha Basu ("I hear she's got a jealous boyfriend"), and Kajol ("she won't shoot in the April heat of Patiala!"). These are all gorgeous and talented Indian actresses. But I made up my mind after getting a phone call from my Delhi soulfriend and social entrepreneur Nanni Singh. That morning, Nanni had read a story about the actor and director Nandita Das. Nandita—star of *Earth* and Merchant-Ivory's *Before the Rains*—was about to take a cricket team of blind Indian kids to Pakistan. The kids would play in different cities and share their vision for peace and their sporting spirit with their Pakistani neighbors. The mention of cricket clinched it for me. Before returning to New York, I called Nandita from the JW Marriott in Mumbai and conveyed the musical spirit of "Ghoom Tana." Our first phone call was as natural a connection between two artists as you could ask for. First Shubha, now Nandita. It was as if I'd known them all my life. Nandita was psyched and connected perfectly with the groove of the project, agreeing to appear in her first music video. To the satisfaction of all Junoonis in Pakistan I managed to find an Indian actress with beauty, brains, boobs, and a heart!

We shot the music video from April 10 to 14, 2004, coinciding with the Good Friday and Easter holidays. Prophet Jesus's timeless message of loving your neighbor was an added inspiration throughout the video shoot in Patiala, which included the Namdar Khan house, thanks to the generosity of Sandeep Singh Sandha and his family. (The Lahore part of the shoot took place later, in July.) The Sandhas gave us total access, as did Captain Amarinder Singh, who literally handed us the keys to the city. Details of the entire project were firmed up by phone calls, e-mails, and text messages. I also funded the whole thing with my own savings because no record company would risk its money on a "peace project" between two enemy countries. I wrote the music and lyrics and recorded the song with a U2-meets-Amir-Khusro-meets-Bollywood vibe in Karachi, Mumbai, and New York. To get a George Harrison feel, I played slide guitar on the track at John Alec's Grand View studios. John co-produced it with me, thus bringing the song full circle to complete my PIA (Pakistani, Indian, and American) roots. Everything was done on instinct and faith, and a tight schedule.

I flew to Delhi from New York on April 9, two months after my first visit to Patiala. I breathed a sigh of relief when I heard from my highly anxious (but highly talented) Pakistani video director Saqib Malik. "Thank God, *yaar*, our Indian visas were finally approved at the last possible moment.

"But everybody at the Indian embassy in Islamabad is very suspicious of this Indo-Pak project," he said. "They're asking, 'what are so many Pakistanis going to be doing in Patiala for four days?'"

That was understandable. After so much war and violence since Partition, one could forgive the Indian immigration authorities for being a little leery about infiltration from the west. But this was a different kind of Pakistani "guerilla" movement into India.

The shooting finally got started in the bustle of Patiala city. Patiala's streets were a writhing mass of bikes, cars, and motor scooters jostling for space among male and female pedestrians in colorful *patkas* and *shalwar kameez*. For the shoot, I wore a green *kurta*, a Lahori vest, and blue jeans, and carried my travel guitar and a knapsack on my shoulder. We were supposed to shoot a scene which involved Nandita. She wore a white *shalwar kameez*, with her hair tied in a pony tail, and drove a Vespa around a narrow, crooked lane in the middle of a crowded women's clothing bazaar. Our first on-camera meeting called for her to accidentally bump into me while riding the scooter. We all thought that would be a simple enough way to get things rolling.

It was anything but. With the film crew in place, Saqib shouted "Action!" Nandita revved up the engine and the scooter moved about an inch forward and then sputtered to a shaky halt. My co-star had a confession to make.

"Salman, I've never actually driven a scooter before in my life," she whispered nervously, as hundreds of expectant fans looked on.

I tried to calm her jangly nerves and said, "You only have to drive 100 feet; how difficult could that be?"

After a moment's hesitation she smiled and said, "Okay, fine, I'll do it. But somebody start this thing for me."

By the twentieth take the crowded bazaar had cleared out in self-preservation because the wild Nandita scooter was on the loose and out of control. Saqib would shout "action" and then immediately take cover as she came racing down the streets of Patiala with a vengeance. On a few occasions, Sanjay and I found ourselves running for our lives as she accidentally accelerated instead of squeezing back the brake handle. As the intended target of her scooter, I could imagine the headlines: "Pakistani musician killed by Indian actress in Patiala"! I'd gladly die for the cause of peace, but this wasn't the kind of sacrifice I envisioned. By the time she got it right, Saqib screamed into the megaphone, "Cut! Print! Take me back home!" None of these bloopers made it into the final product, of course. But maybe it's just as well for Indo-Pak peace that they didn't.

Since the release of the "Ghoom Tana" video and song, I've received a flood of emotional e-mails from Indians and Pakistanis who have journeyed across the border to visit their ancestral birthplaces. I've also met scores of newlywed Indian and Pakistani couples all over the world who have told me they were inspired to tie the marriage knot by "Ghoom Tana"'s message. Top Indian and Pakistani humanitarians, entrepreneurs, and business leaders like Amin Hashwani, Sunil Munjal, and Ajay Khanna co-sponsored screenings of "Ghoom Tana" in Karachi and Delhi which were attended by the entire cast, production teams, movers, shakers, and newsmakers, and diplomats of both countries. On August 14 and 15, 2004, on Pakistan's and India's independence days, the "Ghoom Tana" video and its unlikely story of artists coming together for peace started playing in heavy rotation on Pakistani musical channels (including the historically anti-Indian PTV) and music and news channels in India. I received messages of congratulations from politicians, leaders, and diplomats, including then-President Musharraf. India's former foreign minister Natwar Singh, former foreign secretary Shiv Shankar Menon, and India's top diplomat in Pakistan, T.C.A. Raghavan, all wrote with warm praise.

But the most moving good wishes came from my mother's relatives, like Uncle Latafat, the train survivor, and also the Sikh residents of Namdar Khan Road, Patiala, and Bassi. Throughout the making of the "Ghoom Tana" song and video, I had felt the spirits of Namdar Khan, Aba, Ami Aziza, and my Uncle Farooq cheering and urging me on. My mother wrote a heartfelt letter of thanks to Captain Amarinder, expressing her hope that the vision of compassion and acceptance that "Ghoom Tana" depicted could become a reality for all Indians and Pakistanis in her lifetime. In return, Captain Amarinder and his wife sent a special

Patiala shawl for my mother as a symbol of protection and their shared hopes for the future.

In 1998, Junoon had been banned in Pakistan for singing songs about harmony and conflict resolution. By 2004, our music was the soundtrack to a cross-border celebration. But I wasn't going to rest. There was still another place I wanted the circle of life to take me.

During Junoon's 1998 tour of India, I got tons of e-mails and letters from people in Kashmir, the divided region of the subcontinent. I read them all, one by one, and made a *niyaat* (sacred intention) to one day travel to and perform in the Indian side of the ethereal Kashmir valley. The Kashmiris' gentle Sufi hearts had bled rose-red over the years in the crossfire of Indo-Pak politics. With Pakistan-backed militants on one side of their neighborhood and Indian soldiers on the other, Kashmiris were tired and aching to hear a different kind of music.

Young people in the capital of Srinagar were insisting that Junoon come and play in their city. Their *junoon* became my *junoon*, and I shared their messages of love and yearning with our Indian tour promoter. But he just rolled his eyes.

"I know that Junoon means obsession bordering on madness, but to go to Kashmir to play a rock concert would be the height of lunacy!" he said. "None of us would come back alive, Salman!"

I knew the history of strife-torn Kashmir as well as anyone. It's the core issue of contention between India and Pakistan. Kashmir has a predominantly Muslim population, and it's claimed by both countries as their own property. But even in the zero-sum game of Indo-Pak politics there's room to change the conversation from hate to love. That's what I wanted to do with my guitar—and that's what the kids wanted, too.

"Times will change, Venkat," I told the promoter. "One day Junoon will perform in Kashmir."

Venkat just laughed and shook his head.

"Not in this lifetime, Salman," he said. "Don't let your idealism make you jump off a cliff!"

I had to wait ten years to prove Venkat wrong. The dust of the 1999 war in Kashmir had to settle down, as did the flap over Pakistan's and India's nuclear tests and the fallout of 9/11. There'd also been a change in Junoon's lineup. Ali had embarked on a solo career in 2005 and since

2002, Brian's personal troubles had left him unable to focus on music. But tension was in the air even in May 2008, when I finally set foot in Kashmir with my guitar.

We arrived in Srinagar in late May 2008 at the invitation of the South Asian Foundation and SAF founder and UNESCO goodwill ambassador Madanjeet Singh. Singh, an intrepid octogenarian, had seen Junoon perform at the Nobel Peace Prize ceremony in December 2007, the year Al Gore and Dr. Rajendra Pachauri of the Intergovernmental Panel on Climate Change shared the prize. Like me, Madanjeet had a dream to smell roses and not gunpowder in the valley of Kashmir, and for songs to fill the air once again.

But on May 24, we touched down in a virtual combat zone. I was whisked from the airport to our hotel in a bullet-proof Jeep accompanied by my New Jersey friend and Bengali *tabla* maestro, Pandit Samir Chatterjee; Brooklyn-based drummer Sunny Jain; Canadian bassist Chris Tarry; and my lovely new manager, Samina. A convoy of armed vehicles surrounded us united artists and our entourage. I wanted to smell the fragrant air of the beautiful valley around us. But I couldn't even roll down the windows.

The reason: while thousands of college students wanted us to play, a self-styled group of militants didn't. A day or two before the concert, the United Jehad Council, an umbrella group of Kashmiri militant organizations, had passed a resolution to try to prevent the show from going on. We couldn't play, the militants said, since our concert would have a negative impact on the "disputed status" of Kashmir. Syed Salahuddin, the group's leader, even urged the Pakistani government to stop me from performing—as if Islamabad could have done that! The United Jehad Council wanted to spoil the party for everyone. It was bad enough that they had twisted the meaning of jihad, like others before them. But it got worse.

My chronic case of heartburn surfaced again. Like a few of their unholy predecessors, the United Jehad Council threatened to kill me.

I made it out alive, of course. But the threats against my life especially echoed inside me the afternoon before the show. That evening, all of us in the Junoon party (and nine armed guards) drove up to the Pari Mahal, the angelic abode built by the Mughal prince of peace, Dara Shikoh. Dara, heir apparent of Emperor Shah Jahan, was a Sufi who embodied the all-embracing spirit of Kashmir. The Pari Mahal, Dara's monument to peace, is a series of arched terraces perched high up on a heavenly Himalayan mountain slope. Looking down, I could see our concert stage far below on the eastern edge of the shimmering Dal Lake, the same place where (legend has it) George Harrison received his first sitar lesson from Ravi Shankar. Dara had embarked on a quest for Hindu-Muslim unity but was tortured and beheaded in 1659 by order of his brother Aurangzeb, who eventually became emperor. Dara's sacrifice for loving his neighbors and his quest for spiritual harmony inspired many people, including poets, writers, and musicians like myself. Intolerance had plagued the subcontinent for too long. It was time to confront the ghosts of the past head-on.

The next day at the hotel I sat jamming with Samir, Sunny, and Chris, calming my tense vocal chords and loosening up my restless fingers. The expectant crowds, the Pakistani, Indian and international media hype of the concert, and the UJC's death threats were all swirling around in my head. This was another giant defining moment of my life. What would triumph? The guitars or the guns? Love or hate? Peace or war?

I soon got my answer. By showing up at Junoon's concert, thousands of school and college students voted with their feet and rejected the politics of violence in Kashmir. They sent a clear message to the South Asian Foundation that all Kashmiris deserved to live a life of freedom and dignity. Many of them, girls and boys, jumped over barbed wire and all of them braved the threat of bullets to hear our songs. They walked, hitched rides, and paid scalpers exorbitant sums to come to the venue. They stood for hours in long queues, shrugging off rigorous security checks and the punishing sun. That day nothing was going to dampen their spirits.

A spirited, acoustic bluegrass performance by the The Singhs group warmed up the already bubbling crowd. Then a beautiful Indian woman clad in a white sari went on stage.

"Please welcome for the first time in Kashmir, South Asia's biggest rock band Junoon!" she said.

From that moment on, amidst the roar of the entertainment-starved students, the music possessed the souls of all who had gathered that historic afternoon in Srinagar.

Looking out from the stage I saw screaming and ecstatic kids as well as a VIP cast of South Asian writers, artists, filmmakers, leaders, and even politicians. Like kids in Lahore back in the eighties, Kashmiris were embracing a Rock & Roll Jihad. The UJC was nowhere to be seen. The uncertainty and fear of the previous two days that had gripped all of us just dissipated into the Himalayan ether.

Whatever we sang—"Meri Awaz Suno," Iqbal's "Khudi," Nusrat Fateh Ali Khan's *qawwali*, or Bulleh Shah's poems—the spirits of the people sang louder than us. We played our hearts out, and two hours went by in an instant. Hoarse, high-pitched requests for encores drowned me at the mic as I tried to put a final question to the crowd.

"*Kashmir, bata teri raza kya hai?*" (Kashmir, what destiny do you desire?) I asked.

"*Dosti*"! (Friendship) and "*Sayonee*"! (Soul mate) came the screams for our songs.

As I began to pluck the opening chords of "Sayonee," I gazed out toward the tranquil Dal Lake. I looked up to the west, at the Pari Mahal, and then into the crowd. Some wore *hijabs* and some wore sneakers and all were swaying and dancing like dervishes at the edge of the lake. There were Indians in the audience, and Bangladeshis. There were Afghanis and Pakistanis, and Sri Lankans.

And there were soldiers, uniformed in olive-green and khaki, with their eyes closed and moving to the beat. All were dancing in celebration of peace and oneness. The golden valley of Kashmir was finally echoing with song and laughter. On that blessed day, for a precious few hours, something impossible had become real. The light of hope had begun to burn the veil of darkness.

The sounds of the guitar silenced the guns.

Epilogue

We begin the life that God gave us as seeds. Whether we become musicians, poets, teachers, saints or sinners or soldiers, we are only on this Earth for a short time. The season of the rose won't last forever, as Iqbal wrote. And while on earth, as our inner mystical wheel revolves, we must plant seeds of our own before we return to God.

These days, I'm trying to do my part by planting as many positive seeds as I can. In addition to my work as a musician, I am a documentary presenter, a U.N. HIV/AIDS goodwill ambassador, a speaker, and lately a college professor. I'm still performing my music all over the world—in South Asia, in the U.S., in Europe—and writing new songs. But in the past few years, I've also presented films like *The Rock Star and the Mullahs*, produced and directed by Angus Macqueen and Ruhi Hamid for PBS/ Wide Angle and the BBC. The documentary is about the collision of rock music, politics, and religion in Pakistan—all subjects close to my heart. Working with director Clifford Bestall, I presented the BBC film *It's My Country Too*, which focuses on Muslims living in George W. Bush's post-9/11 America. My song and video "Al-Vida" (Farewell), about a Pakistani woman's fight against HIV/AIDS, helped shine a light on women and HIV/AIDS in Pakistan and in the *desi* diaspora. The "Al-Vida" video reached number one on MTV Desi's charts in 2006. But there's still a lot of work to be done in a region where there's great stigma and discrimination associated with the virus and the disease.

In September 2006 I had the good fortune to meet a peace-mongering Queens College history professor named Mark Rosenblum at a gathering of the Clinton Global Initiative. I was speaking on a panel with my good friends Jeff Skoll of Participant Productions (the production company behind the Oscar winning films *Syriana* and *An Inconvenient Truth*) and Susan Collin Marks of Search for Common Ground (a conflict-resolution nonprofit). At Mark Rosenblum's initiative, I began teaching a course in Muslim music and poetry at Queens College in New York. It's a great gig at an awesome college with students who are as diverse as the planet's population. Only in New York could that be possible. Now, as before, the best way I know how to show people what Islam is really about is through its arts. Nearly ten years after 9/11, it moves my heart to see a mini planet Earth of Queens College students learning the natural intersection of Muslim culture with modern and traditional cultures. It's part of my job to turn them on to the rich and diverse but largely hidden musical heritage of the Muslim world. Mark and I have also put together an interfaith program called Common Chords, which brings together Jewish and Muslim artists, religious leaders and students to come and walk in the other side's shoes. I want to keep cultural connectivity like that going for the rest of my life.

But others will continue to seek to destroy the culture and divine beauty that I and so many others love. I'm writing these lines while traveling between Lahore, Karachi, and Islamabad. Over the past year, parts of Pakistan have come to resemble a horror movie, with the Taliban desperately trying to make inroads further and further into mainstream society. A few weeks before one of my latest visits, the world was shown a sickening video of a young Pakistani girl in a *burqa* being viciously flogged by the Taliban for consorting with a man. A few months before that, the Taliban took over Swat, shutting down girls' schools and destroying movie theaters and music shops. Beating girls, killing and torturing dissenters, cutting up films, and silencing music: that is the extremists' cultural and religious vision of the future of Pakistan and the region. Where the majority of Pakistanis want to grow fragrant flowers, the extremists have sown evil weeds. The Taliban can only be stopped by a united Pakistani civil society (students, lawyers, writers, musicians, teachers, and others) that works with the government, media, and the army to completely reject their vision of hate and violence. Violent extremists are the enemies of Islam and Pakistan.

The Taliban may strengthen and flourish. Or more likely, *inshallah*, their soulless mission of death and destruction will wither and die. Governments will come and go in Pakistan, America, and elsewhere. Darkness and light have alternated for at least the past twenty years in Pakistan, but one thing never changes: the people's spirit. There is now a new generation of Pakistani rock bands and artists, including a growing number of female artists. Women in Pakistani rock and pop were a novelty twenty years ago, but no more. Arts and culture have helped to open the door wider for women. There are also new poets and filmmakers, cricketers, and social workers. Pakistanis dont give up hope—and hope has a wonderful habit of rearing its head when all seems lost: I was dancing in delight like every other Pakistani on June 21, 2009, when the national cricket team came back from the dead to lift the Twenty20 World Cup at Lords Cricket Ground in London. (I was humbled to watch on television the victory celebrations of millions of ecstatic Pakistanis singing "Dil Dil Pakistan" and "Jazba-e Junoon." It would be foolish of me (and beyond the scope of this book) to try to predict Pakistani politics. But I can unequivocally say this: no matter the time, no matter who the politician in power, Pakistanis must always be free to create and compose; be educated; and be entertained by our home-grown music, poetry, films, and art. There's no room in Pakistan for women to be flogged, musicians to be muzzled, cinemas to be locked down, or CDs to be snapped in half. Ever.

That flogging video had a powerful butterfly effect.

I pledged to use all the currency I'd built up in my career to counter the extremists' propaganda of fear and violence. On September 12, 2009, the halls of the United Nations rang out once again with the sounds of unity. Put together by Samina's and my new non-profit, the Salman & Samina Global Wellness Initiative, the "Concert for Pakistan" drew almost 2,000 screaming fans and raised $1 million for rehabilitation of the IDPs and rebuilding girls schools destroyed by the Taliban. I was elated by Jeff Skoll's pledge to help support SSGWI in its mission of social advocacy, and social entrepreneur and business magnate Arif Naqvi and the Aman Foundation came forward to support our humanitarian work. To expand the digital bandwidth of the concert for Pakistan, Chris Gebhardt and TakePart (www.takepart.com/concertforpakistan) took the lead, allowing participants and attendees to share their blogs about a memorable experience.

The spirit of passion is in Pakistanis' DNA. But it's also in the perennial interest of the international community to help see to a thriving arts and culture community in Pakistan, and in the rest of the Muslim world. Artists and humanitarians are the strongest glue between cultures in a world divided by fear and threatened by terrorism. Arts and culture can be mightier than the sword. The people are already going where the leaders should follow. On my tours of the U.S. or Europe, I'll often play before crowds that won't understand the Urdu and Punjabi lyrics I'm singing. But there are scores of people who want to know more about the verses of Bulleh Shah or Iqbal and I'll get flooded with requests for translations or explanations. What gives my audiences and me hope for deeper ties between Islamic and Western culture is that there is love in those lyrics. And there can never be enough love, in any language.

I'm just one person who's trying to live out a journey of light. We can only wake up each day and go out and plow the fields, armed with our God-consciousness and a clear awareness of the purpose of our individual life. In my own case, I try to keep the focus on finding common ground through music and teaching. I plan to keep performing, working with the U.N., and promoting interfaith dialogue and education through our nonprofit organization, Salman and Samina Global Wellness Initiative (SSGWI) around the world. The jihad never ends and my song remains the same. We are all connected and interdependent.

And we all still have so much to teach each other. In 2008, I recorded a song with Melissa Etheridge, a white, Kansas-born lesbian. On the surface we have little in common, but Melissa and I bonded immediately when we met in December 2007 at the Nobel Peace Prize ceremony.

I first heard her sing live from just a few feet away when we were doing sound checks before the Nobel show at the Oslo Spectrum in Norway. I was blown away by the power of Melissa's voice. She and I soon became friends and admirers of each other's music. In January 2008, she invited me to spend a couple of days at her Los Angeles home. Our conversations ran to searching for peace and truth, and how these are universal themes from Rumi to the Beatles. In both East and West, it's poetry and music that unite humanity, not politics, which so often aims to divide and demonize "the Other."

Melissa and I also talked about the children of Abraham: Jesus, Moses, and Muhammad, may God's peace be upon them, and their common spirit of brotherhood and sacrifice. We sat with acoustic guitars and out of that intense talking and jamming came our song "Ring the Bells." "Ring The Bells" is a cry for peace and change in a world of war and chaos.

We launched a "Ring the Bells" peace campaign with our dear friend Deepak Chopra, who supported us through his Alliance for a New Humanity. Participant Productions and Search for Common Ground have also come onboard to make a music video of "Ring the Bells." To heal the deep divisions of race, religion, and region, all of us must ring the bells of peace. All of us must plant the seeds of unity.

Melissa and I began as perfect strangers. But we took each other on a journey into a common space where definitions fell apart. It's the kind of cross-cultural journey I've been taking all my life, and will continue to take. It's the journey my mother took as a fresh-faced AFS student in the 1960s, and the journey that Brian and John Alec made when they came to Pakistan to join their old friend. Anything is possible when we embrace the unknown. When we listen to each other's music and laugh at one another's jokes, we also learn to look at the world through a new lens.

When we see with the heart, all the masks fall down.

Discography & Filmography

All albums, videos, films, and merchandise available from www.junoon.com.

Albums

Vital Signs 1
EMI Pakistan, 1989
Single: "Dil Dil Pakistan"

Junoon (*Obsession*)
EMI Pakistan, 1991
Singles: "Khwab," "Neend Ati Nahin," "Heer"

Talaash (*The Search*)
EMI Pakistan, 1993
Singles: "Heeray," "Talaash"

Inquilaab (*Revolution*)
VCI Records, 1996
Singles: "Jazba-e-Junoon" "Saeein," "Dosti"

Kashmakash (*Introspection*)
VCI Records, 1996
Singles: "Ehtesaab"

Azadi (*Freedom*)
EMI Arabia/VCI Records, 1997
Singles: "Khudi," "Meri Awaz Suno," "Sayonee," "Yaar Bina"

Dosti/Compilation (*Friendship*)
EMI Arabia/Virgin Records India, 1998

Parvaaz (*The Flight*)
EMI Arabia/Lips Records, 1999
Singles: "Bulleya," "Ghoom," "Mitti," "Sajna," "Pyaar Bina"

Millennium 1990–2000
Lips Records, 2000
Singles: "Azadi," "Muk Gaye," "Allah Hu (Live)"

Andaz/Ishq (*Love*)
EMI Arabia/Lips Records, 2001
Singles: "Kaisey Gaon," "Sheeshay ka Ghar," "Dharti key Khuda"

Daur-E-Junoon (*The Era of Junoon*)
Sadaf Stereo, 2002
Single: "Garaj Baras" "Piya (Ocean of Love)," "Pyar hai Zindagi," "Saeein at Roskilde"

Dewaar (*The Wall*)
Sadaf Stereo, 2003

The Best of Junoon
EMI Arabia/Virgin Records India, 2003
Singles: "No More," "Khudi,"

Infiniti
Nameless Sufi Records, 2005
Singles: "Ghoom Tana," "Al-Vida," "Sagar," "Nachoon Gi"

Rock and Roll Jihad
nameless sufi music 2010

Singles

"(What's So Funny 'Bout) Peace, Love and Understanding"
(Theme song for The CW's *Aliens in America*)
CBS Records, 2007
With P.J. Olsson

"Ring the Bells" (from the album *A New Thought for Christmas*)
Island Records, 2008
With Melissa Etheridge

Music for Film and Television Soundtracks

The Princess and the Playboy
Correspondent/BBC, 1996

War and Peace, 2000

Islamabad: Rock City
VH1, 2001

The Rock Star and the Mullahs
PBS/Wide Angle, 2003

It's My Country Too
BBC World, 2005

Sufi Soul
Riverboat, 2005

Aliens in America
The CW, 2007

New Muslim Cool
Specific Pictures, 2009
(For music licensing requests: josh@leopoldmanagement.com)

Documentary Appearances

The Princess and the Playboy (Thea Guest / Jane Corbin)
Assignment/BBC, 1997

War and Peace (Anand Patwardhan), 2000
VH1, 2001

Islamabad: Rock City (Richard Murphy / Lucas Traub)
VH1, 2001

The Rock Star and the Mullahs (Angus Macqueen / Ruhi Hamid)
PBS/Wide Angle, 2003

It's My Country Too (Clifford Bestall / Ruhi Hamid)
BBC World, 2005

Sufi Soul (Simon Broughton / William Dalrymple)
Riverboat, 2005

Websites

www.junoon.com
www.ssgwi.org
www.unaids.org
(All Junoon music available on music sites, including I-tunes)
(All Junoon videos, merchandise, and Salman Ahmad documentaries can be ordered from www.junoon.com or by writing to saminadr@gmail.com)

Acknowledgments

This book would not have manifested itself if I hadn't seen or heard *qawwali*, the Beatles, Led Zeppelin, or Bollywood music. I'm deeply indebted to my wife, Samina, for keeping my old and tattered school and college journals intact despite my best efforts to lose them. Those journals provided the raw material and stream of consciousness to help shape this narrative, and Samina's undying devotion, culinary gifts, and good cheer kept me going through the many difficult and slow grinding days.

Shukriya to my worldly wise literary agent Richard Abate, who introduced me to a wonderful publishing house like Simon & Schuster, and thanks to my incisive and supportive editor and her colleagues Kirsa Rein, Carol de Onís, Jennifer Weidman, Andrew Dodds, and Alison Pantelic.

I'm obliged also for the literary assistance of a wonderful writer and kindred spirit, Robert Schroeder, aka Mojo Chacha, who provided me with excellent writing support and painstaking research and managed to stay calm and professional during my Junooni flights of ideas. Thanks also to the positive support of Amin Hashwani and Todd Patkin, dear friends who are a wellspring of inspiration from across the Arabian sea to the Boston Harbor.

For infusing me with a fresh perspective, many thanks to Jeff Skoll, Walter Parkes, Cory Ondrejka, Peter Singer, Cynthia Schneider, Michael Wolfe, Vatsala, and my sister, Sania.

Some of the bedtime stories that I've told my three sons over the years have found themselves in this book, so a great debt of gratitude goes out to Shamyl, Sherjan, and Imran for being a willing, patient, and critical audience.

Shukriya to Ami and Abu, this book would not be complete without you.

And finally I bow my head to the Almighty without whom nothing is possible: *Allahu Akbar!*

About the Author

Salman Ahmad is a Pakistani-American rock star whose band, Junoon, has sold over 30 million albums. A medical doctor by training, Salman currently travels the globe as a United Nations Goodwill Ambassador, spreading a message of harmony and reconciliation between the West and the Muslim world. He was a featured performer at the 2007 Nobel Peace Prize ceremony, alongside musical superstars such as Alicia Keys, Melissa Etheridge, and Annie Lennox. He currently teaches a course on Muslim music and poetry at the City University of New York's Queens College campus. Salman and his wife, Samina, run a nonprofit organization, SSGWI, which promotes interfaith dialogue and education through arts and culture. Salman spends his free time moving between Pakistan and Rockland County, New York, with Samina and their three sons, Shamyl, Sherjan, and Imraan.

JAICO PUBLISHING HOUSE

Elevate Your Life. Transform Your World.

Established in 1946, Jaico Publishing House is the publisher of stellar authors such as Sri Sri Paramahansa Yogananda, Osho, Robin Sharma, Deepak Chopra, Stephen Hawking, Eknath Easwaran, Sarvapalli Radhakrishnan, Nirad Chaudhuri, Khushwant Singh, Mulk Raj Anand, John Maxwell, Ken Blanchard and Brian Tracy. Our list which has crossed a landmark 2000 titles, is amongst the most diverse in the country, with books in religion, spirituality, mind/body/spirit, self-help, business, cookery, humour, career, games, biographies, fiction, and science.

Jaico has expanded its horizons to become a leading publisher of educational and professional books in management and engineering. Our college-level textbooks and reference titles are used by students countrywide. The success of our academic and professional titles is largely due to the efforts of our Educational and Corporate Sales Divisions.

The late Mr. Jaman Shah established Jaico as a book distribution company. Sensing that independence was around the corner, he aptly named his company Jaico ("Jai" means victory in Hindi). In order to tap the significant demand for affordable books in a developing nation, Mr. Shah initiated Jaico's own publications. Jaico was India's first publisher of paperback books in the English language.

In addition to being a publisher and distributor of its own titles, Jaico is a major distributor of books of leading international publishers such as McGraw Hill, Pearson, Cengage Learning, John Wiley and Elsevier Science. With its headquarters in Mumbai, Jaico has other sales offices in Ahmedabad, Bangalore, Bhopal, Chennai, Delhi, Hyderabad and Kolkata. Our sales team of over 40 executives, direct mail order division, and website ensure that our books effectively reach all urban and rural parts of the country.

SINCE 1946